A PLUM...

LOVE

BARBARA FREDRICKSON, PH.D., is the a... ...is Kenan Distinguished Professor of Psychology and Director of the Positive Emotions and Psychophysiology Laboratory at the University of North Carolina at Chapel Hill. She lives in Chapel Hill, North Carolina, with her family.

Praise for *Love 2.0*

"Read this book and you'll never think about love in the same way again!"
—Sonja Lyubomirsky, Ph.D., author of
The How of Happiness and *The Myths of Happiness*

"A radically new conception of love." —*The Atlantic*

"Barbara Fredrickson drives home the value of being warmhearted, making the scientific case that this variety of positivity benefits our health and our connections, as well as opening our lives to new possibilities. *Love 2.0* is a user-friendly manual for opening our hearts."
—Daniel Goleman, author of *Emotional Intelligence*

"No current book can hold a candle to Fredrickson's *Love 2.0* for its stunning combination of science, wisdom, and poetry. I am tempted to say that there has not been a better book on love since the New Testament."
—George Vaillant, M.D., author of
Spiritual Evolution and *Triumphs of Experience*

"Fredrickson is disassembling centuries of other notions of what love is, how to receive it, how to give it, and why it is so important in distinguishing humans from other mammals on earth." —*National Post*

LOVE 2.0

CREATING HAPPINESS AND HEALTH

IN MOMENTS OF CONNECTION

Barbara L. Fredrickson, Ph.D.

A PLUME BOOK

PLUME
Published by the Penguin Group
Penguin Group (USA) LLC
375 Hudson Street
New York, New York 10014

USA | Canada | UK | Ireland | Australia | New Zealand | India | South Africa | China
penguin.com
A Penguin Random House Company

First published in the United States of America by Hudson Street Press, a member of Penguin Group
(USA) Inc., 2013
First Plume Printing 2014

LIBRARY OF CONGRESS CATALOGING-IN-PUBLICATION DATA
Love 2.0 : how our supreme emotion affects everything we think, do, feel, and become / Barbara L.
Fredrickson.
  p. cm.
 Includes bibliographical references and index.
 ISBN 978-1-59463-099-6 (hc.)
 ISBN 978-0-14-218047-1 (pbk.)
 1. Love—Psychological aspects.   I. Title.
 BF575.L8F72 2013
 152.4'1—dc23   2012018970

Printed in the United States of America
10 9 8 7 6 5 4 3 2 1

Set in Bell MT Std

To you, and to those in whom your love resonates

Contents

PART I

The Vision

CHAPTER 1

Love, Our Supreme Emotion

THE ESKIMOS HAD FIFTY-TWO NAMES FOR SNOW
BECAUSE IT WAS IMPORTANT TO THEM: THERE OUGHT
TO BE AS MANY FOR LOVE.

—Margaret Atwood

onging. You know the feeling. It's that ache of sensing that something vital is missing from your life; a deep thirst for more. More meaning, more connection, more energy—more *something.* Longing is that feeling that courses through your body just before you decide that you're restless, lonely, or unhappy.

Longing like this is not just another mental state. It's deeply physical. Your body craves some essential nutrient that it's not getting, yet you can't quite put your finger on what it is. Sometimes you can numb this ache with a deep dive into work, gossip, television, or gaming. More often than not, though, these and other attempts to fill the aching void are merely temporary distractions. The longing doesn't let up. It trails you like a shadow, insistently, making distractions all the more appealing. And distractions abound—that second or third glass of wine, that stream of texts and tweets, that couch and remote control.

Odds are, food is abundant in your life. And clean drinking water is as close as the nearest faucet and virtually limitless. You have access to reasonably clean air and adequate shelter. Those basic needs have long been met. What you long for now is far more intangible.

What you long for is love. Whether you're single or not, whether you spend your days largely in isolation or steadily surrounded by the buzz of conversation, love is the essential nutrient that your cells crave: true positivity-charged connection with other living beings.

Love, as it turns out, nourishes your body the way the right balance of sunlight, nutrient-rich soil, and water nourishes plants and allows them to flourish. The more you experience it, the more you open up and grow, becoming wiser and more attuned, more resilient and effective, happier and healthier. You grow spiritually as well, better able to see, feel, and appreciate the deep interconnections that inexplicably tie you to others, that embed you within the grand fabric of life.

Just as your body was designed to extract oxygen from the earth's atmosphere, and nutrients from the foods you ingest, your body was designed to love. Love—like taking a deep breath or eating an orange when you're depleted and thirsty—not only feels great but is also life-giving, an indispensable source of energy, sustenance, and health.

When I compare love to oxygen and food, I'm not just taking poetic license. I'm drawing on science: new science that illuminates for the first time how love, and its absence, fundamentally alters the biochemicals in which your body is steeped. They, in turn, can alter the very ways your DNA gets expressed within your cells. The love you do or do not experience today may quite literally change key aspects of your cellular architecture next season and next year—cells that affect your physical health, your vitality, and your overall well-being. In these ways and more, just as your supplies of clean air and nutritious food forecast how long you'll walk this earth—and whether you'll thrive or just get by—so does your supply of love.

It's Not What You Think

To absorb what the new science of love has to offer, you'll need to step back from "love" as you may now know it. Forget about the love that you typically hear on the radio, the one that's centered on desire and yearns for touch from a new squeeze. Set aside the take on love your family might have offered you, one that requires that you love your relatives unconditionally, regardless of whether their actions disturb you, or their aloofness leaves you cold. I'm even asking you to set aside your view of love as a special bond or relationship, be it with your spouse, partner, or soul mate. And if you've come to view love as a commitment, promise, or pledge, through marriage or any other loyalty ritual, prepare for an about-face. I need you to step back from all of your preconceptions and consider an upgrade. *Love 2.0* offers a different perspective—your body's perspective.

If you were asked today, by a roving reporter or an inquisitive dinner party guest, to provide your own definition of love, your answer would likely reflect a mishmash of shared cultural messages and your own deeply personal experiences with intimacy. However compelling your answer, I'd wager that your body has its own—quite different— definition of love. That's what this book is about. Love is not sexual desire or the blood-ties of kinship. Nor is it a special bond or commitment. Sure enough, love is closely related to each of these important concepts. Yet none, I will argue, capture the true meaning of love as your body experiences it.

The vision of love that I offer here will require a radical shift, a departure from what you've come to believe. It's time to upgrade your view of love. Love is not a category of relationships. Nor is it something "out there" that you can fall into, or—years later—out of. Seeing love as a special bond is extraordinarily common, albeit misleading. A bond like this can endure for years—even a lifetime with proper commitment and effort. And having at least one close relationship like this is vital to your health and happiness, to be sure. Even so, that special bond and the commitments people often build around it are better taken as the *products* of love—the results of the many smaller moments in which love infuses you—rather than as love per se. When you equate love with intimate relationships, love can seem confusing. At times it feels great, while at other times it hurts like hell. At times it lifts you up with grand dreams for your future and at other times oppresses you with shame about your inadequacies, or guilt about your past actions. When you limit your view of love to relationships or commitment, love becomes a complex and bewildering thicket of emotions, expectations, and insecurities. Yet when you redirect your eyes toward your body's definition of love, a clear path emerges that cuts through that thicket and leads you to a better life.

There's still more ground to clear. I need to ask you to disengage from some of your most cherished beliefs about love as well: the notions that love is exclusive, lasting, and unconditional. These deeply held beliefs are often more wish than reality in people's lives. They capture people's daydreams about the love-of-their-life whom they've yet to meet. Love, as your body defines it, is not exclusive, not something to be reserved for your soul mate, your inner circle, your kin, or your so-called *loved ones*. Love's reach turns out to be far wider than we're typically coaxed to imagine. Even so, love's timescale is far shorter than we typically think. Love, as you'll see, is not lasting. It's actually far more fleeting than most of us would care to acknowledge. On the upside, though, love is forever renewable. And perhaps most challenging of all, love is not unconditional. It doesn't emerge no matter what, regardless of conditions. To the contrary, you'll see that the love your body craves is exquisitely sensitive to contextual cues. It obeys preconditions. Yet once you understand those preconditions, you can find love countless times each day.

It's difficult to speak of love in scientific terms, I've found, because listeners have so many preexisting and strong beliefs about it. Many of these beliefs reflect our shared cultural heritage, like all those proliferating songs and movies that equate love with infatuation or sexual desire, or with stories that end happily ever after, or even the realistic marriage ceremonies that celebrate love as an exclusive bond and commitment. Other beliefs about love are deeply personal. They reflect your own unique life history, with its interpersonal triumphs and scars, lessons about intimacy learned and not yet learned. Left unaddressed, these preconceptions can derail any serious intellectual discussion of love. They may even keep you from soaking up the full implications of the new findings on it.

This Approach Is Different

The approach I offer weaves together several new strands of science while keeping an eye toward the spiritual and the practical. With roots extending back millennia to your hunter-gatherer ancestors, this approach also casts forward to your future. It envisions your untapped potential for loving and growth, and your ability to create contexts that nurture love and growth in others, and in the generations to come who will inherit whatever world you help to shape.

The bedrock for my approach to love is the science of emotions. For more than two decades, I've investigated that subset of emotions that feel good to you, those pleasing states—of joy, amusement, gratitude, hope, and the like—that simultaneously infuse your mind and body. Odds are you shift into and out of states like these dozens of times each day, sometimes when you're alone, sometimes when you're with others.

What I've found is that even though you experience positive emotions as exquisitely subtle and brief, such moments can ignite powerful forces of growth in your life. They do this first by opening you up: Your outlook quite literally expands as you come under the influence of any of several positive emotions. Put simply, you see more as your vision widens; you see the bigger picture. With this momentarily broadened, more encompassing mind-set, you become more flexible, attuned to others, creative, and wise. Over time, you also become more resourceful. This is because, little by little, these mind-expanding moments of positive emotions add up to reshape your life for the better, making you more knowledgeable, more resilient, more socially integrated, and healthier. In fact, science documents that positive emotions can set off upward spirals in your life, self-sustaining trajectories of growth that lift you up to become a better version of yourself.

These two core facts about positive emotions—that they open you up and transform you for the better—form the two anchor points for my broaden-and-build theory of positive emotions, which I wrote about in my first book, *Positivity*, to show how you can put positive emotions to work as you navigate your days to overcome negativity and thrive.

The word *positivity* is purposefully broad. I chose it to cover the full range of positive emotions and then some. It also spans the psychological conditions that seed your positive emotions as well as their myriad effects—the slowing rhythm of your heart, the opening of your mind, and the relaxed, inviting look on your face. It even encompasses the fruits of positive emotions that ripen for you only a season later— their mounting effects on your relationships, your character, your health and spiritual growth. Here, you could protest and say that I've roped too much into this one term. Yet I see real value in using an encompassing word like positivity. It lassos the fuller dynamic system in which love and other positive emotions operate. Positive emotions are the tiny engines that drive this intricate, ever-churning positivity system. They are the active ingredients that set the rest in motion. Yet when I step back from the proverbial microscope to examine the larger system that orbits around your positive emotions, I see how positive emotions knit you into the fabric of life, the social fabric that unites you with others, and how they orchestrate the ways you grow and rebound through changing circumstances. I needed a new word to encompass that broader system, and that's positivity.

Keeping an eye on this fuller positivity system enables a more precise definition of love, which I provide in chapter 2. Love—like all the other positive emotions—follows the ancestral logic of *broaden and build*: Those pleasant yet fleeting moments of connection that you experience with others expand your awareness in ways that accrue to create lasting and beneficial changes in your life.

The love you crave lies within momentary experiences of connection. Other concepts that go by the word *love* in our shared cultural vocabulary—the all-consuming desire, the exclusive bonds, the commitments to loyalty, the unconditional trust—are best viewed as key players within the larger positivity system that surrounds love. Each in fact grows stronger as your moments of love accumulate: When you've truly connected with someone else, your trust in that person expands, your relationship and loyalty deepen, and you want to spend more good times together. But that's only half the story. The causal arrow also runs in the other direction: Each of these players within the larger positivity system—the desire, bonds, commitments, and trust—also triggers subsequent moments of loving connection. Put simply, it's far easier to connect with another person, when your desire, bond, commitment, or trust is present and strong. So these players are both cause and consequence of loving connections. This is what sustains the complex and dynamic positivity system that forges your often inexplicable ties to family, friends, and community. Love energizes this whole system and sets it into motion.

There's a lot going on here. It's no wonder that love puzzles us. Adding to the confusion, the word *love* is commonly affixed to different parts of the system. So when you tell someone that you love him, you may well be invoking a range of different, albeit closely related concepts. You might, for instance, mean to say that you crave the time you two spend together. Alternatively, you could mean to say that you trust that person and intend to be loyal yourself. Or perhaps professing your love to another serves as a way to elevate that particular relationship as an especially important one in your life, a way to invite or secure that person within your innermost circle. And perhaps most often, your declaration of "I love you" is meant to convey "all of the above." From a practical standpoint, there's certainly nothing wrong with that. I wouldn't ask you to upgrade your vision of love if I didn't see a big payoff for doing so. When we unravel love in chapter 2, you'll begin to understand it in terms that your body knows. For now, suffice it to say that although you may subscribe to a whole host of definitions of love, your body subscribes to just one: Love is that micro-moment of warmth and connection that you share with another living being.

I want to emphasize, though, that love isn't simply one of the many positive emotions that sweep through you from time to time. It's bigger than joy, amusement, gratitude, or hope. It has special status. I call it our supreme emotion. First, that's because any of the other positive emotions—joy, amusement, gratitude, hope, and so on—can be transformed into an instance of love when felt in close connection with another. Yet casting love as shared positive emotion doesn't go nearly far enough. Second, whereas all positive emotions provide benefits—each, after all, broadens your mind-set and builds your resourcefulness—the benefits of love run far deeper, perhaps exponentially so. Love is our supreme emotion that makes us come most fully alive and feel most fully human. It is perhaps the most essential emotional experience for thriving and health.

My approach to love is also different because it crosses emotions science with relationship science. From relationship science, I adopt the idea that love draws you out of your cocoon of self-absorption to attune to others. Love allows you to really *see* another person, holistically, with care, concern, and compassion. Within each moment of loving connection, you become sincerely invested in this other person's well-being, simply for his or her own sake. And the feeling is mutual. You come to recognize that, in this loving moment, this other person is also sincerely invested in *your* well-being; that he or she truly cares for *you*. Relationship scientists cast this sense of mutual care as an abiding attribute of intimate relationships. By contrast, I see mutual care as a momentary state that rises and falls in step with changes in context and emotion.

Truth be told, a happy accident pressed me to see love in a whole new light. I was minding my own business as an emotions scientist about eight years back, testing hypotheses drawn from my broaden-and-build theory. My main goal at the time was to find a way to probe the long-range effects of accumulated positive emotions. Would they build people's resources and transform their lives for the better as the theory predicted? To support definitive claims about cause and effect, I needed an experiment, complete with randomization and rigorous measures. I needed to compare one group of people who increased their daily diets of positive emotions to another group that didn't. The vexing question was *how*? How can people reliably and sustainably increase their daily intake of positive emotions? The methods that I and other scientists had used in the lab to test the short-range effects of positive emotions—the music, the film clips, the cartoons, the unexpected gifts of candy—wouldn't do. They fall flat and lose their charge with repetition. That's because we humans adapt: Even the most potent emotion-eliciting stimulus fades into the background like wallpaper with repeated exposure. After a few failed attempts to develop a viable intervention, I found myself in a yearlong interdisciplinary faculty seminar on integrative medicine. Here is where I was first introduced to the ancient mind-training practice called *metta* in Pali, *maître* in Sanskrit, often translated as loving-kindness, or simply kindness. In Buddhist teachings, loving-kindness is considered one of the four noblest modes of consciousness—the crown jewel, in some traditions. A lightbulb went off for me: This ancient practice, honed over millennia, could help me test my theory. Perhaps training in loving-kindness was the intervention I'd been seeking.

Over the next year, my students and I designed a rigorous and randomized experiment to test the effects of learning to self-generate positive emotions through loving-kindness meditation. My test pilots were reasonably healthy working adults with no particular spiritual orientation. The results were abundantly clear. When people, completely new to meditation, learned to quiet their minds and expand their capacity for love and kindness, they transformed themselves from the inside out. They experienced more love, more engagement, more serenity, more joy, more amusement—more of every positive emotion we measured. And though they typically meditated alone, their biggest boosts in positive emotions came when interacting with others, off the cushion, as it were. Their lives spiraled upward. The kindheartedness they learned to stoke during their meditation practice warmed their connections with others. Later experiments would confirm that it was these connections that most affected their bodies, making them healthier. We also came to discover that other interventions to foster connection—ones that didn't require learning to meditate—could increase people's experiences of love and likewise improve their health. I share all of these change strategies with you in part II.

These discoveries pushed me to rethink love. Taken as a whole, the numbers tell me that when you learn practical ways to generate warm connections with others—through meditation or other means—you step up to a whole new dynamic. Here is where the soft-focus you encounter in typical discussions about love sharpens into high definition. The mysteries that have long been sources both of wonder and exhilaration, as well as confusion and misunderstanding, now give way to practical, evidence-based prescriptions for how to live life well. We know now that a steady diet of love influences how people grow and change, making them healthier and more resilient day by day. And we're beginning to understand exactly how this works, by tracking the complex chain of biological reactions that cascade throughout your body and change your behavior in ways that influence those around you. But even as science unveils the mystery of love, it offers you even more reason to pay attention. I'll show you how love's capacity to nourish, heal, and do good is deeply wired into your biology, and into your ways of relating to others. The sheer complexity of love's biology is reason enough for awe.

When you upgrade your vision of love, you'll be drawn to cherish it all the more. You come to recognize that it deserves greater priority in your life. My doctoral student Lahnna Catalino and I have examined the effects of *prioritizing positivity*. By this we mean the importance you give to your own positive emotional experiences. Do you trust them? Turn toward them? Seek them out and cherish them? Do you use anticipated good feelings as a touchstone when choosing what to do next? Or do you brush good feelings off as trivial, frivolous, or inconsequential? When you learn to prioritize love and other positive emotions, we've found, you actually get more out of them. Your upward spirals lift you higher and faster. With the guidance I've assembled in part II, you'll be set to take off.

That's why I wrote this book. Learning how love works can make a clear difference in your life. It can help you prioritize moments of shared positivity and elevate your faith in humanity. With the greater knowledge of love's inner workings that this book offers, you'll become more efficient at accessing this transcendent state, with all its inherent goodness. Science need not inevitably leave you holding a flat corkboard with a dismembered butterfly pinned to it. Science can also glorify, painting a colorful and multidimensional road map for a more potent life journey, one that eliminates the detours of false hopes, false prophets, false claims, and charts a course toward the real thing. It can leave the butterfly alive and whole and set it free.

Love 2.0: The View from Here

What is love, exactly? What's hidden beneath love's surface? What does love create? How do you unlock more opportunities for it? The new science of love tackles all of these questions and upgrades our vision of love. In chapter 2, I examine your body's definition of love in detail and describe love's necessary preconditions. In chapter 3, I reveal the hidden biological underpinnings of love, and you'll come away with an even deeper appreciation for what love means for your health. In chapter 4, I describe the vast array of benefits that love brings to you.

Part II of this book is all about making changes. You've long admired people skilled at making genuine, heartfelt connections. They seem so perceptive and nimble, so resilient and generous. You've long imagined that being a "grown up" would bestow you with such perspective and grace. Yet age, measured as time since birth, provides no guarantees for maturity or wisdom. In chapters 5 through 9, I offer you explicit guidance on how to seed love more often and more effectively, love for yourself and love for others, through thick and thin, in sickness and in health. You'll come away having learned that love need not remain an unpredictable and elusive state. With practice, you'll find you can generate love anytime you wish. Love will become a renewable resource that you can tap to fuel your own well-being, and the well-being of all those within your radius.

Love is our supreme emotion: Its presence or absence in our lives influences everything we feel, think, do, and become. It's that recurrent state that ties you in—your body and brain alike—to the social fabric, to the bodies and brains of those in your midst. When you experience love—true heart/mind/soul-expanding love—you not only become better able to see the larger tapestry of life and better able to breathe life into the connections that matter to you, but you also set yourself on a pathway that leads to more health, happiness, and wisdom.

CHAPTER 2

What Love Is

As you check out of the grocery store, you share a laugh with the cashier about the face you see peering up at you from the uncommonly gnarly tomato in your basket.

On your way to pick up your mail, you happen upon a neighbor you've not seen in a while and pause to chat. Within minutes you find yourselves swapping lively stories with each other about the fascinations you share.

At work, you and your teammates celebrate a shared triumph with hugs and high fives.

On your morning jog, you smile and nod to greet fellow runners and silently wish them a good day.

You share a long embrace with a family member after a trip that has kept you apart for too many days.

What Love Is

First and foremost, *love is an emotion*, a momentary state that arises to infuse your mind and body alike. Love, like all emotions, surfaces like a distinct and fast-moving weather pattern, a subtle and ever-shifting force. As for all positive emotions, the inner feeling love brings you is inherently and exquisitely pleasant—it feels extraordinarily good, the way a long, cool drink of water feels when you're parched on a hot day. Yet far beyond feeling good, a micro-moment of love, like other positive emotions, literally changes your mind. It expands your awareness of your surroundings, even your sense of self. The boundaries between you and not-you—what lies beyond your skin—relax and become more permeable. While infused with love you see fewer distinctions between you and others. Indeed, your ability to see others—really *see* them, wholeheartedly—springs open. Love can even give you a palpable sense of oneness and connection, a transcendence that makes you feel part of something far larger than yourself.

Then, slowly, this expansive and transcendent feeling fades away, just like any other emotion, be it anger, joy, or sadness. However wondrous, feelings of love sweep through you for only a few moments. No emotion is built to last, not even the ones that feel so good. True, you can learn to coax your fleeting micro-moments of love to linger with you a bit longer, and you can revive them later through conversation. But their duration is best measured in seconds or minutes, not months or years. Love is the ephemeral and precious openness you feel well up in your chest, not a rock-solid ring made of precious metal on your left hand.

The love I speak of here is also far from exclusive. It's not just that unique feeling you reserve for your spouse or your romantic partner. It even extends beyond your warm feelings for your children, parents, or close friends. Love can reach so much further than we typically allow. In fact, no one—young or old, passionate or reserved, single or married—need be excluded. It is love, after all, that energizes that unspoken bond of sameness you sense between you and the person by chance seated next to you on the plane, to whom you've opened up and listened attentively, in that moment when you glance at each other and really see each other, with true respect and appreciation. I'm reminded here of the lyrics that Louis Armstrong's gravelly voice made famous in the late 1960s in "What a Wonderful World": "I see friends shaking hands . . . sayin' 'how do you do?' / They're really sayin . . . 'I love you.'"

Perhaps counterintuitively, love is far more ubiquitous than you ever thought possible for the simple fact that *love is connection*. It's that poignant stretching of your heart that you feel when you gaze into a newborn's eyes for the first time or share a farewell hug with a dear friend. It's even the fondness and sense of shared purpose you might unexpectedly feel with a group of strangers who've come together to marvel at a hatching of sea turtles or cheer at a football game. The new take on love that I want to share with you is this: Love blossoms virtually anytime two or more people—even strangers—connect over a shared positive emotion, be it mild or strong.

To put it in a nutshell, love is the momentary upwelling of three tightly interwoven events: first, a sharing of one or more positive emotions between you and another; second, a synchrony between your and the other person's biochemistry and behaviors; and third, a reflected motive to invest in each other's well-being that brings mutual care.

My shorthand for this trio is *positivity resonance*. Within those moments of interpersonal connection that are characterized by this amplifying symphony—of shared positive emotions, biobehavioral synchrony, and mutual care—life-giving positivity resonates between and among people. This back-and-forth reverberation of positive energy sustains itself—and can even grow stronger—until the momentary connection wanes, which is of course inevitable, because that's how emotions work.

I've come up with a visual metaphor for positivity resonance that likens it to a mirror. This seems apt because a moment of positivity resonance, by definition, involves considerable mirroring at three different levels: You and the other person mirror the positivity in each other's emotional state; you mirror each other's gestures and biochemistry; and you mirror each other's impulse to care for one another. So in a moment of positivity resonance, to some extent, you each become the reflection and extension of the other. Sure enough, when you face a conventional mirror, you meet eyes only with yourself. Imagine, though, facing a mirror straight on and seeing this other person. Before this moment of positivity resonance, the two of you were off doing your own thing—feeling your own emotions, making your own moves, and following your own inclinations. But in this particular moment of connection, your respective feelings, actions, and impulses align and come into sync. For just a moment, you each become something larger than yourself. This is no ordinary moment. Within this mirrored reflection and extension of your own state, you see far more. A powerful back-and-forth union of energy springs up between the two of you, like an electric charge.

Ordinary positive emotions don't resonate like this at all. They are not mirrored back to you. Although the warmth of any positive emotion stretches your mind and spurs you to grow in ways that leave you more resourceful and resilient than before, only love creates such a deep interpersonal resonance. That's because within micro-moments of love, your own positivity, your own warmth and openness, evoke—and is simultaneously evoked by—the warmth and openness emanating from the other person. This shared positivity gets further amplified by the synchronized changes in biochemistry that course through your bodies and the attention you each show the other—the smiles, the leaning in, your verbal and nonverbal expressions of care and concern for each other. These are powerful, energizing moments. Your body was designed to harness this power—to live off it. Your ability to understand and empathize with others depends mightily on having a steady diet of positivity resonance, as do your potentials for wisdom, spirituality, and health.

Odds are, if you were raised in a Western culture, you think of emotions as largely private events. You locate them within a person's boundaries, confined within their mind and skin. When conversing about emotions, your use of singular possessive adjectives betrays this point of view: You refer to "my anxiety," "his anger," or "her interest." Following this logic, love would seem to belong to the person who feels it. Defining love as positivity resonance challenges this view. Love unfolds and reverberates between and among people—*within* interpersonal transactions—and thereby belongs to all parties involved, and to the metaphorical connective tissue that binds them together, albeit temporarily. The biology of love, as you'll see in chapter 3, concurs. Love alters the unseen activity within your body and brain in ways that trigger parallel changes within another person's body and brain. More than any other positive emotion, then, love belongs not to one person, but to pairs or groups of people. It resides within connections. It extends beyond personal boundaries to characterize the vibe that pulsates between and among people. It can even energize whole social networks or inspire a crowd to get up and dance.

Positivity resonance doesn't spring up at random. It emerges within certain circumstances, stemming from particular patterns of thought and action. These are love's bedrock prerequisites. The first precondition is a perception of safety. If you assess your current circumstances as threatening or dangerous in any way, love is not at that moment a possibility for you. Indeed, your brain has been shaped by the forces of natural selection to be exquisitely attuned to threats. Your innate threat detection system even operates outside your conscious awareness. You could be engrossed in conversation, or enjoying a blissful run in the woods, for instance, and still instantaneously spot that writhing snake on your path. Although true threats are rare, not everyone can trust the world this way. People who suffer from anxiety, depression, or even loneliness or low self-esteem perceive threats far more often than circumstances warrant. Sadly, this overalert state thwarts both positivity and positivity resonance. Feeling unsafe, then, is the first obstacle to love.

True Connection Matters

Love's second precondition is connection, true sensory and temporal connection with another living being. You no doubt try to "stay connected" when physical distance keeps you and your loved ones apart. You use the phone, e-mail, and increasingly texts or Facebook, and it's important to do so. Yet your body, sculpted by the forces of natural selection over millennia, was not designed for the abstractions of long-distance love, the XOXs and LOLs. Your body hungers for more. It hungers for moments of oneness.

Feelings of oneness surface when two or more people "sync up" and literally come to act as one, moving to the same hidden beat. You can sync up like this with a stranger just as you can with a lifelong companion. When positivity resonance moves between you and another, for instance, the two of you begin to mirror each other's postures and gestures, and even finish each other's sentences. You feel united, connected, of a piece. When you especially resonate with someone else—even if you've just met—the two of you are quite literally on the same wavelength, biologically. A synchrony also unfolds internally, as your physiological responses—in both body and brain—mirror each other as well.

True connection is one of love's bedrock prerequisites, a prime reason that love is not unconditional, but instead requires a particular stance. Neither abstract nor mediated, true connection is physical and unfolds in real time. It requires a sensory and temporal copresence of bodies. The main mode of sensory connection, scientists contend, is eye contact. Other forms of real-time sensory contact—through touch, voice, or mirrored body postures and gestures—no doubt connect people as well and at times can substitute for eye contact. Nevertheless, eye contact may well be the most potent trigger for connection and oneness.

A smile, more so than any other emotional expression, pops out and draws your eye. That's a good thing, too, because a smile can mean so many different things. Why, for instance, is your new coworker suddenly smiling at you? Is she being sincere or smug? Friendly or self-absorbed? Caring or just polite? Considering that Paul Ekman, the world's leading scientist of human facial expressions, estimates that humans regularly use some fifty different types of smiles, the ambiguity of any given smile becomes more understandable. Plus, the differences between different types of smiles—a friendly smile, an enjoyment smile, a domineering smile, even a fake smile—can be subtle. Whereas scientists like Ekman use deliberate and formal reasoning to detect those subtle differences—most often with the aid of slow-motion video capture—without specialized training, all you have are your gut feelings to figure out what your coworker's smile really means. Yet those gut feelings can be a powerful source of intuition and wisdom if you know how best to access them. Eye contact, it turns out, is crucial. New scientific evidence suggests that if you don't make direct eye contact with your coworker, you're at a distinct disadvantage in trying to figure out what she really feels or means.

Eye contact is the key that unlocks the wisdom of your intuitions because when you meet your smiling coworker's gaze, her smile triggers activity within your own brain circuitry that allows you to simulate—within your own brain, face, and body—the emotions you see emanating from hers. You now know, through this rapid and nonconscious simulation, more about what it feels like to have smiled like that. Access to this embodied feeling, this information springing up from within you, makes you wiser. You become more accurate, for instance, at discerning what her unexpected smile means. You're more attuned, less gullible. You intuitively grasp her intentions. She wasn't being friendly after all, she was gloating. She wasn't looking to connect, but was instead self-satisfied. You don't need to be a cynic to recognize that not all smiles are sincere bids for connection. Some smiles may even be flashed to exploit or control you. Just as you rely on your senses to discern nutritious from rotting food, so, too, can you rely on your senses to help you separate the honest from dishonest invitations for connection.

Once you have made eye contact, your conclusions about your coworker's smile, conscious or not, inform your gut and your next move. Without eye contact, it is much easier to experience misunderstandings, crushed hearts, and exploitation as you over- or under-interpret the friendliness of other people's smiles. You can also miss countless opportunities for life-giving connection. Eye contact helps you better detect the sincere affiliative gestures within a sea of merely polite or decidedly manipulative smiles that bid for your attention. Love, then, is not blind.

Moments of *seemingly* shared positivity abound. You, and those in your midst, can be infused with one form of positivity or another, yet not be truly connected. You and everyone else in the movie theater, for instance, share the positivity emanating from the big screen; you and the person next to you in the lecture hall are fascinated by the same set of new ideas; you and your family members take in the same television comedy. Yet absent eye contact, touch, laughter, or another form of behavioral synchrony, these moments are akin to what developmental psychologists call *parallel play*. They no doubt feel great and their positivity confers broaden-and-build benefits both to you and to others, independently. But if they are not (yet) directly and interpersonally shared experiences, they do not resonate or reverberate, and so they are not (yet) instances of love. The key to love is to add some form of physical connection.

To be clear, the sensory and temporal connections you establish with others through eye contact, touch, conversation, or other forms of behavioral synchrony are not, in and of themselves, love. Even holding hands, after all, can become a loveless habit. Yet in the right contexts, these gestures become springboards for love. The right contexts are those infused with the emotional presence of positivity.

Imagine that instead of me sitting alone at my home office computer searching for words in July 2011 and you sitting (am I right?) who knows where reading these words some years later, that you and I are sitting together at your local coffee shop talking these ideas over. Turns out, you've got a boatload of great questions. It doesn't take long for our shared enthusiasm for what the latest science says about human nature and human potential to take hold of us. Although I'm fairly low-key by nature, this sort of conversation can get me pretty animated. My gestures and smiles convey not only my enthusiasm for the ideas but also my appreciation for your thoughtful questions and examples. I'm attuned to you, sympathetic to your input, and responding to all the subtle cues that reveal how effectively we're communicating.

From my perspective, your smiles, nods, and other gestures of your own positivity and attunement don't just exist "out there" in you. When we meet each other's gaze, they also come to exist, in a very real way, inside me. Within milliseconds my brain and body begin to buzz with your enthusiasm and appreciation, and your attunement to me. The more this happens, the more I come to feel the same way as you, both enthused and appreciative, responsive and sympathetic. Soon enough these feelings surface on my face and emanate through my voice and gestures. As our eyes continue to meet, a parallel simulation process flows forth within you, as the dynamics unfolding within your brain and body begin to pattern mine. A back-and-forth reverberation stretches out between us.

Increasingly, with each passing micro-moment, you and I come to *feel the same way*. We're in sync, attuned. Positivity resonance has established a connection between us, as your and my brain activity and biochemistry increasingly become one and the same. A positivity-infused interweaving of our hearts and minds emerges, a momentary state scientists have called *intersubjectivity*. You can think of this as a miniature version of what *Star Trek*'s infamous Dr. Spock called a *mind meld*. Yet both expressions, in my view, are too focused on the mind, too heartless. For it's vital, too, that the emotional tone of our momentary meld, our interweaving, is warm, open, trusting, and full of genuine care and concern for each other.

Some would call what is happening between us *rapport*. Yet the more I understand the science behind positivity resonance, the more I think this description misleads. *Rapport* sounds optional, superfluous. Something you'd be just as healthy with or without. Given the vital role that positivity resonance plays in our survival, such states warrant elevation. That's why I call them *love*, our supreme emotion. Micromoments like these are those essential nutrients of which most of us in modern life aren't getting enough.

So what's a smile for? Traditional views hold that smiles have evolved to reveal the inner state of the person who smiles. Indeed, when you call a smile a facial expression, you unwittingly subscribe to this view—that certain facial movements universally express a person's otherwise unseen emotions. An opposing view shifts the spotlight onto the *recipient* of a smile and argues that smiles evolved not because they provided a readout of the positive emotion that the smiling person feels, but rather because they evoked a positive emotion in the person who meets the smiling person's gaze. More recently scientists have taken this alternative view a step further, arguing that smiles have evolved to give us an implicit understanding—or gut sense—of the smiling person's true motives. Building on these and other evolutionary accounts, I think it's appropriate to widen the spotlight further still, to illuminate not just either the *smiler* or the *smilee*, but instead the emerging connection between the two people who come to share a smile. One person's sincere, heartfelt smile can trigger a powerful and reverberating state between two people, one characterized by the trio of love's features: a now shared positive emotion, a synchrony of actions and biochemistry, and a feeling of mutual care. Put succinctly, smiles may well have evolved to make love, to create positivity resonance.

Love, then, requires connection. This means that when you're alone, thinking about those you love, reflecting on past loving connections, yearning for more, or even when you're practicing loving-kindness meditation or writing an impassioned love letter, you are not in that moment experiencing true love. It's true that the strong feelings you experience when by yourself are important and absolutely vital to your health and well-being. But they are not (yet) shared, and so they lack the critical and undeniably physical ingredient of resonance. Physical presence is key to love, to positivity resonance.

The problem is that all too often, you simply don't take the time that's needed to truly connect with others. To the contrary, contemporary society, with its fast-changing technology and oppressive workloads, baits you to speed through your day at a pace that's completely antithetical to connection. Feeling pressured to accomplish more each day, you multitask just to stay afloat. Any given moment finds you plotting your next move. What's next on your never-ending to-do list? What do you need and from whom? Increasingly, you converse with others through e-mails, texts, tweets, and other ways that don't require speaking, let alone seeing one another. Yet these can't fulfill your body's craving for connection. Love requires you to be physically and emotionally present. It also requires that you slow down.

My second-born was such a good sleeper that my husband or I could place him in his crib awake and he'd happily drift off to sleep all on his own. Our firstborn was altogether different. He needed to be in our arms while he drifted off. He also needed a particular motion, one that we couldn't achieve in the comfort of a rocking chair, but only by walking. For at least the first year of his life, then, my husband or I would slowly pace across the tiny nursery, holding him in our arms, for up to thirty minutes or more. He trained us well. We learned that we could only place him in his crib after he'd succumbed to a deep sleep. Anything less would lead to another long bout of pacing.

With so many things to juggle as new parents, not to mention our own sleep deprivation, my husband and I began to dread the time-sink of this bedtime ritual. We'd yearn to be released from the shadowy nursery so that we could tackle the mounting dishes and laundry, make headway on a few more work projects by e-mail, or collapse into our own bed. Then, my husband discovered a radical shift that changed everything. He gave up thinking about where else he could be and immersed himself in this parenting experience. He tuned in to our son's heartbeat and breath. He appreciated his warmth, his weight in his arms, and the sweet smell of his skin. By doing so, he transformed a parental chore into a string of loving moments. When my husband shared his secret with me, we each not only enjoyed this bedtime ritual all the more, but our son also fell more swiftly into his deep sleep. Looking back, I now recognize that even though we were physically present with our son as we had walked him to sleep, at first we were not also emotionally present. I have no doubts that infants can pick up on mismatches between their parents' outward actions and inner experiences. In our case, this mismatch had initially prevented the joys and benefits of cross-generational positivity resonance from emerging.

Our boys are now nine and twelve, and their bedtime rituals have changed accordingly. Yet it strikes me that, living less than a mile from our kids' school, my husband and I still have the same opportunity for a walking connection with our kids each day. Yet in the mad dash to get the kids to school on time each weekday, it's easy to find any excuse to drive. We all know the virtues of walking. It's good for our bodies, our brains, as well as the environment. What often goes unrecognized, however, is the good it does for our relationships. It offers up the time, physical copresence, and shared movements to satisfy our and our kids' daily craving for connection. Of course, we can still spoil this chance by being mentally and emotionally elsewhere, by letting headlines, e-mails, and tweets draw us to favor our phones over our kids, for instance. Love grows best when you are attuned to the present moment, your bodily sensations, as well as to the actions and reactions of others. Sadly, when you are more attuned to technology, to-do lists, and mass media than to the unique and wondrous individuals in your day, you miss out.

Made for Love

Upon taking in world news on any given day, you can come away feeling that people in general are more fearful, aggressive, and greedy than ever before. As a global society, we're also feeling more stress, gaining more weight, and being diagnosed with more chronic illnesses year by year. In the United States, life expectancies have actually declined for kids today, relative to their parents, for the first time in centuries. How many of these ills, I wonder, stem from our collective denial of who we are and how we got here?

Like all other living things, you are a collection of cells. The ways your cells form, the ways they operate and grow, and the ways they'll be continually replaced by fresh cells until you take your last breath reflect the deeply encoded ancestral knowledge embedded within your DNA. You are a unique and ingenious animal, to be sure, but an animal nonetheless. Sometimes you forget this basic truth. You can get so caught up in the booming, buzzing world around you that your animal identity slips out of view. You forget how you—and every other human animal—got here, how we collectively arrived in this messy, overtaxed world that we inherited and will one day pass on.

The history of your cells is one of adaptation, of change. Adaptation is both quick and slow. It's quick because in a heartbeat your actions adapt to your ever-changing circumstances—you leap away from dangers, for instance, and lean in toward opportunities. As particular dangers and opportunities recur, your body begins to anticipate them. Springtime, for instance, opens up opportunities to walk barefoot. As you take those opportunities, calluses emerge to protect your feet and your metabolism rises as you become leaner from increased activity. Adaptation is extremely slow, on the other hand, because the wisdom in you that guides your quick responses to dangers, opportunities, and any ensuing physiological adjustments was sculpted, little by little, over millennia by the discerning chisel of Darwinian natural selection. Your animal ancestors were the ones whose quick actions saved their skin. That's how fear, anger, disgust, and other negative emotions evolved over countless generations. Yet your animal ancestors were also the ones whose opportunistic actions added to their reserves of resources—their toolkits—upon which they drew to navigate and survive future threats, so that they might live long enough to successfully raise their young. That's how love and other positive emotions evolved.

Prominent within your ancestor's toolkit—among the life-saving and life-giving resources upon which they could time and again draw—were the strong bonds that they'd forged with those with whom their genetic survival was yoked: their mates, kin, and coalition members. These were the ones in whom they could place their trust and loyalty, the ones to whom they became irresistibly drawn. Without bonds, an ancient animal died young or failed to reproduce. With bonds, an ancient animal stood a chance to become one of your ancestors.

Because bonds made the difference between life and death for your ancestors, so did opportunities to build bonds. Those opportunities presented themselves within safe moments of connection. And just as walking triggers callus formation and raises metabolism, the good feelings that arise when connecting with others trigger biochemical changes that reshape the lenses through which those others are seen, increasing their allure. Ancient animals enticed in this way into repeated moments of positivity resonance built more bonds. It's their

DNA that lives on within your own cells, that forms the wisdom of your body. Love is a product of human evolution. In this very literal way, you were made for love.

This means that you didn't need to learn everything about love anew, from your own firsthand experience. From birth, your body knew how to seek out love, to stoke it, and to gain pleasure and sustenance from it. Your brief yet recurrent blasts of positivity resonance with others accrued to build the very bonds that have kept you alive to this day, enabling you now to be reading these words.

Human culture tempts you to turn away from your animal origins, to divorce yourself from the rat pups that wrestle playfully with one another by day and then later drift peacefully to sleep in one heaping pack, piled one upon the other, or from the zebras that groom each other during quiet moments of safety on the savanna. Yet these ancient, animal forms of love, enacted through touch and mutual care, still live on in you, in your cells. Your thirst for positivity resonance emerges from deep within. Bids for love, to be sure, take new heights in humans. Creatively using uniquely human forms of communication, you can caress your beloved through the spoken words of a poem or inspire him through the rhythms of song and dance. You've got more resources for connection to draw on than does a rat pup or zebra. Yet your need for love is one and the same. Resting in this wisdom you can see past even abundant bickering, nastiness, greed, and fear. You can spot and hone in on life-giving opportunities for positivity resonance. As I'll share in chapter 3, science now reveals that when you become attuned to your body's definition of love, your cells get the message. They defend you from illness and enable you to grow healthier and thrive.

The world you face each day will forever present you with a wild mix of good and bad news. By nature's design, your body is equipped to handle it all—to defend against true threats and to uncover and create nourishing micro-moments of love, not just with mates and kin, but perhaps most consequentially, with those outside your family circle.

More than any other time in human history, after all, your own genetic survival may well hinge on the love you share—and the bonds you form—with complete strangers.

What About Intimates?

Love is a many-splendored thing. This classic saying is apt, not only because love can emerge from the shoots of any other positive emotion you experience, be it amusement, serenity, or gratitude, but also because of your many viable collaborators in love, ranging from your sister to your soul mate, your newborn to your neighbor, even someone you've never met before. Even when you don't share the same language, you and another have so much in common. Barring brain damage or one of a handful of neurological disorders, you each share the nervous and endocrine systems that make positivity resonance possible. Love, then, becomes possible with any human connection.

At the level of positivity resonance, micro-moments of love are virtually identical regardless of whether they bloom between you and a stranger or you and a soul mate; between you and an infant or you and your lifelong best friend. The clearest difference between the love you feel with intimates and the love you feel with anyone with whom you share a connection is its sheer frequency. Spending more total moments together increases your chances to feast on micro-moments of positivity resonance. These micro-moments change you. They forge new coalitions with strangers, advance your acquaintanceships into friendships, and cultivate even deeper intimacy in your most cherished relationships. Each micro-moment of positivity resonance knits you in a little tighter to the social fabric of your community, your network of relationships, and your family.

Whereas the biological synchrony that emerges between connected brains and bodies may be comparable no matter who the other person may be, the triggers for your micro-moments of love can be wholly different with intimates. The hallmark feature of intimacy is *mutual responsiveness*, that reassuring sense that you and your soul mate—or you and your best friend—really "get" each other. This means that you come to your interactions with a well-developed understanding of each other's inner workings, and you use that privileged knowledge thoughtfully, for each other's benefit. Intimacy is that safe and comforting feeling you get when you can bask in the knowledge that this other person truly understands and appreciates you. You can relax in this person's presence and let your guard down. Your mutual sense of trust, perhaps reinforced by your commitments of loyalty to each other, allows each of you to be more open with each other than either of you would be elsewhere.

Within these safe environs of intimacy, love can spring up in the most unlikely moments. More than a decade ago, for instance, I was driving through my then-hometown with my husband, finding my way to a corner store I'd been to only once or twice before. Coming up on the back side of the store, I turned left into what I figured was the back entrance, planning to make my way around the parking lot to the storefront. Only it wasn't really an entrance. It was just a short gravel road that led nowhere. I stopped the car and stared at the distant storefront. I'm sure I was only frozen like that for a matter of seconds, but my husband found it amusing. "Stuck on a gravel road?" he chided. We shared a laugh at my stunned response. I can't tell you how many times in the years since Jeff has resurrected this phrase to gently tease me for being a bit slow to figure out an unexpected situation. Knowing me so well, he gets that surprises can make me deer-in-the-headlights stuck for a moment (or six). Yet instead of taking this recurrence as a character flaw to overlook, or as cause for annoyance or criticism, he has made it our running inside joke. Ever an alchemist, he transforms predicaments like these into micro-moments of love. Love that not only brings me swiftly back into action but also reinforces the safety of our bond.

This silly example points to yet another thing that your intimates uniquely offer you: shared history. Earlier this year I took a late-night cab ride at a conference with my former office mate from graduate school, whom I'd just run into for the first time in nearly a decade. Although we'd lost touch for so long, within a matter of minutes, we were laughing uproariously in the back of that cab about old times, conjuring up our old goofy sayings and antics. In the short commute to our respective hotels we were transported back to the late 1980s as well, and to the fun times we'd had together. Wiping the tears of laughter away as we said our good-byes, we dreamed up ways we might reconnect again in the future.

Your intimates offer you history, safety, trust, and openness in addition to the frequent opportunity to connect. The more trusting and open you are with someone else—and the more trusting and open that person is with you—the more points of connection each of you may find over which to share a laugh, or a common source of intrigue, serenity, or delight.

What About Babies?

Appreciating the deeply shared understanding and care that supports the micro-moments of love you feel with intimates can make you wonder whether newborns have the wherewithal to truly engage in love. While (most) parents love (most of) their newborns, are their newborns truly capable of loving them back? With their limited capacities, how can newborns muster up the selfless focus on others seemingly required by love? The trick is, they don't need to muster at all. Under the right prenatal conditions, newborns arrive thirsty for connection with caring adults, trusting and open. From close range, they seek out your eye contact, body contact, and even synchronize their movements, to the extent they can, with yours. Ever the empiricist, I tested this claim out within minutes after my first son was born. As I held him skin to skin on my chest, we simply gazed at each other. Then I stuck my tongue out at him. It didn't take but a moment for him to mirror me by sticking out his own tongue. I replicated my experiment some three years later when my second son was born and got the same result, a silly mother-son synchrony immortalized both times by my husband on film.

Recasting love as positivity resonance makes it easy to identify micro-moment after micro-moment of love blossoming between infants and their responsive caretakers. Developmental science has shown that the attentive, infant-caregiver dance is absolutely vital to normal human development. As we'll see in chapter 3, infant-caregiver synchrony runs deeper than visible behaviors; it coordinates biological synchrony as well. Babies live off this stuff. We all do. Like babies, we were all designed to thrive on love. Positivity resonance is a vital nutrient.

This makes the fate of babies who, for whatever reasons, are deprived of positivity resonance all the more heart-wrenching. Sadly, not all children have the loving nourishment they need. Some, even as their other physical needs are met—for shelter, food, clothing, and such—have far too little experience sharing positive emotions with others. Love's absence, research shows, can compromise nearly all aspects of children's development—their cognitive and social abilities, their health. At one extreme, the stark and pervasive deprivation experienced by Romanian orphans reveals the painfully long shadow cast by early emotional neglect. Even among those orphans adopted and raised by loving Western families, developmental problems can persist for decades. More commonplace and poignant, however, is the unintentional emotional neglect that emerges within ordinary, even financially prosperous families.

A huge untreated source of such neglect comes from depression, which is estimated to affect 10–12 percent of postpartum moms, yet is similarly harmful when it plagues fathers or other infant caregivers.

Widely viewed as a disorder of the positive emotional system, depression smothers the sparks of positivity and positivity resonance like a heavy, wet blanket thrown over a waning campfire. It flattens people's emotional experiences. Do you know the feeling of the lead apron the dental assistant drapes over you before an X-ray? Well, imagine all your clothes were made of that leaded material. How sluggish would that make you? How unmotivated to move? Your biggest wish when feeling depressed can be just to curl up alone in your bed. Sleep may be the only relief in sight. Now imagine caring for a newborn in this depressed state. Sure, you'd muster up the energy to change diapers and provide necessary feedings. But studies show that what a depressed caregiver does not do well is synchronize. Depression itself slows down your body movements and speech output. For the infant in your care, this translates into less behavioral contingency between the two of you, and less predictability. When synchrony does emerge, odds are it's laced not with positivity, but negativity—be it anger or indifference. Depression, then, not only impairs your ability to experience and express your own positive emotions but also impairs your ability to connect with the preverbal being in your care. With the two key scaffolds of positivity and connection missing, positivity resonance—so badly needed for both of you—simply can't emerge.

The damages done to the developing child have been duly cataloged by developmental scientists. The list includes long-lasting deficits that can derail kids well into adolescence and beyond, first, in their use of symbols and other early forms of cognitive reasoning that undergird successful academic performance, and next, in their abilities to take other people's perspectives and empathize, skills vital to developing supportive social relationships. More generally, behavioral synchrony between infant and caregiver sets the stage for children's development of self-regulation, which gives them tools for controlling and channeling their emotions, attention, and behaviors, tools vital to success in all domains of life.

The range of lifelong benefits that lovingly reared infants extract from the recurrent micro-moments of positivity resonance they share with attentive caregivers shines a spotlight on the immense value of these fleeting and subtle states. Although the typical springboards for the loving moments you share with intimates are surely different from the peekaboo games infants play with their caregivers, this painstaking infant research underscores that a deep or complex understanding of the other is hardly necessary for love. Any moment of positivity resonance that ripples through the brains and bodies of you and another can be health- and life-giving, regardless of whether you share history together. Studies of successful marriages also bear this out. Couples who regularly make time to do new and exciting things together—like hiking, skiing, dancing, or attending concerts and plays—have better-quality marriages. These activities provide a steady stream of shared micro-moments of positivity resonance. Intimacy and shared history are hardly preconditions for taking a hike.

Love 2.0: The View from Here

Love is different from what you might have thought. It's certainly different from what I thought. Love springs up anytime any two or more people connect over a shared positive emotion. What does it mean, then, to say that I love my husband, Jeff? It used to mean that eighteen plus years ago, I fell in love with him. So much so that I abandoned my crusty attitude toward marriage and chose to dive right in. I used to uphold love as that constant, steady force that defines my relationship with Jeff. Of course that constant, steady force still exists between us. Yet upgrading my vision of love, I now see that steady force, not as love per se, but as the bond he and I share, and the commitments we two have made to each other, to be loyal and trusting to the end.

That bond and these commitments forge a deep and abiding sense of safety within our relationship, a safety that tills the soil for frequent moments of love. Knowing now that, from our bodies' perspective, love is positivity resonance—nutrient-rich bursts that accrue to make Jeff, me, and the bond we share healthier—shakes us out of any complacency that tempts us to take our love for granted, as a mere attribute of our relationship. Love, this new view tells us with some urgency, is something we should recultivate every morning, every afternoon, and every evening. Seeing love as positivity resonance motivates us to reach out for a hug more often or share an inspiring or silly idea or image over breakfast. In these small ways, we plant additional seeds of love that help our bodies, our well-being, and our marriage to grow stronger.

And here's something that's hard to admit: If I take my body's perspective on love seriously, it means that right now—at this very moment in which I'm crafting this sentence—I do not love my husband. Our positivity resonance, after all, only lasts as long as we two are engaged with each other. Bonds last. Love doesn't. The same goes for you and your loved ones. Unless you're cuddled up with someone reading these words aloud to him or her, right now, as far as your body knows, you don't love anyone. Of course, you have affection for many, and bonds with a subset of these. And you may even be experiencing strong feelings of positivity now that will prime the pump for later, bona fide and bodily felt love. But right now—within this very moment that you are reading this sentence—your body is loveless.

Moreover, love, as you've seen, obeys conditions. If you feel unsafe, or fail to find the time or contexts to truly connect with others, the delicate pas de deux of positivity resonance won't commence. Beyond these obstacles, something more insidious may also be barring you from love. It's your reaction to the L-word itself. Although you may be intrigued by the concept of positivity resonance, when it really comes down to it, you might hesitate to call that feeling love. You'd rather reserve this powerful word for your exclusive relationships—to describe your relationship to your spouse, your mother, or your kids—or at most for the micro-moments of positivity resonance you experience within those exclusive relationships. Some of my descriptions of love may have even drawn you to balk: Do I really need to call that moment of positive connection I just had with my coworker *love*? Was that *love* I just felt when I shared a smile with a complete stranger? Using the L-word to describe these sorts of connections makes you uneasy, uncomfortable. You'd prefer not to see them that way. Why not just say that you "got along" or "enjoyed each other's company"? Does it really do any good to call this nonexclusive stuff *love*?

Obviously, I think it does. The scientific understanding of love and its benefits offers you a completely fresh set of lenses through which to see your world and your prospects for health, happiness, and spiritual wisdom. Through these new lenses you see things that you were literally blind to before. Ordinary, everyday exchanges with colleagues and strangers now light up and call out to you as opportunities—life-giving opportunities for connection, growth, and health, your own and theirs. You can also see for the first time how micro-moments of love carry irrepressible ripple effects across whole social networks, helping each person who experiences positivity resonance to grow and in turn touch and uplift the lives of countless others. These new lenses even change the way you see your more intimate relationships with family and friends. You now also see the rivers of missed opportunities for the true love of positivity resonance. You now know how to connect to and love these cherished people in your life more and better. Viewing love as distinct from long-standing relationships is especially vital as people increasingly face repeated geographical relocations that distance families and friends. Falling in love within smaller moments and with a greater variety of people gives new hope to the lonely and isolated among us. Love, I hope you see, bears upgrading.

I'm not worried about any surface resistance to using the L-word.

The terminology you use is not what matters. What matters is that you recognize positivity resonance when it happens as well as the abundant opportunities for it, and that, more and more frequently, you seek it out. I offer the next chapter, on the biology of love, to stimulate an even deeper appreciation for how much your body needs, craves, and was designed to thrive on this life-giving form of connection.

CHAPTER 3

Love's Biology

THE SOUL MUST ALWAYS STAND AJAR, READY TO
WELCOME THE ECSTATIC EXPERIENCE.

—Emily Dickinson

It's all too tempting, especially in Western culture, to take your body to be a noun, a thing. Sure, it's a living thing, but still, like other concrete things that you can see and touch, you typically describe your body with reference to its stable physical properties, like your height, your weight, your skin tone, your apparent age, and the like. A photo works well to convey these attributes. You recognize, of course, that five years from now, today's photo will seem a bit outdated. By then, your body's physical properties might shift a bit—you might, for instance, become a little shorter, a little heavier, a little paler, or look a little older. Still, you're comfortable with the idea that your body remains pretty much the same from day to day. It has constancy.

Yet constancy, ancient Eastern philosophies warn, is an illusion, a trick of the mind. Impermanence is the rule—constant change, the only constancy. True for all things, this is especially true for living things, which, by definition, change or adapt as needed in response to changes in context. Just as plants turn toward the sun and track its arc from dawn to dusk, your own heart alters its activity with each postural shift, each new emotion, even each breath you take. Seen in this light, your body is more verb than noun: It shifts, cascades, and pulsates; it connects and builds; it erodes and flushes. Mere photographs fail to capture these nonstop and mostly unseen churning dynamics. Instead, you need movies. Increasingly, scientists work to capture these and other dynamic changes as they unfurl within living, breathing, and interacting bodies. True, scientists need to understand form as well as function, anatomy as well as physiology, nouns as well as verbs. Yet when it comes to love, verbs rule. Positivity resonance lies in the action, the doing, the connecting. It wells up, like a wave forming in the ocean, and then dissipates, like that same wave, after its crash. To fully appreciate love's biology, you'll need to train your eye to see this ever-shifting ebb and flow.

Taking cues from what leading neuroscientist Stephen Porges calls the *social engagement system*, I describe love's biology as a system, a whole comprised of several interacting parts. You can think of love, or positivity resonance, as one of the more complex and recurrent *scenes* nested within the *act* of your day, which is in turn nested within the *play* of your life. As with any scene in a play, the drama of love has its own cast of characters. Here I turn the spotlight on three main biological characters: your brain; one particular hormone, oxytocin, which circulates throughout your brain and body; and your vagus nerve, the tenth cranial nerve that runs from deep within your brain stem down to your heart, lungs, and other internal organs. Other characters step onto the biological stage to deliver their own lines, to be sure, but these three are primary players in love's biology.

Although always on stage, these main characters deliver their lines quietly, most often fully outside of your conscious awareness. As you move through your day, these biological characters—your brain, your oxytocin, and your vagus nerve—are ever responsive to set changes. As you interact with one person after another, they gently nudge you to attend to these others more closely and forge connections when possible. They shape your motives and behaviors in subtle ways, yet ultimately, their actions serve to strengthen your relationships and knit you in closer to the social fabric of life. In the sections that follow, I'll shine the spotlight on each of these three main characters in turn, to help you see how each forges and supports those life-giving moments of positivity resonance for which your body thirsts.

Love on the Brain

When you and another truly connect, love reverberates between you. In the very moment that you experience positivity resonance, your brain syncs up with the other person's brain. Within each moment of love, you and the other are on the same wavelength. As your respective brain waves mirror one another, each of you—moment by moment—changes the other's mind.

At least this is what I've been telling you. How do you know it really happens? You can't see this brain synchrony surface in real time after all. What you'd need is some way to peer inside two people's heads while they chatted so that you could tell whether their respective brain activity really does march along in time together. This would tell you whether they really "click." Only with this sort of X-ray vision could you decide whether love is better described as a solo act—an emotion contained within the boundaries of the person feeling it—or a duet or ensemble, performed by a duo or group. That sort of X-ray vision sounds like science fiction.

Yet turning science fiction into science fact is what scientists and engineers love most. Breakthrough work by neuroscientist Uri Hasson, of Princeton University, has done just that. He and his team have found ways to measure multiple brains connecting through conversation. The obstacles they faced to do this were large. First, brain scanners are loud machines—no place to carry on actual conversations. Second, they're also extraordinarily expensive, both to buy and to use. Almost all brain imaging studies thus scan just one person's brain at a time. Yet with clever engineering and clever experimental logistics, Hasson's team cleared both obstacles. They created a custom optic microphone that canceled out the noise of the scanner without distorting the delicate brain signals his team sought to capture. The logistics feat was to mimic a natural conversation by pulling it apart in time.

Suppose, for a moment, you were stranded at the airport last week. Your plane to Miami was delayed for hours. Bored with your reading and web-browsing, you got to talking to another stranded passenger, a lively young college student on her way home for break. You'd been chatting back and forth for a while, every so often, meeting eyes and sharing smiles. The conversation was very natural, like you were friends already. Somehow or another, she got to telling you about her crazy high school prom experience. In great detail, she launched into how she happened to have two dates to the same prom; how she ended up having only five minutes to get dressed and ready for the prom after a full day of scuba diving; how, on her way to after-prom festivities, she crashed her boyfriend's car in the wee hours of the morning; and then how she completely lucked out of getting ticketed (or arrested!) by the officer who witnessed her accident. She's a good storyteller: You hung on her every word. Fifteen minutes melted away as she shared all the twists and turns of her hapless prom night. It's clear, too, that you both enjoyed the chance to connect, rather than read, while you waited for your plane together.

Okay, now it's time for a set change: Instead of in an airport terminal, this conversation actually unfolded in a brain imaging lab at Princeton University. And instead of you sitting side by side with your impromptu friend, Hasson's team actually invited her to visit the lab weeks ago, and they audio-recorded her entire prom story while scanning her brain's activity with functional magnetic resonance imaging (fMRI). You're here lying in the scanner today, listening to her story over fancy headphones, while Hasson's team records your own brain activity. After you get out of the scanner, they ask you to report on what you heard in as much detail as possible. This takes a while; hers was a long, circuitous story after all.

Hasson's team later looked at the extent to which your brain activity mirrored hers. They painstakingly matched up each specific brain area across the two of you, time-locked your respective scans, and looked for "coupling," or the degree to which your brains lit up in synchrony with each other, matched in both space and time.

It turns out that the brain coupling evident between you two is surprisingly widespread. In other words, speaking with and listening to the human voice appear to activate much of the exact same brain activity at pretty much the same time. Keep in mind that—despite your new friend's gift for storytelling—this was still a pretty artificial conversation. Isolated inside the brain scanner across different days, you never actually got to see each other's gestures, meet each other's eyes, or even take turns speaking. You only listened to her voice over headphones. The brain coupling that would emerge in real time with the full and animated dialogue that could well spring up between the two of you if you were in fact seated side by side in the airplane terminal is likely to be far more extensive. Yet hearing someone's voice offers an important channel of sensory and temporal connection, because voice can convey so much emotion. By contrast, consider how little brain coupling would emerge if the connection between the two of you were to be further reduced, for instance, if you only read her story, at your own pacing and presumed intonations, or only heard *about* her story, as in my thumbnail depiction of it a few paragraphs back.

Forget the idea of a few isolated mirror neurons. So-called mirror neurons refer to a microscopic brain area that Italian neurophysiologists found to "light up" both when a monkey reaches for a banana and when that same monkey sees a person reach for a banana. The discovery of mirror neurons was a huge breakthrough because it told us that taking some action and seeing someone else take that same action are far more alike than previously thought. This means that when you know something—like why that person who just walked into your office is smiling—you know it because your brain and body simulate being in that person's shoes, in their skin. Your knowing is not just abstract and conceptual; it's embodied and physical. Yet it seems now that the concept of isolated mirror neurons was just the tip of the unseen and enormous iceberg. What Hasson and his team uncovered was far more extensive neuronal coupling than previously imagined. Far from being isolated to one or two brain areas, really "clicking" with someone else appears to be a whole brain dance in a fully mirrored room. The reflections between the two of you are that penetrating and widespread.

It turns out that you weren't the only one listening to your new friend's prom story. Hasson's team invited ten other people to have their brains scanned while listening to the very same audio-recording of her story that you heard. Whereas you listened attentively to everything she said, others didn't so much. Those differences showed up clearly when you were each asked to recount her story afterward. By tallying up the matches between her original, impromptu prom story and each listener's retelling of it, Hasson's team rank-ordered the whole set of listeners by how well they understood the story. Those differences in comprehension reflect the success or failure of communication—how thoroughly information from her brain was transferred to your brain, and to the brains of the other listeners. Strikingly, Hasson's team discovered that the degree of success in communication predicted the degree of brain coupling between speaker and listener, and did so in surprising ways.

Most of the time, across most brain areas, listeners' brains mirrored the speaker's brain after a short time lag, around one to three seconds later. It only makes sense, after all, that the speaker leads this dance, since the story is hers and she chooses her words before you and the others hear them. In other cases, though, this neural pas de deux between speaker and listener showed hardly any lag at all—the respective changes in brain activity were virtually synchronized. Your particular case was different, however. Recall that you were the one who grasped your new friend's story better than anybody. You hung on every word and picked up every detail of it, even the seemingly inconsequential ones. Your more complete grasp of her story went hand in hand with something truly remarkable: Your brain activity actually *anticipated* her brain activity by a few seconds in several cortical areas. Excellent communication, it thus seems, doesn't simply involve following along very closely. It also involves forecasting. Once you were in sync and on the same page with your new friend, enjoying her and her story, you could even anticipate what she'd say next, or how she'd say it. Your brain could anticipate her brain's next move.

Brain coupling, Hasson argues, is the means by which we understand each other. He goes even further to claim that communication—a true meeting of the minds—is a single act, performed by two brains. Considering the positivity resonance of love, what I find most fascinating about these findings is that a key brain area that showed coupling in Hasson's speaker-listener study was the insula, an area linked with conscious feeling states. Evidence for synchrony in two people's insulae suggests that in good communication, two individuals come to feel a single, shared emotion as well, one that is distributed across their two brains. Indeed, in other work, Hasson and colleagues have shown that people's brains come particularly into sync during emotional moments. Neural coupling, then—really understanding someone else—becomes all the more likely when you share the same emotion. Even more so than ordinary communication, a micro-moment of love is a single act, performed by two brains. Shared emotions, brain synchrony, and mutual understanding emerge together. And mutual understanding is just steps away from mutual care. Once two people understand each other—really "get" each other in any given moment—the benevolent concerns and actions of mutual care can flow forth unimpeded.

As you move through your day, quite naturally you move in and out of different scenes. Each scene, of course, has its own script. For perhaps most of your day, you're pretty much caught up in your own thoughts and plans, oblivious to the presence or feelings of anyone nearby. Your brain, in such moments, is doing its own thing. But in those rarer moments when you truly connect with someone else over positivity—by sharing a smile, a laugh, a common passion, or an engaging story—you become attuned, with genuine care and concern for the other. You empathize with what they're going through, as your two brains sync up and act as one, as a unified team.

Neural coupling like this is a biological manifestation of oneness. Laboratory studies have already shown that when positive emotions course through you, your awareness expands from your habitual focus on "me" to a more generous focus on "we." When you're feeling bad— afraid, anxious, or angry—even your best friend can seem pretty remote or separate from you. The same goes for when you're feeling nothing in particular. Not so, when you're feeling good. Under the influence of positive emotions, your sense of self actually expands to include others to greater degrees. Your best friend, in these light-hearted moments, simply seems like a bigger part of you.

Hasson's work suggests that when you share your positive emotions with others, when you experience positivity resonance together with this sense of expansion, it's also deeply physical, evident in your brain. The emotional understanding of true empathy recruits coinciding brain activity in both you and the person of your focus. Another telling brain imaging study, this one conducted by scientists in Taipei, Taiwan, illustrates self-other overlap at the neuronal level. Imagine for a moment being a participant in this study. While you are in the fMRI brain scanner, the researchers show you a number of short, animated scenes and ask you to picture yourself in these scenes. Some of these scenes depict painful events, like dropping something heavy on your toe or getting your fingers pinched in a closing door. What the brain images show is that, compared to imagining neutral, nonpainful situations, imagining yourself in these painful situations lights up the well-known network of brain areas associated with pain processing, including the insula, that area linked with conscious feeling states. When you are later asked to imagine these same painful events happening to a loved one—your spouse, your best friend, or your child, for instance—these same brain areas light up. By and large, then, your loved one's pain *is* your pain. By contrast, when you imagine these painful events happening to complete strangers, a different pattern of activation emerges altogether, one that shows little activation in the insula and more activation in areas linked with distinguishing and distancing yourself from others, and actively inhibiting or regulating emotions, as if to prevent their pain from becoming your pain. At the level of brain activity during imagined pain, you and your beloved are virtually indistinguishable.

Whereas the Taipei research team defined love to be a lasting loving relationship (what, for clarity's sake, I call a bond), the work from Hasson's team at Princeton tells me that neural synchrony and overlap can also unfold between you and a complete stranger—if you let it. Positivity resonance between brains, as it turns out, requires only connection, not the intimacy or shared history that comes with a special bond. Even so, the distinctions revealed in the Taipei study, between imagining your loved one's pain and imagining a stranger's pain, underscore that stifled emotions and guarded personal boundaries, while at times necessary and fully appropriate, can also function as obstacles to positivity resonance. As we'll see in the next section, your attunement to various opportunities for positive connection with others is supported not just by neural synchrony, but by the hormone oxytocin as well.

Biochemistries in Love

Oxytocin, which is nicknamed by some the "cuddle hormone" or the "love hormone," is actually more properly identified as a neuropeptide because it acts not just within your body but also within your brain. Oxytocin has long been known to play a key role in social bonding and attachment. Clear evidence of this first emerged from experiments with a monogamous breed of prairie voles: Oxytocin, when dripped into one animal's brain in the presence of the opposite sex, creates in that animal a long-lasting preference to remain together with the other, cuddled up side by side, behavior taken as evidence that oxytocin sparked the formation of a powerful social bond between them. In humans, oxytocin surges during sexual intercourse for both men and women, and, for women, during childbirth and lactation, pivotal inter-personal moments that stand to forge new social bonds or cement existing ones. The natural blasts of oxytocin during such moments are so large and powerful that for many years they all but blinded scien-tists to the more subtle ebb and flow of oxytocin during more typical day-to-day activities, like playing with your kids, getting to know your new neighbor, or striking a deal with a new business partner. Technical obstacles also needed to be cleared. Decades after oxytocin's role in monogamous prairie voles had been amply charted, scientists studying human biochemistry still struggled to find ways to reliably and nonin-vasively measure and manipulate oxytocin during natural behavior. Scientific understanding of oxytocin's role in your everyday social life could not advance without more practical research tools at hand.

Dramatic new evidence of oxytocin's power to shape your social life first surfaced in Europe, where laws permitted the use of a synthetic form of oxytocin, available as a nasal spray, for investigational pur-poses. Among the first of these studies was one in which 128 men from Zurich played the so-called trust game with real monetary outcomes on the line. At random, these men were assigned to either the role of "investor" or the role of "trustee," and each was given an equivalent pot of starting funds. Investors made the first move in the game. They could give some, all, or none of their allocated funds to the trustee. During the transfer of funds, the experimenter tripled their investment while letting the trustee know how much the investors had originally transferred. Trustees made the next move. They could give some, all, or none of their new allotment of funds (the investors' tripled investment plus their own original allocation) back to investors. The structure of the game puts investors, but not trustees, at risk. If an investor chose to entrust the other guy with his investment, he risked receiving nothing in return if the trustee chose to selfishly keep the entire monetary gain for himself. But if the trustee was fair, they could each double their money.

Prior to playing this trust game, using a double-blind research design, participants received either oxytocin or an inert placebo by nasal spray. The effect of this single intranasal blast of oxytocin on the outcome of the trust game was dramatic: The number of investors who trusted their entire allotment to their trustee more than doubled. Interestingly, related research using this same trust game showed that the mere act of being entrusted with another person's money raises the trustee's naturally occurring levels of oxytocin, and that the greater the trustee's oxytocin rise, the more of his recent windfall he sacrificed back to the investor. The neuropeptide oxytocin, then, steers the actions of both the investor and the trustee, shaping both trust and reciprocity. These findings suggest that through synchronous oxytocin surges, trust and cooperation can quickly become mutual.

Since the original study on oxytocin and the trust game was published in *Nature* in 2005, variations on it have abounded. We now know, for instance, that oxytocin doesn't simply make people more trusting with money, it also makes them far more trusting—a whopping 44 percent more trusting—with confidential information about themselves. Interestingly, the simple act of sharing an important secret from your life with someone you just met increases your naturally circulating levels of oxytocin, which in turn raises your confidence that you can trust that person to guard your privacy. Thankfully, we also know that oxytocin does not induce trust indiscriminately, making people gullible and therefore open to exploitation. The effects of oxytocin on trust turn out to be quite sensitive to interpersonal cues, like those subtle signs that tip you off that another may be the gambling type or irresponsible in other ways. Rest assured, then, if oxytocin spray were to be aerated through your workplace ventilation system, you'd still maintain your shrewd attunement to subtle signs that suggest whether someone is worthy of your trust or not.

Researchers have since moved on to examine the effects of oxytocin on people's sensitivities to the subtle social cues that signal whether or not trust is warranted. From this work, I can tell you that, under the influence of oxytocin, you attend more to people's eyes and become specifically more attuned to their smiles, especially subtle ones. Perhaps because of the closer attention you pay to peoples' smiles and eyes, you become a better judge of their feelings and view people on the whole as more attractive and trustworthy. You also become particularly sensitized to environmental cues linked to positive social connections—for instance, to words like *love* and *kissing*. Researchers who have combined the use of oxytocin nasal spray (versus placebo) with brain imaging have also learned that oxytocin modulates the activity of your amygdala, the subcortical structure deep within your brain linked to emotional processing. Specifically, under the influence of a single blast of oxytocin nasal spray, the parts of your amygdala that tune in to threats are muted, whereas the parts that tune in to positive social opportunities are amplified. Reflecting these negativity-dampening effects, a single shot of oxytocin can also help you glide through stressful social situations, like giving an impromptu speech or discussing a conflict-ridden topic with your spouse. If you were to face these difficulties under the influence of oxytocin, studies suggest, you'd have less cortisol, the so-called stress hormone, coursing through you, and you'd behave more positively, both verbally, by disclosing your feelings, and nonverbally, by making more eye contact and friendly gestures. Related research shows that behaving kindly in these ways also raises your naturally occurring levels of oxytocin, which in turn curbs stress-induced rises in heart rate and blood pressure, reduces feelings of depression, and increases your pain thresholds.

More generally, oxytocin has been cast as a lead character in the mammalian *calm-and-connect* response, a distinct cascade of brain and body responses best contrasted to the far more familiar *fight-or-flight* response. Let's face it, meeting new people can be a little scary at times. Think back to what it was like for you on your first day at a new school or in a new job. You're suddenly thrown in with people you'd never heard of before. Even if a new person seems friendly, it's hard to know his true motives. Will he help you? Or will he instead take advantage of you in one way or another? Human greed, after all, runs rampant and can yield all manner of exploitation. Oxytocin appears both to *calm* fears that might steer you away from interacting with strangers and also to sharpen your skills for *connection*. As I've mentioned, though, oxytocin is far from blind. It indeed heightens your attunement to cues that signal whether others are sincere or not. Through eye contact and close attention to all manner of smiles—and the embodied simulations such visual intake triggers—your gut instincts about whom to trust and whom not to trust become more reliable. Rather than avoid all new people out of fear and suspicion, oxytocin helps you pick up on cues that signal another person's goodwill and guides you to approach them with your own. Because all people need social connections, not just to reproduce, but to survive and thrive in this world, oxytocin has been dubbed "the great facilitator of life."

It, too, can jump the gap between people such that someone else's oxytocin flow can trigger your own. A biochemical synchrony can then emerge that supports mutual engagement, care, and responsiveness.

The clearest evidence that oxytocin rises and falls in synchrony between people comes from studies of infants and their parents. When an infant and a parent—either mom or dad—interact, sometimes they are truly captivated by each other, and other times not. When an infant and parent do click, their coordinated motions and emotions show lots of mutual positive engagement. Picture moms or dads showering their baby with kisses, tickling their baby's tiny fingers and toes, smiling at their baby, and speaking to him or her in that high-pitched, singsong tone that scientists call *motherese.* These parents are superattentive. As they tickle and coo they're also closely tracking their baby's face for signs that their delight is mutual. In step with their parent's affectionate antics, these attentive babies babble, coo, smile, and giggle. Positivity resonates back and forth between them. Micro-moments of love blossom.

Of course, not every infant-parent interaction is so rosy. Some pairs show little mutual engagement. Some moms and dads rarely make eye contact with their infants and emit precious little positivity, either verbally or nonverbally. These pairs are simply less attuned to each other, less connected. And in those rare moments when they are engaged, the vibe that joins them is distinctly more negative. They connect over mutual distress or indifference, rather than over mutual affection.

It turns out that positive behavioral synchrony—the degree to which an infant and a parent (through eye contact and affectionate touch) laugh, smile, and coo together—goes hand in hand with oxytocin synchrony. Researchers have measured oxytocin levels in the saliva of dads, moms, and infants both before and after a videotaped, face-to-face parent-infant interaction. For infant-parent pairs who show mutual positive engagement, oxytocin levels also come into sync. Without such engagement, however, no oxytocin synchrony emerges.

Positivity resonance, then, can be viewed as the doorway through which the exquisitely attuned biochemical tendencies of one generation influence those of the next generation to form lasting, often lifelong bonds. Knowing, too, that oxytocin can ebb and flow in unison among non-kin—even among brand-new acquaintances just learning to trust each other—micro-moments of love, of positivity resonance, can also be viewed as the doorways through which caring and compassionate communities are forged. Love, we know, builds lasting resources. Oxytocin, studies show, swings the hammer.

This core tenet of my broaden-and-build theory—that love builds lasting resources—finds support in a fascinating program of research on . . . rodents. It turns out that rat moms and their newborn pups show a form of positive engagement and synchrony analogous to that of human parents with their infants. Sensitive parenting in a rat mom, however, is conveyed by her attentively licking and grooming her newborn pups. When a rat mom licks and grooms her pup, it increases the pup's sensitivity to oxytocin, as indicated, for instance, by the number of oxytocin receptors deep within the pup's amygdala, as well as within other subcortical brain regions. Sure enough, these well-groomed—or I dare say well-*loved*—rat pups grow up to have calmer demeanors; they're less skittish, more curious. The researchers can be certain that it's the experiences of loving connection that determine the brain and behavioral profiles of the next generation (that is, their oxytocin receptors and calm demeanors)—and not simply shared genes—because cross-fostering studies show the same patterns of results. That is, even when a rat mom raises a newborn pup that is not her own, her maternal attention still forecasts that pup's brain sensitivity to oxytocin and whether it grows up to be anxious or calm.

Touring Vagus

Who you are today is also shaped by the third biological character that I want you to meet: your tenth cranial nerve. This key conduit connects your brain to your body and is also called your vagus nerve (sounds like Vegas, as in Las Vegas). It emerges from your brain stem deep within your skull and, although it makes multiple stops at your various internal organs, perhaps most significantly it connects your brain to your heart. You already know that your heart rate shoots up when you feel insulted or threatened—registering the ancestral fight-or-flight response—but you may not know that it's your vagus nerve that eventually soothes your racing heart, by orchestrating (together with oxytocin) the equally ancestral calm-and-connect response.

Keeping in mind that love *is* connection, you should know that your vagus nerve is a biological asset that supports and coordinates your experiences of love. Completely outside of your awareness, your vagus nerve stimulates tiny facial muscles that better enable you to make eye contact and synchronize your facial expressions with another person. It even adjusts the minuscule muscles of your middle ear so you can better track the other person's voice against any background noise. In these exquisitely subtle yet consequential ways, your vagus nerve increases the odds that the two of you will connect, upping your chances for positivity resonance.

Scientists can measure the strength of your vagus nerve—your biological aptitude for love—simply by tracking your heart rate in conjunction with your breathing rate. Specifically, I can look at the degree to which your heart rate, as tracked by sensors placed on your lowest ribs, is patterned by your breathing rate, as revealed by an expandable bellows that encircles your rib cage. This pattern is called *vagal tone*. Like muscle tone, the higher your vagal tone, the better.

In addition to putting the brakes on the big jumps in your heart rate that may be caused by stress, fear, or exertion, your vagus nerve also increases the routine efficiency of your heart, beat by beat, or more precisely, breath by breath. The human heart rate tends to run fairly high, as if we're always on guard for the next danger that might be hidden around the corner. When you're breathing in, a fast heart rate is an efficient heart rate. After all, each successive heartbeat during an in-breath circulates more freshly oxygenated blood throughout your brain and body. Yet when you're breathing out, a fast heart rate is not all that helpful because your supply of freshly oxygenated blood is waning. Here again, your vagus nerve steps in to help out. It can very gently apply the brake on your heart while you exhale, slowing your heart rate down a small degree. In turn your vagus nerve can gently let up on the brake while you inhale, letting your naturally high heart rate resume to grab all the oxygenated blood that it can get. This creates a subtle yet healthy pattern of cardiac arrhythmia: Your heart rate speeds up a bit when you inhale and slows down a bit when you exhale. This is the pattern that reflects your vagal tone, the strength or condition of your vagus nerve. It characterizes the nimbleness with which your primitive, nonconscious brain holds the reins on your galloping heart.

I give you this quick tour of vagus because this conduit within you, between your brain and your heart, has a story to tell about how attuned you are to sources of love in your midst. It even makes a quiet prediction about what illnesses may beset you and how long you're likely to live. Your biological propensities for love and health, as we shall see, are intimately intertwined. Measured at rest, vagal tone also tends to be extraordinarily stable over time. For most people, it remains roughly the same year after year, rhythmically channeling them toward loneliness or social prosperity, sickness or health.

That's because people with higher vagal tone, science has shown, are more flexible across a whole host of domains—physical, mental, and social. They simply adapt better to their ever-shifting circumstances, albeit completely at nonconscious levels. Physically, they regulate their internal bodily processes more efficiently, like their glucose levels and inflammation. Mentally, they're better able to regulate their attention and emotions, even their behavior. Socially, they're especially skillful in navigating interpersonal interactions and in forging positive connections with others. By definition, then, they experience more micro-moments of love. It's as though the agility of the conduit between their brains and hearts—as reflected in their high vagal tone—allows them to be exquisitely agile, attuned, and flexible as they navigate the ups and downs of day-to-day life and social exchanges. High vagal tone, then, can be taken as high loving potential. Indeed, this is what doctoral student Bethany Kok and I have found: Compared to people with lower vagal tone, those with higher vagal tone experience more love in their daily lives, more moments of positivity resonance.

You might now be wondering whether you're one of the lucky ones blessed with high vagal tone. If you are, that's great. Yet even if you're not advantaged with high vagal tone today, the latest science gives plenty of reason for hope. Just as you can build muscle tone through regular physical exercises, you can build vagal tone through regular emotional exercises of the kind I share in part II of this book. The key, once again, is the power of love.

My students and I work together in what I call the PEP Lab, or the Positive Emotions and Psychophysiology Laboratory. Not long ago, we conducted an experiment on the effects of learning the ancient mind-training practice of loving-kindness meditation. Our study participants visited the PEP Lab at the University of North Carolina one by one, and we measured their vagal tone while they sat and relaxed for a few minutes. At the end of this initial laboratory testing session, we instructed participants how to log on to the study website each evening to record their emotions and social connections of the day. A few weeks later, by random assignment, we determined which participants would learn loving-kindness meditation and which would not. All would continue to monitor their day-to-day emotions and social connections using our study website. Months later, weeks after the meditation workshop ended, one by one we invited all participants back to the PEP Lab, where we again measured their vagal tone under the same resting conditions as before.

In May 2010, I had the immense honor of presenting the results of this experiment directly to His Holiness the Fourteenth Dalai Lama. A handful of scientists were invited to a private meeting to brief His Holiness on their latest discoveries about the effects of mind-training. After briefly describing to His Holiness the functions of the vagus nerve and the concept of vagal tone, I shared what my team and I had discovered in this most recent study: that vagal tone—which is commonly taken to be as stable an attribute as your adult height—actually improves significantly with mind-training. Here is your evidence-based reason for hope: No matter what your biological capacity for love is today, you can bolster that capacity by next season.

For it was those study participants who had been assigned at random to learn loving-kindness meditation who changed the most. They devoted scarcely more than an hour of their time each week to the practice. Yet within a matter of months, completely unbeknownst to them, their vagus nerves began to respond more readily to the rhythms of their breathing, emitting more of that healthy arrhythmia that is the fingerprint of high vagal tone. Breath by breath—loving moment by loving moment—their capacity for positivity resonance matured. Moreover, through painstaking statistical analyses, we pinpointed that those who experienced the most frequent positivity resonance in connection with others showed the biggest increases in vagal tone. Love literally made people healthier.

Upward Spirals Unleashed

It's time now to step back from isolated scientific findings and take in the big picture. Recall that your body's positivity resonance operates within a much larger system. Along with love and all the other positive emotions, this system also includes your enduring resources—your physical health, your social bonds, your personality traits, and your resilience. Having assets like these certainly makes life easier, and more satisfying. In addition, though, such resources also serve as booster shots that increase the frequency and intensity of your micro-moments of positivity resonance. Love built those resources in you, and those resources in turn boost your experiences of love. This is not a simple case of cause and effect. The causal arrow instead runs in both directions at once, creating the dynamic and reciprocal causality that drives self-sustaining trajectories of growth. Through love, you become a better version of yourself. And as your better self, you experience love more readily. It is in this dance between your enduring resources and your micro-moments of love that life-giving upward spirals are born.

Looking out from this more encompassing vantage point, let's revisit the scientific findings I shared with His Holiness the Dalai Lama. By learning how to self-generate love, you can raise your vagal tone. And with higher vagal tone, your attention and actions become more agile, more attuned to the people in your midst. You become better able to forge the interpersonal connections that give rise to positivity resonance. Through vagal tone, then, love begets love.

Likewise, evidence suggests that positivity resonance raises your oxytocin levels. And under the influence of oxytocin, you grow calmer, more attuned to others, friendlier, and more open. Here, too, your skills for forging connections sharpen, which increases your ability to cultivate positivity resonance. Through oxytocin as well then, love begets love.

Recall, too, that positive connections with others create neural coupling, or synchronous brain activity between people. With repetition, positivity resonance also produces structural changes in the brain, for instance, rendering the threat-detecting amygdala more sensitive to the calming influence of oxytocin. While much of the work on neuroplasticity—the brain's capacity to change with experience—comes from research on nonhuman animals, tantalizing evidence has also recently emerged from studies of humans. Becoming a parent, for instance, not only opens the door for parent-infant positivity resonance but also appears to usher in structural changes in brain regions that facilitate positivity resonance. This research shows how love reroutes the neural wiring of your brain, making it more likely that you'll have healthy habits and healthy social bonds in the future. Through brain plasticity, too, then, love begets love.

Plasticity, or openness to change, characterizes your body's cells as well. New cells are born within you all the time. Even now, as you take time to read this book, new cells are coming online within you, taking their predetermined place within the massive orchestra of communication and mutual influence that you call your body. Yet not everything about the birth of your new cells is scripted in advance by your DNA. Some aspects are open to contextual influences signaled by the changing biochemicals that course through you. If you feel lonely and disconnected from others, for instance, your circulating levels of the stress hormone cortisol will rise. Your cortisol levels, in turn, signal your immune system to alter the way your genes are expressed in your next-generation white blood cells, specifically making them less sensitive to cortisol. When this happens, studies show, your inflammatory response becomes more chronic, less responsive to cues that a crises situation has subsided. This is how, over time, chronic feelings of loneliness can weaken people's immune systems and open the door to inflammation-based chronic illnesses, like cardiovascular disease and arthritis. The data go further to suggest that *feeling* isolated or unconnected to others does more bodily damage than *actual* isolation, suggesting that painful emotions drive the bodily systems that in turn steer you toward dire health outcomes. By tracking how your emotions—and the biochemical changes they trigger—alter gene expression within your immune system, the tools of molecular biology now show how a lack of love compromises your immunity and your health.

Even so, there is ample reason for hope. In countless social exchanges each day, your potential to alleviate loneliness with love is enormous. Your biology, as we have seen in this chapter, enacts your experiences of love. Even so, you have more control over your biology than you realize. Once you grasp the pathways and common obstacles to love, you gain a measure of control over the biochemicals that bathe your cells. To a considerable extent, you orchestrate the messages that your cells hear, the messages that tell your cells whether to grow toward health or toward illness. My collaborators and I are just beginning to chart the ways that oxytocin and other ingredients that make up love's biochemistry trigger healthy changes in gene expression that may foster physical and mental well-being. Also through the plasticity of your cells, we hypothesize, love begets love.

All of love's unseen biological transformations—in your brain rhythms, your blood stream, your vagus nerve, and your cells—in turn ready you to become even more attuned to love, better equipped, biologically, to cultivate moments of positivity resonance with others. This latent biological upward spiral is a powerful force: Love can affect you so deeply that it reshapes you from the inside out and by doing so alters your destiny for further loving moments. With each micro-moment of love, then, as I feature in chapter 4, you climb another rung on the spiraling ladder that lifts you up to your higher ground, to richer and more compassionate social relationships, to greater resilience and wisdom, and to better physical health.

Love 2.0: The View from Here

Put simply, your body was designed for love, and to benefit from loving. Human bodies become healthier when repeatedly nourished by positivity resonance with others, with the result that human communities become more harmonious and loving. This clear win-win arrangement is written into our DNA.

Everyday micro-moments of positivity resonance add up and ultimately transform your life for the better. You become healthier, happier, and more socially integrated. Your wisdom and resilience grow as well. Having more resources like these in turn equips you to experience micro-moments of love more readily and more often, with further broaden-and-build benefits. Your body, as biology has it, energizes and sustains this upward spiral. The unseen and heretofore unsung biology of love affects everything you feel, think, do, and become.

This isn't all about you, though. Love, as we've seen, is not a solo act. The benefits that unfold from love for you, then, also unfold for all those who are party to positivity resonance. Seen from this vantage point, emotional and physical health are contagious. Indeed, studies of actual social networks show that, over time, happiness spreads through whole communities. Your friend's coworker's sister's happiness actually stands to elevate your own happiness.

The new science of love makes it clear that your body acts as a verb. Sure enough, some aspects of your body remain relatively constant day in and day out, like your DNA or your eye color. But your brain continually registers your ever-changing circumstances and in turn orchestrates the flux of biochemicals that reshape your body and brain from the inside out, at the cellular level. Your body takes action. Most notably, it broadcasts everything you feel—your moments of positivity resonance or their lack—to every part of you, readying you for either health or illness and rendering you either more or less equipped for loving connection.

I hope you've found it mind-opening to zoom in on the biology of love in action—the ways positivity resonance can synchronize your brain and oxytocin waves with those of another, and how, over time, it can build the capacity of your vagus nerve, which points you toward physical health, social skill, and overall well-being. Touring love's biology, I've found, can help ground an otherwise nebulous concept, a concept all too often draped in a gauze of rainbows, unicorns, and cupids taking aim at cartoon hearts. Even so, a fully upgraded view of love can't stop with biology. It demands that you zoom out as well, to appreciate the ways that love also infuses all that lies beyond your physical body, its effects on your actions and relationships, your wisdom and your spiritual potential. For it is these more encompassing changes that spring up in love's path that can motivate you to create a better life for yourself. Before moving on to part II, then, in which I offer practical guidance on how to seed love more readily, I want to show you what's new in the bigger picture that is emerging from the science of love—a picture that shows exactly how creating more positivity resonance in your life influences all that you feel, think, do, and become.

CHAPTER 4

Love's Ripples

YOU ARE MADE IN THE IMAGE OF WHAT YOU DESIRE.

—Thomas Merton

So far I have urged you to look at love differently, to envision and appreciate it from your body's perspective, as micro-moments of positivity resonance. In this chapter, we'll continue to unwrap love's many gifts as I take you deeper into the science of love. You'll come away with an appreciation for love's mind-set and actions, as well as the long-term growth it nourishes.

Learning to see love's ripple effects can be a lifeline. The signs of love, which for your ancestors were perhaps among the most enticing objects in the landscape, can be so subtle by modern standards that you can miss them completely. If you rush through your morning routine, for instance, inhale breakfast and brush your teeth while driving to work, plow through your in-box and mushrooming to-do list, run to meeting after meeting right up to the end of your workday, race through the grocery store, fix a quick dinner for your kids, send them off to bed, only to collapse in your own bed to fret about the marathon day you face tomorrow, how do you find the time or the energy to kindle those fragile states of positivity resonance?

Thinking

Nearly sixty years ago, a decade before the counterculture of the 1960s erupted throughout the United States and beyond, Aldous Huxley famously described his first experience with psychedelic drugs, in his controversial 1954 book, *The Doors of Perception*. The book's title cast back to the metaphorical language of English poet and printmaker William Blake's 1790 book, *The Marriage of Heaven and Hell*, and inspired the name of the 1960s American rock band the Doors. Blake wrote:

> If the doors of perception were cleansed every thing would appear to man as it is, infinite. For man has closed himself up, till he sees all things through narrow chinks of his cavern.

Building on Blake's metaphor, Huxley likened the human brain to a reducing valve. It functions to limit your awareness to only those perceptions, ideas, and memories that might be useful for your survival at any given moment, eliminating all else. Although narrowed awareness prevents you from becoming overwhelmed by a flood of images and impressions, to some extent, it can become an overlearned habit, a self-limiting cavern. By comparing—through the use of language—your own reduced experiences of the world to the reduced experiences of others, you can become convinced that your limited awareness represents the reality of the world. Huxley writes:

> Most people, most of the time, know only what comes through the reducing valve and is consecrated as genuinely real by the local language. Certain persons, however, seem to be born with a kind of bypass that circumvents the reducing valve. In others temporary bypasses may be acquired either spontaneously, or as the result of deliberate "spiritual exercises," or through hypnosis, or by means of drugs.

Huxley's hypothesis that the doors of perception can temporarily swing open wider than usual—even seemingly spontaneously—is now confirmed by brain imaging experiments. Importantly, however, you don't need drugs, hypnosis, or lofty spiritual experiences to open those doors. Sometimes all it takes is a little positivity.

Through functional magnetic resonance imaging (fMRI), we can track dynamic changes in blood flow within people's brains as they perform various mental tasks. Ample past work of this sort pinpoints a distinct brain area that reacts to human faces (the extrastriate fusiform face area, or FFA) as well as a separate brain area that reacts to places (the parahippocampal place area, or PPA). A clever experiment capitalized on this knowledge of brain specificity by asking study participants to decide whether each successive face, shown to them in a central location across a series of slides, was male or female, and to ignore all else. This task was simple; the right answer was always abundantly clear. What made the study more interesting was that each face was embedded within a larger picture of a place, specifically the curb shot of a house, much like you might see in a real estate ad. In theory, if the doors of perception were opened wide, the conjoint images used in this task (that is, the faces nested within houses) would excite both the face (FFA) and the place (PPA) areas of the brain. If the doors of perception were largely closed, however, perhaps only the face area of the brain would become activated.

At random, blocks of these conjoint images were preceded by positive, neutral, or negative images, all rather mild. The images used to create positive emotions, for instance, showed cute puppies or delectable desserts. By tracking blood flow within the FFA and PPA, the researchers could thus compare how wide or narrow each participant's perceptual field of view was under the influence of different emotional states. The results were clear. Negative emotions narrowed people's perception, reflected by significantly reduced blood flow within the PPA. Put differently, when feeling bad, people were great at following the task instructions—they ignored all that surrounded the faces so thoroughly that their brains barely registered the presence of the houses. The results for neutral states were much the same. By contrast, positive emotions broadened perception, as reflected by increased blood flow within the PPA. In other words, on the heels of seeing puppies or cake, people's brains registered both the faces and the houses that encircled them. When feeling good, these data suggest, you can't help but pick up more of the contextual information that surrounds you. In Huxley's terms, positive emotions provide a temporary bypass that circumvents the reducing valve. This brain imaging study provides solid evidence that your doors of perception open wider than usual under positivity's influence.

A related and fascinating series of studies tested stroke patients beset with brain lesions that produce visual neglect, or the inability to perceive and act on information presented within the visual field opposite the brain lesion. A patient with lesions in his right parietal cortex, for instance, is literally unaware of images and words presented within his left visual field. Using both controlled behavioral tasks as well as brain imaging, researchers discovered that when such patients listen to pleasant music, they overcome their loss of awareness. That is, they are temporarily able to see and act on information that simply doesn't register for them while not listening to music, or when listening to music they don't like.

One point I wish to make here is that your experiences of love and other positive emotions need not bowl you over to bust open your perceptual gates. Studies like these show that far less intense positive emotional experiences—like taking in inspiring images or listening to upbeat music—open those same doors. What Huxley described as temporary and spontaneous bypasses that circumvent the reducing valve turn out to be the orderly perceptual byproducts of commonplace positive emotions. Indeed, with the emotional know-how I offer you in part II, you'll be able to infuse any day or activity with expanded modes of consciousness.

As positive emotions open your doors of perception, you become better equipped to connect with others. Your mind's typical modus operandi, after all, is to be rather self-centered. Your thoughts tend to revolve around what you yourself need and want, and your own concerns. Self-absorption can become ever more extreme when you feel threatened in some manner. By contrast, my collaborators and I have conducted experiments that show how when you feel good, you see beyond your cocoon of self-interest to become more aware of others, more likely to focus on their needs, wants, and concerns, and to see things from their perspective.

Once you actually forge a connection with someone else to create a shared moment of positivity resonance, the doors of perception widen further, in unique ways. First and foremost, you come to view one another as part of a unified whole—a single "us" rather than two separate "me's." And compared to other positive emotions, love stretches your circle of concern to include others to a greater degree. Love carries its characteristic *care* and *concern* for others, a warmth and genuine interest that inspire you to extend your trust and compassion to them. In fact, a recent attempt to pinpoint the most essential feature of love— a feature that spans all varieties of love, from romantic to parental to platonic—identifies such care and concern, expressed abstractly as your "investment in the well-being of another, for his or her own sake," as an essential, always-present fingerprint of love. Love's characteristic care and concern drive you to attend more closely to other people's needs and help you vigilantly take in and evaluate incoming information so that you can protect them from harm. Love also leaves you with more positive automatic reactions to the persons with whom you've shared micro-moments of positivity resonance the next time you meet, an implicit goodwill that paves the way for future experiences of positivity resonance with them. Indeed, studies show that as you learn to cultivate micro-moments of love more readily, your everyday interactions with friends and coworkers become more lighthearted and enjoyable.

Simply put, love changes your mind.

Doing

If, like me, you are a product of Western culture, odds are you tend to see the mind and body as rather separate. "Thinking" seems like one thing, and "doing" quite another. Yet this sharp distinction is only an illusion. New science makes clear that each is cut from the same cloth. Knowing then that love alters your mind's modus operandi, swinging open your doors of perception wider, allowing you to recognize your unity with others, care for them, and capitalize on your combined strengths, should make it easier to understand how love alters your gestures and actions. For just as neuroscientific studies show that positive emotions open your perceptual awareness, kinematic studies by my collaborator Melissa Gross show that they also open your torso, literally expanding the (rib) cage in which your heart sits. When your mind and body are infused with good feelings, those feelings lift and expand your chest, a subtle nonverbal gesture that makes you more inviting to others, more open for connection.

Genuine good feelings also open up your face, as your lips stretch up and open into a smile, raising your cheeks to create (or deepen) the crow's feet at the corners of your eyes.

Any positive emotion can draw you to smile and carry yourself with a more open posture. And so any positive emotion can be taken by those around you as a sign to relax and connect. When someone feels safe enough to accept that invitation and joins you with his or her own heartfelt good feelings, love's positivity resonance fires up. The nonverbal gestures unique to these shared micro-moments of love eluded scientists for decades. In part, this reflected early methodological choices, like overreliance on posed expressions and still photographs. More recently, scientists have taken a more holistic and dynamic look at the spontaneous nonverbal expressions that flow between two people engaged in ordinary conversations infused with mutual positivity. Widening their approach has enabled scientists to uncover the unique nonverbal fingerprint of love.

Love, this new evidence shows, is characterized by four distinct nonverbal cues. The first cue, not surprisingly, is how often you and the other person each smile at each other, in the genuine, eye-crinkling manner. A second cue is the frequency with which you each use open and friendly hand gestures to refer to each other, like your outstretched palm. (Hostile hand gestures, like pointing or finger-wagging, are by definition excluded from this category of gestures.) A third cue is how often you each lean in toward each other, literally bringing your hearts closer together. The fourth cue is how often you each nod your head, a sign that you affirm and accept each other.

Taken together, these four nonverbal cues—smiles, gestures, leans, and nods—both emanate from a person's inner experiences of love and are read by others *as* love. Love, displayed in this way, also matters. It has force. It forecasts not only the social support people feel in their relationships but also how they deliver direct criticism, which (as I describe in a later section) has been found to predict the long-term stability of loving relationships. These four nonverbal gestures are thus a dependable and consequential sign of love.

Other nonverbal gestures can also reveal love—literally if the timing is right. For instance, when people come together and connect, their actions often come into sync, so that their hand movements and facial expressions mirror each other to a certain degree. Spontaneously synchronized gestures like these can make two separate individuals come to look like one well-orchestrated unit. This phenomenon extends beyond pairs: Just as birds migrate in flocks and fish swim in schools, large groups of people at times spontaneously move in synchronized ways. You can begin to appreciate how a football game or a concert can trigger positivity resonance on a grand scale. Through intense synchronized cheers, chants, marches, or dance, these and other ways of keeping in time together forge deep feelings of group solidarity—even throughout an entire arena.

I experienced this powerfully when I attended my first major college football game, late in August 1995, in one of the world's largest outdoor stadiums, the University of Michigan's beloved "Big House," which seats more than one hundred thousand. I was new to the University of Michigan faculty and not a sports fan of any sort. Even so, a colleague of mine urged my husband and me to attend the opening game of the football season, because "that's what we do here." So we went, not expecting anything in particular. The game—the Pigskin Classic against the University of Virginia and debut for new head coach Lloyd Carr—turned out to be one for the record books. Although Michigan had been favored, well into the fourth quarter, the Virginia Cavaliers had the Wolverines shut out at 0–17. Somehow, though, the Wolverines pulled off two touchdowns that put the score at 12–17. Yet their failure to kick in extra points would leave them needing yet another touchdown to win the game. With fewer than three minutes remaining, they scrambled to make several attempts, each one thwarted by the strong Virginia defense. Then, with just four seconds left on the clock, Michigan quarterback Scott Dreisbach threw a Hail Mary pass to Mercury Hayes. This was clearly the Wolverine's last hope, and the stadium fell into near-silence with the tension of it all. Running deep into the end zone, Hayes caught the ball with his left foot just brushing the turf before sheer momentum forced him out of bounds. It was an absolutely unbelievable touchdown! Coach Carr's new team had achieved the biggest Wolverine comeback to date. The stadium exploded into celebratory cheers, high fives, and backslapping hugs. Virtually every *body* present was part of one massive burst of celebration. I've never experienced anything like it in my life—before or since. More than one hundred thousand people—all strangers to us at the time—were sharing the same boisterous euphoria (save for a few Cavalier fans). I'd easily call it mass positivity resonance. And what a conversion experience: From that moment on, I was a die-hard Michigan football fan. For the first time in my life, I devoured the sports pages, donned maize and blue, and fretted if I had to miss a game. That single game cemented me within my new community.

Even far subtler forms of behavioral synchrony than this can change people. Suppose from where you sit on your front porch, you spot two of your neighbors chatting near their mailboxes. Although you can't quite make out what they're saying, their gestures make clear that they're engaged in a lively exchange. As one raises her brows in disbelief, so does the other. Moments later, each touches her own face, one after the other. My doctoral student Tanya Vacharkulksemsuk has painstakingly coded behavioral synchrony like this as two strangers meet for the first time. What we've learned is that when people move together as one orchestrated unit, they later report that they experienced an embodied sense of rapport with each other—they say they felt alive, connected, with a mutual sense of warmth and trust as they conversed. Other studies concur. When synchrony is surreptitiously produced in experimental studies—by having people walk, tap, sing, sway, or rock together in time—it breeds liking, cooperation, and compassion, as well as success in joint action. By now, you'll recognize these various effects as pointing to positivity resonance, your body's definition of love. From the research you read about in chapter 3, you can also bet that the synchrony between your chatting neighbors runs deeper than what you can see with your own eyes. Odds are that their synchronized gestures both reflect and trigger synchrony in their brain and oxytocin activity as well.

Next I turn to the ripples that love spreads out over time. As you experience positivity resonance more often, day in and day out, it affects all that you become.

Becoming

Becoming Us. Consider your closest relationships—with your best friend, your spouse, your parent, or your child—the people with whom you feel so interwoven that you freely use words like *we* and *us* in everyday conversation. Yet those words didn't always fit. Even your closest relationships had a starting point prior to which *us* didn't apply. Odds are, positivity resonance was part of the origin story for each important relationship that you have today. Think back to those origins for a moment. Was the emotion you first shared together playful amusement or raucous joy? Was it mutual fascination or awe? Or was it instead a peaceful moment of serenity or shared relief? Maybe it was some other flavor on the positivity menu. Although it might be easier to call up the day you first met or "clicked" with your best friend or spouse, the generation-spanning bonds you share with a parent or child were also forged through accumulated micro-moments of felt security and affection, communicated variously through synchronized gaze, touch, and vocalizations. One after the other, micro-moments of positivity resonance like these formed the pathways toward the relationships that you now take for granted as the most solid sources of comfort, support, and companionship in your life.

The study that Tanya Vacharkulksemsuk conducted with me, described above, tells us that as relationships are first budding, two people begin to share not only their emotions but also their motions. Spontaneously and nonconsciously, they begin to gesture in synchrony, as a unified duo. Indeed, these nonverbal signs of unity forecast a shared subjective appreciation of oneness, connection, and an embodied sense of rapport. The more that positivity resonance orchestrates shared movements between people, the data show, the more likely a relationship is to take root. Following this logic further, some choices for first dates are better than others. Dancing or canoeing (assuming you each take up an oar) could be better bets for bonding than simply catching a movie or sharing a meal. The same would go for galvanizing a work team. Whether it's through initial icebreaker activities, a nature retreat, or ritualized ways of sharing good news and appreciations, the platforms you create for shared motions and positive emotions are what allow a team to gel.

The glue that positivity resonance offers isn't just for connecting once-strangers at the start of new relationships. It also further cements long-standing ties, making them even more secure and satisfying. Art and Elaine, a married couple living in Long Island, New York, learned this fact in a surprising way. They saw a poster in town recruiting couples to join a study on the "factors that affect relationships." Motivated more by curiosity than the promised thirty dollars, they called to sign up. They got more curious when the person on the phone asked them about a range of medical conditions that might prevent them from engaging in physical or aerobic activity. Their curiosity rose still higher when they met the researcher at the designated lab room on campus. It was set up more like a gymnastics room, with a large gymnasium mat rolled out across the floor, covering about thirty feet. Halfway down the mat, another fat mat was rolled up like a barricade, about three feet high. As part of the study, the researcher asked Art and Elaine to complete surveys and discuss a few topics together, like their next vacation and a future home improvement project, which she videotaped for later analysis. These tasks seemed simple enough and not altogether unexpected in a study of relationships. Yet they were flabbergasted when the researcher directed them to their next task. Indeed, their curiosity about the room setup erupted into outright chuckles of disbelief as the researcher used Velcro bands to tie Art's and Elaine's wrists and ankles together. She told them that their task was to crawl on their hands and knees as fast as they could to the far end of the mat and back, clearing the barrier in each direction. All the while, they'd need to hold a cylinder-shaped pillow off the floor without using their hands, arms, or teeth. If they could complete this absurd task in less than a minute, she told them, they'd win a bag of candy, something she said few couples before them had done.

It didn't take long for Art and Elaine to discover that they could only hold the pillow up by pressing it between their torsos, which made their bound-crawling all the more challenging. The whole event was hilarious. They toppled over several times, laughing uncontrollably. By their third attempt, they finally got their limbs into sync. They beat the clock and won the prize—all smiles and (once unbound) high fives!

It turned out that other couples who'd signed up for the study didn't have nearly as much fun as did Elaine and Art. By the flip of a coin, some couples got the same silly crawling assignment they did, whereas other couples were assigned to a far more mundane and slow-paced crawling task: Never bound by Velcro, each member of these couples took turns crawling very slowly across the mat, while rolling a ball ahead of them. Their snail's pace was enforced by a metronome, no less! What the researchers hypothesized—and would find here and in their other experiments—is that couples who were at random assigned to the fun-filled task that required both touch and behavioral synchrony actually came to love each other more deeply; they reported greater relationship quality on the follow-up surveys and showed more accepting and fewer hostile behaviors in their follow-on discussions. Engaging in this silly, childlike activity together actually deepened loving feelings and strengthened bonds, even in long-standing intimate relationships. Experiments like these explain the observation I made back in chapter 2, that couples who regularly do new and exciting (or even silly) things together have better-quality marriages.

At times, the impetus for sharing a positive emotion with a loved one might be some external activity, like a trip, or the silly assignment Art and Elaine were given in that laboratory study. Perhaps more frequently, however, there isn't any jointly experienced external trigger at all. Instead, one or the other of you starts the ball rolling by bringing your own positive emotion to your partner. Suppose your partner comes home after a long day at the office with good news to share about a breakthrough at work, or some recognition he or she received for a recent accomplishment. Through the well-worn lenses of self-absorption, you might take such disclosures as simply your partner's way of explaining his or her own good mood. Or more cynically, you might take it as bragging. Yet through the lenses of connection, you're more likely to recognize disclosures like these as opportunities for positivity resonance, or new chances to stoke love and its benefits.

Whether or not the feeling of love ensues, studies of couples show, hinges a lot on how you respond to your partner's positive expressions. Do you lean in toward them? Or do you shy away? Do you meet them in kind, expressing your own genuine positive emotions in turn? Or do you shrug them off as irrelevant or point out the potential downsides? Researchers who have carefully coded couples' responsiveness to each other in situations like these find that those who capitalize on each other's good fortunes, by responding to their partner's good news with their own enthusiasm and outward encouragement, have higher-quality relationships. They enjoy more intimacy, commitment, and passion with each other, and find their relationship to be more satisfying overall. In other words, when one partner's good news and enthusiasm ignites to become the other partner's good news and enthusiasm as well, a micro-moment of positivity resonance is born. Studies show that these moments of back-and-forth positivity resonance are not only satisfying in and of themselves, providing boosts to each partner's own mood, but they also further fortify the relationship, making it more intimate, committed, and passionate next season than it is today. Another person's expression of positivity, from this perspective, can be seen as a bid for connection and love. If you answer that bid, the ensuing positivity resonance will nourish you both.

Two ways to fortify your intimate relationships, then, are to bring your own good news home to share, and to celebrate your partner's good news. Regardless of who initiates, the key is to connect to create a shared experience, one that allows positivity to resonate between you for a spell, momentarily synchronizing your gestures and your biorhythms and creating the warm glow of mutual care. Sharing or celebrating the joy of some personal good fortune is certainly not the only way to foster the micro-moments of love that strengthen relationships. Any positive emotion, if shared, can do the same.

In collaboration with my colleague Sara Algoe, for instance, I've explored how kindness and appreciation flow back and forth in couples, creating tender moments of positivity resonance that also serve to nourish intimacy and relationship growth. In particular, we've examined how people habitually express appreciation to their partners. We learned from this work that some people tend to say "thanks" better than others. Genuine feelings of appreciation or gratitude, after all, well up when you recognize that someone else went out of his or her way to do something nice for you. Another way to say this is that the script for gratitude involves both a *benefit*, or kind deed, and a *benefactor*, the kind person behind the kind deed. Whereas many people express their appreciation to others by shining a spotlight on the benefit they received—the gift, favor, or the kind deed itself—we discovered that, by contrast, the best "thank-yous" simply use the benefit as a springboard toward shining a spotlight on the good qualities of the other person, their benefactor. Done well, then, expressing appreciation for your partner's kindness to you can become a kind gesture in return, one that conveys that you see and appreciate in your partner's actions his or her good and inspiring qualities.

How did we know that this is the best way to convey appreciation? Because compared to expressions that merely focus on benefits, those that also focus on benefactors make the partner who hears that "thanks" feel understood, cared for, and validated. And this good feeling—the feeling that their partner really "gets" them and cherishes them—allows people to walk around each day feeling better about themselves and better about their relationship. And in six months' time, it forecasts becoming even more solid and satisfied with their relationship.

Saying "thanks" well then isn't just a matter of being polite, it's a matter of being loving, and becoming a stronger version of what together you call "us."

Becoming Resilient. How do you handle stress and strain? Do you at times feel shattered by adversity? Crushed during hard times? After an emotional hurricane hits, do you wallow in negativity or stumble about to pick up the pieces of your former self? Or perhaps, based on past experience, you've tried to steel yourself against any future emotional disasters by increasing the heft of your defensive armor. Maybe you find the prospects of being shattered so disturbing that you've striven to be bulletproof.

By and large, your protective armor works well. It shields you from routine emotional blows and keeps you from crumbling into self-pity or otherwise becoming devastated by negativity. Yet this sort of self-protection comes at a price. It can shield you from the especially good stuff as well. Sure enough, within your own walled-off cavern, you can and do readily experience genuine positive emotions, say, of interest, pride, inspiration, or peace. Yet your ability to share these good feelings with others is compromised. Put differently, in making yourself bulletproof you may also numb yourself to possibilities for true connection. Being less able to connect, in turn, shuts you and your body out from registering and creating opportunities for positivity resonance, which are both life-giving and health-conferring.

To be sure, there are more ways to face emotional storms than to be flattened by or impervious to them. For more than a decade, my students and I have studied the psychological habits of resilient people. These are the ones who, when faced with emotional storms, bend without breaking and bounce back to weather the next storm even better equipped than they were for the last.

Resilient people, our studies have shown, are emotionally agile. They neither steel themselves against negativity, nor wallow in it. Instead, they meet adversity with clear eyes, superbly attuned to the nuances of their ever-changing circumstances. This allows them to effortlessly calibrate their reactions to their circumstances, meeting them with a fitting emotional response, neither overblown nor insensitive. When the circumstances warrant, they can be moved to tears or shaken. They don't defend themselves against bad feelings like these. Yet neither do they overly identify with them. Rather, their negative emotions rise up, like an ocean wave, and then dissolve. Strong emotions move through them, which allows them to move on in their wake.

What allows resilient people to be so agile? As I detailed in *Positivity*, their agility stems from their steady diet of positive emotion. Each successive experience of positive emotion, after all, gives them a fresh experience of openness. Resilient people come to better register and appreciate the larger contexts of life, which allows them to respond to emotional upsets with more perspective, flexibility, and grace. Our data indeed show that life gets better and better for people who experience more positive emotions than others, not simply because positive emotions feel good, but because good feelings nourish resilience. Being better equipped to manage inevitable ups and downs is what makes life itself more satisfying. Resilient people are more hopeful, more excited to rise up to challenges, more appreciative of their many blessings. These positive emotions, our lab experiments show, help flush out any lingering aftereffects of negativity within you. They dismantle or undo the grip that negative emotions can gain on your mind and body alike, the grip that—when too long-lasting—can make you vulnerable to illness and even early death.

The science of resilience has deepened considerably within the last decade. We've seen not only a groundswell of scientific interest in the topic but also a fundamental shift in how resilience is viewed. Before, experts saw resilience in the face of adversity as a rare human feat; we now know that, in the context of a well-functioning emotion system, resilience can be normative, or standard. We also now know that people's levels of resilience are not set in stone, or DNA. They can be improved through experience and training. So as you practice the skills, detailed in part II of this book, to increase your daily diet of positivity resonance, you'll become more resilient, too, better able to adapt to life's inevitable upsets and adversity.

Resilient people don't go it alone. Even as kids, they were especially adept at using humor to get others to smile or laugh along with them. In these and other ways, resilient kids are adept at stoking positivity resonance with their friends and caretakers. Developmental psychologists contend that resilient kids cultivated this capacity through their experiences of sensitive parenting as infants. Some parents, more than others, are adept at interpreting and matching their infant's ever-changing emotional states. They can smoothly repair their infant's distress to create micro-moments of positivity resonance. These more sensitive and attuned parents help their children to develop their own store of self-soothing techniques, coping mechanisms that ultimately allow the children to become ever more self-sufficient as they grow older. Resilience, then, doesn't just originate from positive emotions; it originates from positivity resonance.

More often than not, you don't face stress and adversity by yourself, alone. You face it together with others. Divorce strains entire families after all; earthquakes rock whole communities; wars upend entire nations; and increasingly, an economic collapse can strain an entire planet. When resilient, you know just when to lend a hand, an ear, or a shoulder, and just when to seek out these and other sources of comfort and steadiness from others. Resilience, then, is not simply a property of individuals. It's equally a property of social groups—of families, communities, nations, even the entire global community. Facing tough times together and well, researchers suggest, requires precisely that suite of personal and collective resources that micro-moments of positivity resonance serve to build. Social resilience becomes all the more likely when you and those with whom you share fate—at home, at work, or in your community or nation—are able and motivated to connect with one another, to take one another's perspectives, and to communicate care and respect just as readily as you recognize it when others convey their positive regard to you. Such emotional agility and fluid communication within groups isn't easy to achieve, of course. Any brief reflection on politics, gossip, or any manner of nitpicking can remind you how easy it is to smother the openness, tolerance, and trust needed to support social resilience. Yet knowing that successive moments of positivity resonance shore up and strengthen these necessary resources can help you see that social resilience emerges in the wake of love.

Close study of what makes some marriages more resilient than others bears this out. John Gottman, perhaps the world's leading scientific expert on emotions in marriage, tells couples that they can "bank" their shared positive emotions to help them through later tough times. Through decades of meticulous research, Gottman discovered that couples who experience higher ratios of positive to negative emotions with each other are better able to navigate disagreements and upsets. When discussing difficult topics, for instance, they tend to refrain from mirroring each other's distress and negativity with their own. Instead, they de-escalate any conflict (or potential conflict) by meeting their partner's negativity with something altogether different, often making some caring, affirming, or lighthearted comment or gesture that creates space for reflection. Put differently, couples with rich recent histories of positivity resonance are better equipped to defuse the emotional bombs that threaten them both.

You can "bank" positivity resonance and draw on it later because momentary experiences of love and other positive emotions build resources. In other words, the small investments you deposit in the so-called bank don't just sit there. They accumulate, earn interest, and pay out dividends in the form of durable resources that you can later draw on to face future adversity. Moreover, just as money earned in one arena can be spent in other arenas, the positivity resonance that you create in certain relationships can build personal resources—values, beliefs, and skills—that help you navigate all manner of social upsets and difficulties. Having a loving marriage, then, can help you be more resilient in your work team. Sharing more moments of positivity resonance in schools and neighborhoods, for instance, may help whole nations be more resilient during tough times.

Resilience matters now more than ever, both your personal resilience, as well as the collective resilience that you cultivate within your family, your community, your nation, and our world. No matter how resilient you are today, higher levels of resilience are readily within your grasp. That's because genuine positive emotions are available to you at any time. And when you connect with others over these good feelings, you create a positivity resonance that energizes and strengthens the metaphorical connective tissue that binds you. Love and resilience are renewable resources.

Becoming Wise. Imagine having at your fingertips all the knowledge and experience to allow you to properly discern which of the many paths ahead of you to take. Imagine how it would feel to so readily grasp just the right thing to do and the right way to do it. You can accept yourself fully, even in light of your shortcomings and missteps. You're able to shake free of your nagging self-criticism, worry, and rumination and enjoy the added mental capacity that this escape frees up. And you can now fully take in the whole of your surroundings. You effortlessly assess the core meanings of your current circumstances, as well as its more subtle, seemingly insignificant, details. Imagine not having to puzzle through how to make a good first impression, or how to add value to a group process. You can now understand the wide variety of people in your midst—and truly accept them. You intuitively understand their unique perspectives, know just what they want and need, and how best to connect with them. Imagine being able to glide through rough terrain—even complicated entanglements marked by suffering, uncertainty, or both—instinctively knowing how to move forward, while calming hearts and allaying fears, your own and those of others present.

We call people who meet these ideals wise. They have what

scientists call "expertise in the fundamental pragmatics of life." They judiciously draw on their past experiences and values to arrive at practical and fitting courses of action for themselves and others in nearly any situation. They not only grasp the human condition and the meaning of life but are also able to translate these lofty philosophical insights into down-to-earth plans and advice. Wise people, studies show, are especially discerning because they are able to see holistically and integrate seemingly contradictory perspectives to achieve balance and well-being in everyday life.

Broadened awareness, or being able to "see the big picture" and "connect the dots," can thus be viewed as a core facet of wisdom. The tightly controlled laboratory experiments (described earlier in this chapter) convincingly reveal that the scope of your awareness changes dynamically over time, depending on your current emotional state. Your awareness narrows with negative emotions and broadens with positive ones. It's when feeling good, then, that you're best equipped to see holistically and come up with creative and practical solutions to the problems you and others are facing.

Your wisdom, then, ebbs and flows just as your emotions do. Let's face it, sometimes you're just not able to access and integrate all the knowledge and experience you've gained over the years. Think back to when you've made your most unwise choices, and odds are you'll uncover images of yourself during particularly strained times— stressed beyond your limits, overwhelmed, in pain, wholly alone, or otherwise adrift from the moorings of your most-cherished values. By opening the doors of perception, positive emotions provide you with the much-needed space to recognize disparate points of view and weigh your various options for action.

Positivity resonance allows you access to the wisdom of your past experiences and, more generally, makes you intellectually sharper. Spend just ten minutes in pleasant conversation with someone else and your performance on a subsequent IQ test gets a boost. Conversing with valued others makes you wiser on the fundamental pragmatics of life as well. Suppose you've been called on to offer advice. Say an older colleague of yours at work confides in you that he hasn't achieved what he had once planned to achieve. What would you advise him to do and consider? Or your fourteen-year-old niece calls you to say that she absolutely wants to move out of her family home immediately. What would you advise her to do and consider? While your off-the-cuff advice to these troubled souls may not be altogether bad, studies suggest that you'd be considerably more pragmatic and discerning if you could first discuss these dilemmas for a few minutes with someone whose perspective you really value, say your spouse, your best friend, or a mentor, and then think about the situation a bit more on your own. More generally, studies show that positivity resonance unlocks collective brainstorming power, making it easier for you to solve difficult problems when working and laughing together with others, compared to when you face those problems alone. Love, then, defined as positivity resonance, momentarily expands your awareness, which boosts your IQ and unlocks your wisdom.

Beyond these momentary effects, however, positivity resonance also triggers enduring, long-term gains in cognitive abilities and wisdom. The more frequently older adults connect with others, the lower their risks for cognitive decline and Alzheimer's disease. Yet love isn't just about staving off age-related cognitive decline. Scientists have also demonstrated clear links between how often people connect socially with friends, neighbors, and relatives, and their lab-tested cognitive functioning, even in far younger people who are in their twenties or thirties. One way that your recurrent connections with loved ones make you lastingly wiser is by giving you inner voices to consult. Suppose you're called on to navigate some particularly difficult life dilemma, your own, or that of a close confidant. You yearn to talk matters over with your mentor, spouse, or best friend. Yet, for whatever reason, you can't get a hold of these valued others—perhaps they're traveling, busy, or even deceased. Research shows that simply imagining having a conversation with them is as good as actually talking with them. So consult them in your mind. Ask them what advice they'd offer. In this way, a cherished parent or mentor, even if deceased, leaves you with an inner voice that guides you through challenging times. Your past moments of love and connection make you lastingly wiser.

A sizable grain of truth, then, lives on in the closing lines of English poet John Masefield's poem "Biography" in which he muses on how his own life's meaning will be utterly missed by historians who reduce his life "to lists of dates and facts" without knowing "the golden instants and bright days":

> *Best trust the happy moments. What they gave*
> *Makes man less fearful of a certain grave,*
> *And gives his work compassion and new eyes.*
> *The days that make us happy make us wise.*

Becoming Healthy. Love is not a magic bullet. You can no more expect to become healthier through a single, isolated micro-moment of positivity resonance than you can by eating just one piece of broccoli per year. Yet just as a steady diet of a wide range of fresh fruits and vegetables does indeed make you healthier, so does a steady diet of a wide range of loving moments.

Some of the most direct causal evidence that love improves your bodily systems in lasting ways comes from that experiment that recently emerged from my PEP Lab, first described in chapter 3. People in that study were randomized to either learn how to self-generate love more frequently or not. Participants' daily reports of love and social connection diverged across the two groups, and these differences accounted for significant improvements in people's resting levels of vagal tone. Random assignment to the "love" condition, we learned, lastingly benefits the functioning of the physical heart.

Your vagal tone is a key indicator of the health of your parasympathetic nervous system. It helps down-regulate your racing heart so that you can regain calm after a fright or take advantage of a much-needed break in the action. With heart disease being by far the leading cause of death in the United States, your physician can use knowledge of your vagal tone to forecast with some accuracy your likelihood of heart failure, as well as your odds of surviving such a catastrophic health event. Your vagal tone also reflects the strength of your immune system, with a particular tie to chronic inflammation, a known risk factor for not only heart failure but also stroke, arthritis, diabetes, and even some cancers. What our experiment suggests, then, is that by learning to love more frequently, you reduce your risks for many of the worst health conditions that we all dread.

Currently, my PEP Lab is pushing to learn even more about the biological pathways that account for the various health benefits of loving connections by investigating how love changes you at the cellular level. We now periodically draw blood from all our study volunteers and, in collaboration with UCLA genomics expert Steve Cole, we're tracking how random assignment to the "love" condition changes the ways people's DNA gets expressed within their cells. Past work discovered that chronic loneliness—a persistent yearning for more positivity resonance—compromises the ways a person's genes are expressed, particularly in aspects of the white blood cells of the immune system that govern inflammation. We're testing the hypothesis that learning to increase the frequency of loving connections alters gene expression in ways that fortify disease resistance and in turn keep people in good health.

Insight into how everyday moments of love register and resonate within the human body helps make sense of the groundswell of evidence that links experiences of positive social connections to health and longevity. Mountains of research have documented that people who have diverse and rewarding relationships with others are healthier and live longer. A more recent wave of longitudinal studies specifically ties positive emotions to healthy longevity. These studies suggest that a lack of positivity resonance is in fact more damaging to your health than smoking cigarettes, drinking alcohol excessively, or being obese. Specifically, these studies tell us that people who experience more warm and caring connections with others have fewer colds, lower blood pressure, and less often succumb to heart disease and stroke, diabetes, Alzheimer's disease, and some cancers. Many of the key conditions that threaten to set you back or shorten your life can thus be staved off by upgrading how and how frequently you connect with others.

Love 2.0: The View from Here

Love, as we've seen here, ripples out through space and time. In a moment of positivity resonance, studies show, your awareness automatically expands, allowing you to appreciate more than you typically do. Also quite automatically, your body leans in toward and affirms the other person, and begins a subtle synchronized dance that further reinforces your connection. Over time, these powerful moments change who you are. They help expand your network of relationships and grow your resilience, wisdom, and physical health.

These ripples don't just affect you. They also affect the people with whom you share your moments of positivity resonance. So as you upgrade your view of love and learn to cultivate more micro-moments of it, you not only get benefits, you give benefits. This repeated back-and-forth sharing, however small or subtle, helps establish and strengthen healthy communities and cultures.

"You are made in the image of what you desire," Thomas Merton said. My aim in writing this book is to open your eyes to the wisdom of this claim and the scientific evidence that backs it up. Although a single desire may seem fleeting and ephemeral, when repeated and repeatedly acted on, desires become powerful, life-shaping forces. A single gust of wind, after it moves on, hardly alters the shape of a tree. Yet when you find all the trees in a given area leaning decidedly to the west, you can see the lasting effects of the prevailing winds. The new science of positivity resonance tells us that when you make love your prevailing desire, you remake whole domains of your life. You become appreciably and enduringly different, and better. You uplift others, helping them become different and better as well. My hope is that digesting the science I offer you here in part I has awakened your desire for love, for more positivity resonance in your day. You now know how deeply and pervasively love affects you. Now you are ready to begin making the changes—even very small adjustments—that will help you foster more and better loving moments. In part II, I offer you guidance for doing just that.

The Guidance

CHAPTER 5

Loving Kindness

LOVE DOESN'T JUST SIT THERE, LIKE A STONE;
IT HAS TO BE MADE, LIKE BREAD;
REMADE ALL THE TIME, MADE NEW.

—Ursula K. Le Guin

Here, in part II, I invite you to reconsider love in both personal and practical terms. In your own life, when, where, and with whom do you feel it? What opportunities for love, as yet untapped, can you identify?

In this and each of the following chapters, I get specific. I describe a range of activities that you can use to expand love's radius in your own life.

Because my own research program has uncovered considerable evidence over the past decade on the benefits of meditation, I offer at least one meditation practice in each of the next four chapters. But don't worry. If you suspect that meditation is not for you, I've got plenty of other practices for you to try. I call these "micro-moment practices" because they describe consequential shifts in attention and awareness you can make within a micro-moment.

You need not like or even try every practice I describe. Indeed, I suspect that you won't. Yet please be open to experimenting. Take time to observe how the practices affect you and your interactions with others. Find one or more practices that really resonate for you. Then, identify a recurring daily event that can serve as your cue to engage in each chosen practice. "If I'm walking from my car into work," for instance, "then I'll practice celebratory love." Study after study shows that making concrete "if . . . then" plans like this dramatically increases people's success at self-change. Consider, too, whether you might benefit from making your self-reflections more formal, by using the positivity tracking tools I've made available on the website that accompanies this book, at www.PositivityResonance.com.

In any case, be ready to see changes. Your potential for love is virtually unbounded. I see at least two reasons for this. First, positive emotions are ubiquitous. Despite the hardwired human habit of scanning current circumstances for sources of danger and negativity, positive emotions are what most people feel most frequently. This tendency toward positivity reflects the reassuring fact that most moments are indeed benign. Right in this moment, for instance, as you are reading this sentence, I suspect that you're sitting fairly comfortably and that no one is inserting pins into your eyes. So what's not to like about the present moment? Relax and enjoy it. Look around and you'll come to realize that you can increase your ratio of positive to negative emotions even further by becoming more attuned to the sources of positive emotion in your midst, be they a welcomed sense of safety, a shimmer of beauty, or a small gesture of kindness.

The second reason your potential for love is nearly limitless is that social interactions are also ubiquitous. Like bees and ants, we humans are ultrasocial creatures. Your life is embedded within increasingly vast networks of relationships, social ties, and broader communities. Just count up the number of people you see or communicate with on any given day. Your tally includes not only family and friends after all but also team members and other work associates, neighbors, and acquaintances, the employees and fellow customers at any business you happen to visit, and more. Love can infuse and nourish all of these connections—even whole networks of people—just as it infuses and nourishes your own body and mind.

At the heart of love is a feeling—a feeling with both physical as well as mental components. Physically, your whole body feels relaxed, with a warmth and openness in your chest, as if your heart were stretching open to let in or embrace another being. This is the feeling that makes you want to move in closer, to listen and observe more carefully. Mentally, you yearn for good fortune for others. You wish them well with great sincerity. You also wish to show how much you care, to enact tenderness and concern. We've all experienced love like this at one time or another. It's that warm and tender feeling you have when you first hold a newborn, or greet a cherished friend after many months, or even years, apart. Some of this tenderness, along with its associated impulse to show care and concern, is even released when you come across a kitten, puppy, or other baby animal. Think here of a time when some small creature drew a slow "Awwww . . ." out of you. If you're like many people, you recognize this tender feeling rolling through you mostly when you're with loved ones. Indeed, scientists from Darwin to Ekman suggest tenderness like this honors familial bonds. Yet by now I hope you're recognizing that your potential for micro-moments of love is far greater. Each time you encounter another—or yourself—you have the opportunity to do so with tenderness and warmth, and with relaxed openness and goodwill. The goal of this chapter, and indeed part II of this book, is to provide specific tools for expanding the circle of those with whom you share the warmth and tenderness of love.

Preparatory Practices

As you read through part II, you'll notice that most of the practices that I recommend to seed love are solo activities. They are activities you can undertake completely on your own, just by redirecting your attention, or taking time for self-reflection, or meditation. How can these practices work, you may wonder, if love is only experienced in connection with others? Why not dive right into interventions that alter how you interact with others, such as that you smile, nod, or lean in toward them more often, or mirror their gestures?

Two reasons, actually. The first concerns sincerity. I suspect you've encountered people who, in the course of doing their jobs, have been told to "smile at the customers" or "act cheerfully." While they (and their superiors) may have the best intentions, what emerges on these workers' faces and in their gestures from following these decrees often feels distinctly forced, or "put on." Your gut tells you that they don't really mean it, that they don't truly care about you, personally. It's easy to become cynical about such gestures. You wonder, what are they trying to sell me? Your suspicion puts you on guard, bracing to avoid any unwanted influence. Studies have indeed documented clear differences between genuinely heartfelt smiles and the so-called social or unfelt smiles that these workers put on like a uniform. Beyond the fact that genuine smiles uniquely activate the cheek-raising muscles that create (or deepen) crow's feet at the corners of people's eyes, genuine smiles also differ in timing from forced or insincere smiles. Sincere smiles tend to arise and then fade away in the span of a few seconds. Insincere smiles, by contrast, are either flashed more quickly, in less than a second, or worn for longer durations, like makeup or a mask. Basically, you, like most people, are not altogether good at putting on a smile in the absence of genuine positive feeling. You are, however, exceptionally good at detecting insincere smiles in others, especially (as discussed in chapter 2) when making eye contact.

So one reason to begin with love-seeding activities on your own, rather than in social interactions proper, is to avoid the predictable boomerang effect of trying too hard to adjust your nonverbal actions. To be successful, you'll need to cultivate genuinely positive social sentiments from the inside out. People familiar with "method acting" know this well. Instead of mimicking the outward emotional gestures of the character he or she aims to portray, a method actor works to recall and then relive an emotional event from his or her own life that corresponds to the emotion the character is intended to experience. This makes the resulting portrayal appreciably more organic and genuine.

The motto of my home state of North Carolina is: "To be, rather than to seem," or in Latin, *Esse quam videri.* This aspiration comes from the first-century BCE musings of Cicero, the famous Roman philosopher and statesman. Writing "On Friendship" Cicero made the case that without virtue, friendship is impossible. True friendship, as Cicero saw it, was actually rather rare "for there are not so many possessed of virtue as there are that desire to seem virtuous." Strikingly, the definition of friendship that emerges from Cicero's writings bears resemblance to positivity resonance as I've articulated it throughout this book (especially in chapter 2). Friendship, to Cicero, involves complete sympathy in all matters, together with goodwill, affection, and kindness. This sort of heartfelt connection with others is not possible without sincerity. Flattery, or "false statements . . . framed purposely to satisfy and please," according to Cicero, is inherently damaging. Contemporary science concurs. Feigned positivity resonance creates a toxic insincerity that is damaging perhaps most severely to the person who initiates it. To *be* loving rather than to *seem* loving is an aspiration truly worthy of your time and energy.

The second reason that most of these practices begin in solitude is that genuinely positive social sentiments take time to cultivate. There's often quite a thicket of self-absorption that needs to be cleared before the fragile shoots of loving tenderness can emerge. Solo activities are vital for this. While these activities do not directly create positivity resonance, they can set the table for an eventual feast of love. I call these practices preparatory. They condition your mind, heart, eyes, and ears to be more prepared for positivity resonance when true connections become possible. With these practices, you become poised to capitalize on opportunities for love when they arise, rather than remain oblivious or blind to them. Intervening off-line, prior to your interactions with others, may in fact be the best route for creating positivity resonance in its most natural form, guided by your own open heart. As Cicero phrased it, "Unless you see an open bosom and show your own, you can have nothing worthy of confidence, nothing of which you can feel certain, not even the fact of your loving or being loved, since you are ignorant of what either really is."

Reflecting on Social Connections

The first tool for experiencing more moments of love is one that we discovered completely by chance. It entails simply reflecting, at the end of each day, on the three longest social interactions you've had that day, and asking yourself how "connected" and "in tune" you felt with the people with whom you spent your time. These people could be family, friends, coworkers, or completely new acquaintances, and it doesn't matter whether the same person shows up in more than one interaction. Merely reflecting on whether your potential moments for positivity resonance were in fact realized seems to serve as a gentle reminder about your ever-present capacity for love.

My students and I first included a brief nightly reflection task like this in one of our many longitudinal studies a few years back. We'd originally included it to track group differences in our participants' experiences of social connection. We expected that, compared to the people in our wait list control group, those who were randomly assigned to learn loving-kindness meditation (LKM) would report more day-to-day social connections alongside more day-to-day positive emotions. They did. What we didn't expect was that our control group—those who simply completed the daily surveys yet did not learn LKM—would also show increases over time in both social connections and positive emotions. We'd never seen this before. Across several past longitudinal studies in which we'd asked people to provide daily reports of their emotions, we'd never seen improvements simply due to the act of regularly reflecting on feelings. But in this study, we did. The only difference was that we'd added the social connection questions. With these two questions added to the very end of the daily report form, upward spirals emerged for our control participants as well.

Even more remarkable, increased feelings of social connection forecast changes in the functioning of people's physical hearts, as registered by increases in their vagal tone. If it weren't for this pronounced effect, we might have dismissed the result as mere wishful thinking or the possibility that our study participants simply got wind of our interests (in social connection and positive emotions) and told us (through their daily reports) what they thought we wanted to hear. Yet the fact that reflecting on social connection appeared to penetrate the body to affect enduring heart rhythms made us take a closer look.

This surprise finding inspired a key part of my student Bethany Kok's dissertation. To gather definitive data on whether the one-minute thought exercise of considering how "close" and "in tune" people feel when interacting with others in fact generates important emotional and biological changes, Bethany randomly assigned working adults to reflect daily either on their social connections in this manner or on the three tasks on which they spent the most time that day and to evaluate how "useful" and "important" those tasks had felt to them. Remarkably, here again, we observed increases in day-to-day positive emotions and end-of-study vagal tone, but only in the group assigned to reflect on social connections. Clearly something powerful was embedded within this simple thought exercise.

Bethany and I suspect that the real active ingredient runs deeper than merely the end-of-the-day reflection. We speculate that the daily question serves as a subtle cue that reminds people that each of their social interactions is indeed an opportunity for something more than just an exchange of goods or information. With this in mind, people may begin to approach each interaction with a bit more presence, aiming to cultivate heartfelt connection rather than miss out on it. This speculation merits direct test, because it's also possible that people don't change their behaviors at all, but simply become more sensitive to the positive connections that already exist for them, more likely to notice and prioritize them.

I encourage you to try this exercise out for yourself. A small shift in attention like this could well lead to large changes in your overall health and well-being.

Try This Micro-moment Practice: Reflect on Your Social Connections

Each night, for a few weeks, review your entire day and call to mind the three longest social interactions you had that day. Thinking of these three interactions all together, consider how true each of the following two statements is for you:

- During these social interactions, I felt "in tune" with the person/s around me.
- During these social interactions, I felt close to the person/s.

Rate the truth of these two statements on a scale from 1 to 7, on which 1 = *not at all true*, and 7 = *very true*. You may record your responses anywhere, for instance in a notebook or computer spreadsheet that you create. Or you can use the online recording tools on the website that accompanies this book by visiting www.PositivityResonance.com. One benefit of recording your responses online is that you can also choose to rate your emotions each day, and thereby, as the weeks progress, you can see whether your positivity ratio rises in step with your greater attention to social connections.

Donna's Story

Not long ago, I shared this preliminary finding on the impact of merely reflecting on social connections with Donna, a friend of mine who for years has been trying out new tools for increasing well-being. At the time, Donna had been facing a series of setbacks and disappointments at work and had lost some close, work-based friendships. Being single, she also felt emotionally isolated. With her stress levels at an all-time high, she was losing sleep, feeling lethargic, and had little remaining self-confidence. She was feeling her absolute worst at a time when she needed a lot of strength just to get through a workday. Over breakfast, I shared with her that Bethany and I had serendipitously stumbled upon what we thought might be a bouillon cube version of our loving-kindness interventions: a condensed, minute-long thought exercise that might well yield comparable results.

Having tried out several other positive psychology interventions, Donna was immediately curious. She asked more about the technique. I shared that what our participants had done was extraordinarily simple—just answer those two questions about their three longest social interactions of the day. Donna soaked up our fresh data with great interest and wondered how her own life might be different if her three longest interactions each day were life-giving rather than life-draining, sources of strength rather than disappointment. Right then, she transformed our accidental finding into her own, self-styled well-being intervention. She set herself a new goal of seeking out at least three interactions each day that held positivity resonance. While she could hardly control the influx of uncertainty and setbacks in her day-to-day life, she could strive to cultivate more loving connections each day.

As someone who lives alone, Donna's new goal was challenging to pull off. But the initial payoff was high enough to keep her engaged. While she'd never kept up with the "three good things" exercise commonly used in positive psychology, in which you write down at the end of each day three things that went well that day and consider why each happened, she did stick with her own "three loving connections" exercise. Several weeks later she wrote me a note to say that she found it made a "huge difference" in her life. She also found that love breeds confidence and strength. The more loving interactions she had, the better prepared she was to face her difficult days at work.

Donna observed that her self-styled "three loving connections" activity did two things for her. First, it made her look for people she enjoys being with and inspired her to enhance those relationships. She shared with me, for instance, that after a particularly stressful day, she now would often call her twentysomething niece, just to see what she's been up to lately and share some giggles. As her phone calls to her niece became more frequent, their relationship grew deeper and stronger. Other family and friends became closer and her relationships with them became more healthy and helpful. The other effect of her "three loving connections" activity was that she now found herself looking for ways to make the difficult relationships in her life better. Her positive and powerful relationships with family and friends had become the new normal in her life, and she strove to make even the difficult relationships in her life better. She had a strong foundation of loving relationships to support her in this endeavor.

I had the chance to have lunch with Donna nearly a year later. I asked how she was doing, and she said she was doing great. Her demeanor concurred. She seemed far more relaxed and cheerful than she had during that breakfast at which I first shared with her my lab's serendipitous discovery. Later, I learned that setbacks and disappointments were still streaming into her life. As I listened to her recount them, I thought they might even be worse. The difference, she said, was that now she was able to let these recurrent sources of negativity simply roll by. They didn't get under her skin. With her decisive focus on cultivating three loving connections each day, she'd created more spaciousness in her mind and generosity in her heart for facing these ongoing difficulties. Although still single, she discovered that love comes in many different forms. She knew she was a special part of her family, even if they were miles away. She had also cultivated special relationships with a few families in her neighborhood. And she had found that not all of her work relationships were doomed to be difficult, but discovered some good friends there, also.

Try This Micro-moment Practice: Create Three Loving Connections

Recall how energizing and rewarding it can be to really connect with somebody, sharing a flow of thoughts and feelings with ease. As your day unfolds, seek out at least three opportunities to connect with others like this, with warmth, respect, and goodwill. Opportunities may spring up at home, at work, in your neighborhood, or out in your community. Wherever you are, open toward others, freely offering your attention, creating a sense of safety, through eye contact, conversation, or, when appropriate, touch. Share your own lighthearted thoughts and feelings, and stay present as the other person shares theirs. Afterward, lightly reflect on whether that interchange led you to feel the oneness of positivity resonance, even to a small degree. Creating the intention to seek out and create more micro-moments of loving connection can be another tool for elevating your health and well-being.

Loving-Kindness Meditation

Back in chapter 1, I first underscored the power of a particular meditation practice, known as loving-kindness meditation, or LKM. LKM is an activity, honed over millennia in various Buddhist traditions, designed to condition your heart to be more open and loving. Although Buddhist in origin, LKM can be used to deepen any faith tradition, or be practiced without one. Here, throughout part II, I show you the ropes for how to practice LKM yourself. In each chapter, I introduce one or more facets of LKM, each designed to stretch your goodwill in new directions. Before I turn to the first meditation activity, however, I offer a few framing thoughts to help you get the most out of LKM, especially if you are completely new to it. As a preparatory tool for creating positivity resonance, LKM is well worth trying out. My research program confirms that it can open up many fresh possibilities for you.

First and foremost, LKM helps you recondition your habitual ways of responding to others. Odds are you cruise through much of your day wrapped up in a cocoon of self-absorption, tightly woven with all of your wishes, plans, and goals of the moment. You consider what you'll wear, eat, and do, and where you'll go. You prioritize things on your to-do list. You puzzle over what you'll say in an upcoming encounter that you suspect may be difficult. You, after all, are the lead character in the play that is your own day and life. Others play bit parts. They are not particularly consequential to the overall arch of your plotline, and by consequence they often undergo little character development in the script that your mind follows. You sometimes even treat them as though they were mere props, inanimate objects that populate the setting, yet bear no real importance to you or your day. Why wouldn't it be this way? The play is all about you.

You see where the illustration is going. Each person is, after all, the star of his or her own play and day. If you dropped the script of your own day and picked up the script of another person's day, this other person would suddenly undergo considerable character development. You'd come to appreciate his or her own wishes, plans, and goals. You'd understand that this person isn't merely a bit part or prop, but rather fully human, like you. Just like you, this person is full of yearnings and strivings, hopes and insecurities. This is true of every person. It's equally true of all those with whom you cross paths, as well as all those you'll never meet, not even once.

LKM opens the doors of perception to break you out of your cocoon of self-absorption and restore others to their full humanity. It challenges your natural tendency to treat others like props or thinly developed characters who play only bit parts in your own self-centered play. By widening your awareness, LKM opens your eyes, mind, and heart to seeing others more fully, with warmth, kindness, and tender wishes for their well-being. The practice expands your outlook in ways that help you create the safety and connection between you and another that can seed positivity resonance.

Like other meditation practices, LKM involves quiet contemplation in a seated posture, often with eyes closed and an initial focus on the breath and the heart region. You might start by setting an alarm to chime softly after ten or so minutes, so that you can experiment without concern for the time. As the practice becomes more familiar and comfortable, you can experiment with longer meditation times, aiming for twenty to twenty-five minutes of daily practice whenever possible. I'm not suggesting that you become a monk. Keep in mind that randomized controlled trials from my lab and others have revealed a wide array of benefits after just a few months of practicing LKM for an average of sixty minutes a week, which translates into three to four times a week for just fifteen to twenty minutes each.

LKM is a bit like guided imagery, although the practice targets loving feelings more than visual images per se. You encourage those warm feelings to rise up by repeating a set of phrases—silently, to yourself—each of which is a wish for another's well-being. To some, LKM may at first blush seem fake, like saccharin, or unrealistic. Or it may feel forced, like your smile when you're getting your passport picture taken. These are understandable misimpressions of the practice. Although it may seem as though your goal in LKM is to fabricate positivity, the truth is, that's not even possible. You can no more conjure up an emotion directly out of thin air than you could right now, sitting as you are, conjure up pain in your left shin. What you can do, however, is set the stage for positivity. You do this by contemplating certain thoughts and wishes and then being open to the positive sentiments that may arise out of those thoughts and wishes. You set your intentions and then see what follows from that.

Some people, when they first learn of the science of positive emotions, think they should make their motto "Be positive." I advise against this, strongly. When you enact this motto, even with good intentions, you can inadvertently create a toxic insincerity that is harmful to both you and others. It's like papering over the messy reality of being human with a simple yellow smiley face. Indeed, studies show that striving too hard for happiness backfires. Better than making your motto "Be positive" is to lightly adopt the mind-set of positivity. I find "Be open" to be a better motto. It can serve as a touchstone for attitude adjustment in most every circumstance.

Openness is especially important to the practice of LKM. Although you might begin a session of LKM intending to create warm and tender feelings of care, it's important not to cling to this goal too tightly. The idea is, instead, to be open to whatever arises. Sometimes it may actually feel as though your heart is expanding within your chest, overflowing with tenderness and concern for others. Other times you might feel next to nothing. Both responses are normal. The best way to avoid the damaging effects of insincere positivity, or an oppressively saccharin LKM session, is to accept whatever feelings authentically arise within you. Pay special heed to the feelings that arise from within your body. Your mind, after all, can all too readily fall into a trap of wishful thinking. You may so dearly wish to feel loving feelings that your mind fools you into thinking that you do. Your body isn't so tricky. As you practice LKM, learn to trust the sensations within your body more than the thoughts within your mind.

Sometimes people new to LKM are suspicious of the intent of the practice. It can seem naïve, or like magical thinking. They wonder, "Do people really believe that simply thinking these wishes instantly erases all troubles? Doesn't this whole enterprise hinge on the metaphysical? If so, why should I waste my time with it?" From the perspective of emotions science, LKM is not the least bit supernatural. I can assure you, based on solid empirical evidence, that whatever positive feelings you generate in LKM are likely to imbue the rest of your day with more positivity as well. This greater positivity can show up as more openness in your posture, breathing, and body comportment, and on your face, openness that can be readily spotted by those with whom you interact or cross paths. Since nonverbal gestures are contagious, your openness also allows others to become more open and relaxed. Meeting each other with openness like this increases the odds that the two of you will come into sync. LKM also shows up in the sense you make of each new circumstance that you encounter. You're more likely to see things in a good light, give the benefit of the doubt, and be optimistic about the future and others' potential. Your intonation becomes more upbeat and inviting. Well after you practice LKM, your verbal and nonverbal behavior may remain changed such that others feel a greater sense of safety in your presence, more likely to open up and connect. The pathways through which LKM seeds subsequent moments of positivity resonance are wholly physical. There is no need to invoke magical thinking or the metaphysical to explain its downstream effects.

Another way to ward off insincerity or any seeming naïveté when practicing LKM is to balance the practice with equanimity, the wisdom of the big picture. When you step back and take in the big picture in a balanced way, it's easier to see that all people are alike in the ways that matter most. All have wishes, feelings, and yearnings—to feel secure and happy, and to experience ease as their day unfolds. From this vantage point, you can gently remind yourself how interconnected you are with everyone else who walks this earth: how your and each person's separate pursuits of safety, happiness, and ease are in actuality intertwined and interdependent.

You can also remind yourself of the truth of suffering. Suffering exists. No matter how many warm wishes you cultivate, conditions in this world are such that people to whom you offer loving-kindness inevitably suffer from time to time. It can be helpful to allow your recognition of the inevitability of suffering to surface, while at the same time registering the abundant sources of safety for both you and others. Holding suffering and safety side by side helps you maintain your resilience in the face of suffering, so that you don't become shattered or overcome by it. It is into this larger context of acceptance—acceptance of similarity, interconnection, and of suffering and safety—that you can offer the wishes for happiness and well-being that are central to LKM.

Cultivating the wisdom to put your LKM practice into balanced perspective protects its sincerity and keeps it real. Absent the backdrop of this wisdom, you might notice yourself becoming too attached to the prospect that your wishes will come true. You may come to feel that the people who you contemplate *will* feel safe, happy, healthy, and at ease. Or you might slip into feeling that these wishes must come true: that your own pursuit of happiness somehow hinges on it. These sorts of yearnings are not helpful. They reflect attachments to a certain outcome or way of being, rather than openness to whatever arises or is. Know that clinging to any sort of fixed idea that your wishes need be fulfilled is not the state you seek. Such desires masquerade as the state you seek, but miss the mark altogether.

Far more important than reading or talking about LKM, however, is the time and energy you devote to practicing it. When you're ready to dive in, read the following passages a few times, and then put the book down and experience it yourself.

Try This Meditation Practice: Loving-Kindness

Find a quiet place where you are unlikely to be interrupted. If you're in a chair, scoot back in your seat so that the lowest part of your spine is well supported and straighten your spine up toward the sky. Lean forward from the back of the chair just a bit. Relax your shoulders and pull them back slightly. This position allows you to expand your rib cage in all directions when you breath, creating more spaciousness around your heart. Place your feet flat on the floor, so that the heels and balls of your feet make equal connection with the ground. Rest your palms gently on your thighs. If sitting like this doesn't appeal to you, find any other position that makes you feel both alert and relaxed and that allows your chest to expand. Once you are physically comfortable, let your eyes drift closed. Or, if you find that awkward, set your gaze lightly on a spot on the floor in front of you, or on a simple, peaceful object.

Bring your awareness to the sensations of your own heart. Breathe to and from your heart. Notice how each breath brings new energy to your heart and allows your heart to send life-giving oxygen coursing throughout your body. Rest in this awareness for several breaths. Now, in this quiet moment, visualize someone for whom you already feel warm, tender, and compassionate feelings. This could be your child, your spouse, even a pet—someone whom the mere thought of makes you smile. Let his or her smiling face surface in your mind's eye. As you take in that image, with the lightest mental touch, briefly call to mind this loved one's good qualities. Your goal is to rouse warm and tender feelings naturally, by visualizing how connecting with this loved one makes you feel.

Once these tender feelings have taken root, creating genuine warmth and kindness in you, gently repeat the traditional phrases of LKM, silently to yourself, in some form or another. The traditional phrases go something like this:

May this one (or I, we, he, she, or they) feel safe.
May this one feel happy.
May this one feel healthy.
May this one live with ease.

The words themselves are not as critical as the sentiments and emotions they evoke. You can rephrase the statements in ways that serve to stir your heart the most. You might try extending the phrases ever so slightly to draw out the intent of each wish more fully.

May they feel safe and protected, like a child in her mother's arms.
May they feel happy and peaceful.
May they feel healthy and strong.
May they live with ease.

Although your mind may pull you to race ahead, try to reflect on these phrases slowly, at your heart's pace. Silently say no more than one phrase to yourself with each breath cycle. Visualize what the fulfillment of each wish would look like. How would the loved one's face and body posture appear? What energy would be created? In the space between breaths, pause just a moment to feel your heart and body. Really notice them. Discover what sensations arise in you. As you repeat the phrases for this loved one in particular, you might imagine seeing your good wishes moving from your heart region to his or hers, perhaps as a wave, a beam of light, or a slowly unfurling golden ribbon.

After you've slowly and steadily repeated the phrases for this particular loved one for a few minutes, gently let go of his or her image and simply hold the warm and tender feelings in your heart region.

Next, radiate your warm and friendly feelings to someone else, perhaps to another person that you know well. Visualize this person's face, and gently and briefly call to mind his or her good qualities. Now again, with this new person in mind, slowly repeat the classic LKM phrases, or your own renditions of them. Visualize how this person would appear if each wish were to come true for him or her, pausing just a moment between each phrase to notice how your body responds.

As you continue to practice, gradually call to mind all your friends and family, as a group. Wish them all well through your body's appreciation of the classic LKM phrases. Next, welcome in all the people with whom you share a connection—even remote connections, like the service person you reached on your last call for tech support. Use the phrases to extend your goodwill as far as you can.

As you end your meditation, gently remind yourself that you can generate these feelings of kindness and warmth anytime you wish. By taking time with this activity, you've begun to condition your emotions to more readily do just that. You'll now be better prepared to experience true connection with others.

Beginning a meditation practice is a very personal project. People differ in the kinds of external support they need to get started and to stay with it. The most important step to take is to allocate time to practice. Keep in mind that our research shows that just sixty minutes a week can make a noticeable difference in your life. You might thus choose to set your alarm for ten minutes earlier each morning to practice with the LKM phrases completely on your own. If you find yourself losing focus, you can follow any number of guided meditations until your focus and follow-through become stronger. I've included a few such guided meditations free for you to download at www.PositivityResonance.com. Other great meditation aids are also available, and I point out a few of my favorites under Recommended Reading in the back of this book. I also highly recommend taking a meditation class or workshop. Ask for one at your local hospital, gym, or wellness center.

Love 2.0: The View from Here

Love is not simply something you stumble or fall into. While love can certainly catch you by surprise, like a sudden rain, unlike the weather, you can also seed and cultivate the conditions for love all on your own. All it takes is that you develop an eye and a feel for love and for the contexts in which you might seed it. Slow down and prepare your own heart and mind to be truly open to others. Reflect on moments of connection, actively seek these moments out, or condition your heart with the time-tested good wishes of loving-kindness meditation. Try these practices and watch what then unfolds between you and others, using your own body as your tuning fork to spot love's presence. With any of the practices that I offer in this chapter, you take steps toward shifting your attention away from yourself and toward others, a shift that in itself opens countless opportunities for love.

Notice how this shift feels inside your body. Notice how energized you get in a bona fide moment of positivity resonance. Conversations become deeper and more meaningful, connections stronger. You'll begin to see each new interaction as an opportunity, not as an obligation or obstacle. Your more open stance will be amply reinforced by the positive feelings that you share in the brightened moments spent with others.

Aware now of the ingredients and potency of positivity resonance, you have new lenses through which to view each and every encounter you have with others. True, you are unlikely to elevate all of your interpersonal encounters into moments of positivity resonance. After all, you can only reshape your side of each interpersonal interchange. So don't judge yourself against unrealistically high standards. Do notice, however, whether you've been able to upgrade one, two, or even three ordinary interchanges each day into acts of love. These are the small changes that can add up to big improvements in your health and happiness.

CHAPTER 6

Loving Self

I EXIST AS I AM, THAT IS ENOUGH.
IF NO OTHER IN THE WORLD BE AWARE I SIT CONTENT.
AND IF EACH AND ALL BE AWARE I SIT CONTENT.

—Walt Whitman

The old saying tells us that we can't love others unless we first love ourselves. It's true. Even though love is defined throughout this book as moments of positivity shared between and among people, the positivity shared between knower and known—between *I* and *me*—provides a vital foundation for all other forms of love. We first need to accept ourselves fully, as worthy partners in positivity, before we can freely enjoy the many other fruits of positivity resonance that we can share with others.

Like all forms of positivity resonance, self-love requires both safety and connection. Either of two obstacles may stand in the way. For some people, both obstacles are fused together into one mammoth and seemingly insurmountable boulder. The first is self-diminishment, or not believing yourself to be worthy of love or acceptance. At an implicit, unspoken level, you may dismiss your good qualities as insignificant and stay locked in on your shortcomings. You may feel it necessary to fill those gaps in your character before you can fully accept and love yourself. You may think, "If only I were _____." You can fill in the blank with any of your usual suspects, those ideals against which you judge yourself: "thinner, kinder, wealthier, smarter, more energetic, more productive, more organized, more successful, more thoughtful . . ." Then you wait. You withhold love from yourself until you meet those unspoken preconditions. But the waiting never ends, and the self-love never flows.

The second obstacle to self-love presents as self-aggrandizement, or believing oneself to be more special or more deserving than others. Or perhaps you're not so busy comparing yourself favorably to others, but rather you see yourself as especially capable or triumphant. Your self-esteem is high. This is a devious obstacle to circumnavigate because it masquerades as self-love. Sure as day it's positive. Even so, a telltale sign that these positive self-descriptions fall short of true self-love is that they are guarded very tightly. As you shield your positive self-views from the light of contradictory evidence, a brittle narcissism emerges. Although narcissism like this is often taken as excessive self-love, in truth it's something else altogether. In believing yourself to be especially deserving and discerning, or especially wonderful—even at a deep, unspoken or unrecognized level—the slights and shortcomings that all people face as they navigate the social world become magnified out of proportion, viewed as threats or insults to your character. If this is your obstacle, your happiness hinges on whether others treat you in just the right way, or show you the proper form of respect by turning a blind eye to your shortcomings. In truth, self-aggrandizement is often a defense—a protective armor donned to cover up a more negative view of self. It can be self-diminishment in disguise.

Both obstacles to the safety and connection necessary for self-love—self-diminishment and self-aggrandizement—deny the wisdom of sameness and oneness. At a core, spiritual level, there is no social topography, no hierarchy that ranks people from more to less deserving. The truth is you are neither beneath nor above others. Brain disorders aside, all people are fundamentally the same when it comes to their ability to think, to feel, and to yearn for love. All are equally deserving of acceptance, respect, and love, even with their many shortcomings. You are no exception. Just like everyone else, you deserve your own love.

So what happens if you give in? If you accept yourself, right at this moment, just as you are, without preconditions of any sort? Can you, as Walt Whitman suggests, be content with yourself as you are right now, whether fully isolated, or scrutinized by millions? This chapter describes a range of practices that can unlock this greater openness to who you actually are, openness that begets kindness and self-love. These practices coax you to more fully accept and appreciate who and how you are right now, failures and shortcomings and all. I describe both the formal practice of loving-kindness meditation as well as more informal practices, each of which allows you to experiment with self-love. These practices are not self-indulgent, navel-gazing escapes from reality. Like positivity resonance, they build your foundation for health and well-being. Indeed, studies show that self-directed, self-compassionate love is far more vital to your health and happiness than is oft-touted high self-esteem.

Where to Start?

Although people don't differ in their worthiness of their own love, they differ a great deal in their ability to offer it. For many people—and you may be one of them—offering warmth and tenderness to yourself feels more than a little bit awkward. For whatever reasons, you simply may be unaccustomed to fully accepting and caring for yourself as you are.

This may be a particular hang-up for those of us born and raised in cultures that foster deflating self-criticism, puffed-up self-aggrandizement, or both. Initial research bears this out. Kristin Neff, a developmental scientist at the University of Texas at Austin who has pioneered scientific assessment of a form of self-love that she calls *self-compassion*, has found this to be the case. Her research shows that people in cultures—like the United States—that are heavy on both self-deprecation and high self-esteem show lower levels of self-love and by consequence experience higher rates of depression and dissatisfaction with life. By contrast, people in cultures—like Thailand—where Buddhism infuses more self-acceptance into daily life show higher levels of self-love and by consequence seem to suffer less depression and dissatisfaction.

Indeed, lore among those who teach LKM is that barriers to self-love are particularly high among Western students. Sharon Salzberg, cofounder of the Insight Meditation Society, in Barre, Massachusetts, is perhaps the leading Western teacher of LKM. It's no overstatement to say that she is the person most responsible for first bringing the practice of LKM from the East to the West, having first encountered this ancient practice in India in the 1970s and then practicing it intensively in Burma in the 1980s. I'm lucky to be able to draw on Sharon's deep expertise while I craft my experiments on LKM's effects, as she serves as a consultant on my research grants.

Sharon tells me that Western students frequently encounter difficulties or resistance when encouraged to direct loving-kindness toward themselves. Some even fall asleep at this stage. Others quit altogether, judging themselves to be incapable of it. Making matters worse, in traditional LKM formats, the self is an early, or even the first, focus. Before moving on to offering loving-kindness to others, the traditional sequence is to first offer loving-kindness to oneself. For many, this becomes a seemingly insurmountable obstacle.

Noting this, Sharon offers a story about the first time she met His Holiness the Fourteenth Dalai Lama. It was back in 1979 on his first trip to the West. As part of his visit, he came to her center in Barre and gave a talk to the group of students who'd been sitting a meditation retreat there. One student raised his hand to confess that he'd been practicing LKM for some weeks and had come to the conclusion that he was incapable of directing love to himself. Sharon recounted how stunned and puzzled His Holiness was. "You're wrong!" he told the student, albeit in his characteristic light and loving tone. "You have Buddha nature!" he proclaimed, referring to the possibility of awakening that is ever-present in all people. The ability to direct warmth and tenderness to the self was apparently a nonissue for him and to those he most frequently taught.

Sharon also tells me that the reason that the traditional Buddhist practice of LKM begins with the self is because the self is presumed to be an easy target for love. Indeed, wishing oneself well was thought to be as natural as breathing, or as seeking out food when hungry or water when thirsty. Having practiced the skill of cultivating loving-kindness for the easy targets, like a cherished teacher or mentor, a dear friend, or oneself, students will then have developed key skills before they approach the harder targets, like unknown or difficult people. The logic is not to slam those new to the practice with the hardest parts first, but rather to build their skills gradually, starting with easy targets and working up to the more difficult ones.

Accordingly, if you find that directing love toward yourself is especially problematic, you might consider whether to practice with easier people first. Perhaps start with a teacher or mentor to whom you feel especially grateful, or a friend who the mere thought of can melt your face into a smile. After you've spent considerable time—perhaps even weeks—practicing cultivating warm and tender feelings for these people, then you can begin experimenting with cultivating warm and tender feelings for yourself. You may in fact be your own most "difficult" person on which to focus in the next stage of your practice. If so, you're in good company. That's a common experience. Rest assured, the order of targets to which you direct your warm wishes matters far less than the time and energy you devote to developing this habit and skill. Your aim is simply to condition your heart to be more comfortable and familiar with warm and tender sentiments.

Sidestep Obstacles to Self-Love

As I introduced the practice of LKM in the previous chapter, I suggested that you lightly reflect on the good qualities of the person or people for whom you are extending your good wishes. Here I expand on the logic of this. As you visualize a particular person, gently name what's good about him or her: "Generous." "Kind." "Accepting." "Honest." "Grounded." "Inspiring." You don't need a long list, one or two traits will do. Let yourself begin to see these one or two traits not simply as labels, affixed to these people in superficial ways, but rather as deep expressions of who they are in this world, of who they've been to you. Here you might lightly visualize the particular actions of this person that exemplify each trait. Keep in mind that calling up another's good qualities does not require you to deny or disguise his or her bad qualities or shortcomings. Rather, it's simply an invitation to shift your focus in this moment toward the good and be open to it. Think of it as turning toward the light, just as a sunflower tracks the position of the sun. It's not that the sunflower is unaware of darkness, but rather that, in moments of daylight, it finds more energy—quite literally—in the light. You can, too.

When you're ready to practice directing loving-kindness to yourself, you can follow these same steps. See yourself, in your mind's eye, from a cherishing observer's perspective. This is not the time to imagine yourself as you looked the last time you had your portrait taken, whether in posed formality or orchestrated informality. Instead, see yourself just as you are, holistically, without any pose or intended impression to create. Imagine yourself as you are now dressed and sitting. Or perhaps you can build a mental self-image based on a truly candid snapshot that someone else took of you while you were going about your business, completely unaware of the camera. Once you have this mental image of yourself in mind, lightly name a few of your good qualities. "Caring." "Curious." "Hopeful." "Creative." "Patient." Consider whatever comes to mind right now. There's no need for this to be some final "best" description of your character. Simply use the good qualities that come to mind as a springboard for your tenderness and warmth, a way to remind yourself of your neglected strengths.

What if no good qualities come to mind? No need to worry. That happens to people. It's completely normal. In her first book, simply entitled *Lovingkindness*, Sharon Salzberg speaks of "relearning loveliness," drawing her phrasing from the beloved poem "Saint Francis and the Sow," in which American poet Galway Kinnell describes how Saint Francis gently put his hand on the forehead of a sow to remind her "in words and in touch" of her value. Sometimes, you can forget your own loveliness. You forget the many, many reasons for which you wholly deserve love. Your loveliness isn't about outward beauty. As Kinnell's poem reminds, a pig is hardly what you'd imagine first when considering what's lovely. And yet, through the sow's actions—through the generosity she offers in the simple gesture of feeding her offspring— the sow *is* lovely, fully lovely, from snout to tail. When you recognize how your own actions have contributed to the greater good, you, too, can relearn your own loveliness. As you recognize your own value and value-added, as Kinnell puts it, you open as a flower, "from within, from self-blessing."

If you have difficulty summoning your good qualities, try sidestepping this obstacle by imagining how those who care for you might see you. Be like Saint Francis to the sow. Imagine for a moment stopping the busy pace of your daily life. See yourself stopped, freeze-frame, in the midst of your daily activities. Now imagine: Approaching you in this freeze-framed moment is someone who cares for you, someone who, at one time or another, has appreciated you and shown you warmth. This could be a mentor or a dear friend, your partner, parent, or another loving relative, either alive now, or long gone. Imagine that this person's intention is to remind you of your long-forgotten loveliness. Perhaps like Saint Francis, he or she rests a hand on your brow and reminds you, in words and in touch, of your good qualities. What would he or she say? What would you remember? What image of yourself would emerge?

Try This Meditation Practice: See Yourself as the Target of Others' Love

You can circumnavigate your own particular obstacles to self-love by visualizing the cherished people in your life themselves engaged in the well-wishing that typifies LKM, whether or not they have actually practiced this technique formally. Imagine all your beloved mentors and friends, all your treasured family members, standing in a circle around you. You are now the center of each one's attention and loving regard, the hub of this imagined social gathering.

Just as, in LKM, you extend your own wishes for each of them to feel safe, happy, healthy, and at ease, the feeling is often mutual. These other people wish for you to feel safe, happy, healthy, and at ease. Visualize how it is that you might be represented in each of their minds and hearts. On to which of your good qualities would they shine a light? Gently hold those descriptions of you that surface in your mind and let them soak in. Recall your many actions that underlie these characterizations of you. Allow yourself to see those actions as deep indicators of your worth. Draw sustenance from the positive regard in which these cherished others hold you. Relax yourself into its warmth, feeling the safety and security it offers you. Now visualize the unfurling of good wishes emanating from each person's heart to yours. Like the spokes of a wheel, these wishes connect the outer ring of your circle of supporters to you, its hub. At this point, you might visualize all of those gathered speaking the classic phrases of LKM in unison, with your own name inserted:

May you, [your name here], feel safe and protected.
May you, [your name], feel happy and peaceful.
May you, [your name], feel healthy and strong.
May you, [your name], live with ease.

Adopting this loving observers' perspective on yourself can offer an "appreciative jolt" that allows you to see—and truly feel—how it is that you add value to those around you. From this perspective, you can better discern your good qualities. Of course, you still have your own unique set of less-than-good qualities as well. If your mind gets pulled toward those, gently invite yourself to table those shortcomings for now. You can always examine them later. This is a rare moment to spotlight the good in you and you don't want to miss it.

Another way to bypass your obstacles to self-love is to visualize yourself together with any or all of these individuals and to speak the phrases of LKM as "we":

May we feel safe.
May we feel happy.
May we feel healthy.
May we live with ease.

You can think here of the good qualities that you and this other person (or persons) share, and visualize the good wishes that emanate from your heart as surrounding and infusing the two (or more) of you. You might find that thinking of yourself together with these cherished others provides a more comfortable stepping stone on the path leading you to direct love toward yourself.

Even if you have a hard time populating the circle with people who you know appreciate you, you can populate it with any or all of the people around the globe who have—or have ever—practiced the ancient technique of LKM. After all, each one of these people—whether an aging widow in Thailand, a thirtysomething prisoner in Texas, or His Holiness the Dalai Lama himself—has practiced extending the wishes of loving-kindness to all people, because all people yearn for and deserve to feel safe, happy, and healthy, and to live with ease. Perhaps it can help you to visualize yourself as tucked into the masses of humanity for which others have extended their earnest expressions of love.

Loving-Kindness for Yourself

When you're ready—perhaps after you've eased your way in by sidestepping your own obstacles using one or more of the strategies just described—try experimenting with directing full-on loving-kindness toward yourself, following the ancient traditions of LKM. Again, it can be tempting to avoid or minimize this portion of the practice, for all the same reasons previously discussed. Stay alert to the possibility that you may disguise your neglect of self-love as humility or as selfless compassion for others. These rationalizations can be common. Move past them. The idea here is simply to experiment with and explore self-love using your personal experiences as your data. As you experiment, notice areas of resistance and become curious about them. Although by definition, areas of resistance beg you to turn away, decide in advance instead to hang in with them. Witness how you experience resistance and even lean in toward it. I can guarantee there's more to learn by leaning in than from turning away. When you avoid a challenge like this, you forfeit opportunities for experiential learning that yields wisdom. Yet when you approach these areas of resistance, your return on this investment is better awareness and understanding, both of yourself and of love.

Knowing that it can be all too easy to zoom past using yourself as your target as you begin your LKM practice, you might decide up front that you'll focus exclusively on yourself for several weeks. Even mark off this time on your calendar. This is in fact how LKM has been taught to the participants in my team's research studies. The very first guided meditation our study participants are offered focuses exclusively on the self, and they are instructed to stay working with this particular meditation daily, for the first two weeks. This is not self-indulgence. Rather, many LKM teachers find that exploration of self-love provides a solid foundation from which to later expand love's reach. You can use this reasoning if you need to justify this level of self-focus to yourself: Self-focus has been part of LKM practice for millennia, and it will help you deepen your skills for extending your experiences of love to many, many others.

You can start in small ways simply by becoming aware of your body. Your body has its own pace, your mind another. Simply attending to your body coaxes you to slow down. Once you tune in to your physical sensations, you might discover a need to shift positions, stretch, or give yourself a few minutes of massage. Doing so is a form of self-love that instantly creates more comfort and ease. Just as eye contact is a key channel for making a connection with another person, awareness of your own body sensations is a key channel for self-love. It's the platform from which you can offer yourself compassionate attention.

Try This Meditation Practice: Self-Love

Find a comfortable place to sit where you won't be disturbed. If you're in a chair, make your way to the back of the chair so that your lower back is well supported. Ground both of your feet flat on the floor. Sit upright, with your spine, neck, and the crown of your head pulled skyward. Gently pull your shoulder blades backward and downward, raising your rib cage slightly. These postural shifts will create a true physical openness for your heart, an openness consistent with the positive emotions you aim to cultivate. Gently lower your gaze to reduce visual distractions. If you're comfortable, close your eyes.

Begin by taking two or three deep breaths, and bring your awareness to your heart. Visualize how each in-breath affects your heart physically. Remind yourself how your heart is nestled between your two lungs. Consider how each in-breath gently massages your heart, in a tender, cradling embrace. Begin now to breathe normally, making no special effort to breathe in any particular way. Continue to rest your awareness on your heart. Consider how each in-breath nourishes you, as your heart drinks in precious oxygen. This passage of oxygen— from the nearby air, through your lungs and then into your beating heart and bloodstream—is the most basic and constant connection between you and the world around you. This simple action of breathing knits together all that is within you with all that lies beyond your skin. Each new breath thus creates a unity of life and community as all people alike share the nourishment that the earth's atmosphere freely offers. All drink from the same well. Simply witness yourself, now, drinking in oxygen from the well of life that surrounds you.

When you're ready, check in with how your body is feeling today, at this very moment. Are you experiencing any aches and pains? Any worries or areas of tension? Or are you excited, caught up in eager anticipation of something new? Whatever the feeling, there's no need to push it aside. Pleasant or not, let the feeling in. Accept it as part of what it means to be you at this moment. Meet the feeling with curiosity and openness. Explore it. Note how this feeling registers in your body and how those bodily feelings change—subtly—from one moment to the next. Whether your current experience is pleasant or unpleasant, just witness and accept it. Whether events in your life are presenting you with good or bad fortune these days, just witness and accept those events. See them as part of the inevitable ups and downs that all people experience, no matter what part of this earth they call home. And just as surely as all people face good and bad fortune, and experience pleasant and unpleasant emotions, all people—all the world over—yearn to feel good, safe, peaceful, and healthy.

Alongside this awareness of suffering's inevitability and the fundamental sameness of all people, you can choose to wish yourself well. You deserve this kindness as much as anyone. Now, put your intention for this particular practice session, whatever it is, into words. This will shine a light on the path you choose and help you get back on it when your mind inevitably strays.

Begin by lightly calling to mind your own good qualities. If it helps, briefly visualize an event that exemplifies one of those good qualities. No need to launch an exhaustive hunt for the "best" good quality or the "best" exemplifying event. Just lightly accept whatever good quality or instance of it that comes to mind. No need to judge or rate it. Simply let it remind you of what's good in you, what touches your heart about yourself. Then, gently offer the classic wishes of loving-kindness to yourself, choosing phrasings of these classic sentiments that best speak to your heart.

May I feel safe and protected.
May I feel happy and peaceful.
May I feel healthy and strong.
May I live with ease.

See yourself as being a dear friend to yourself. It may help to first conjure up the feelings of warmth and tenderness you might feel toward a small child, or a kitten, as innocent as these small creatures can be. Experience how your face softens or your heart expands in their presence. Now imagine directing these same feelings of warmth and tenderness toward yourself.

May I feel safe.
May I feel happy.

May I feel healthy.

May I live with ease.

Between each phrase, pause for just a moment and drop your aware-ness down to your body, to your heart in particular. Note and accept whatever sensations arise there. Know that this practice session is more than the mere repetition of phrases. The phrases simply open the door to a chance for you to condition your heart to be more open, more accepting, and kinder. Staying aware of your heart region allows you to witness this conditioning as it unfolds.

At one moment or another, you'll discover that your attention has strayed from the phrases. This may happen quite a lot. Don't worry. It's normal. Simply begin again by gently bringing your awareness back to the phrases. There's no need to berate yourself for losing your focus. Indeed, each new moment of beginning again presents another oppor-tunity for experimenting with the spirit of loving-kindness. Can you acknowledge your departure from your intended path while at the same time gently returning to it? What would it take to do so with a kind and loving sentiment toward yourself? Can you set aside all harshness?

As you come to the end of this practice session, know that it's com-pletely natural for you to treat yourself kindly and wish yourself well, even though you may forget to do so quite often. Know that you can generate this tender and loving attitude toward yourself anytime you wish, just by reminding yourself that this stance exists, and how at ease it makes you feel. Sure enough, difficulties and obstacles to your happiness will still arise. Suffering happens. But now you know that you need not add to that suffering by treating yourself harshly. Indeed, you can reduce your suffering considerably at any time by reminding yourself of the ancient and ageless wishes of LKM.

As your practice of LKM turns inward, toward yourself, be aware that this may also be a good time to begin (or resume) writing in a journal.

Whenever possible, just after your meditation practice session, allow yourself an additional five to ten minutes to journal the stream of your consciousness. Doing so creates the time and space for you to reflect on any associations or insights that arise for you as you begin to give yourself this new kindhearted attention. What does it feel like to create these warmer, more open sentiments toward yourself? How do these sentiments make your body feel? What markers of resistance become apparent for you? What happens when you experiment with bringing your awareness—even your breath—to those areas of resistance? How do they respond? Do they tense up further? Or do they soften? Simply observe what your inner experience is like for you today. What flavors does it offer you? Are you full of feeling? Or are you numb? Brimming with energy, or worn down? Know that any of these responses are normal and just describe what you feel. See where this recognition leads you.

If you find that you'd like additional structure as you begin experimenting with offering loving intention and attention to yourself, you can access the guided meditation on self-love that I've made available on www.PositivityResonance.com. All of the resources on this website are free for you to use and I hope you will find benefit in them. I also highly recommend that you seek out a local teacher. Nothing quite compares to having someone with more experience offer her or his own way of seeing and speaking about your journey as it unfolds. As with all teachings, adopt what resonates within you, making it your own, and leave the rest as you found it. Like everyone else, myself included, you are the keeper of the eclectic wisdom you've absorbed from a long succession of teachers, including those with and without that formal title.

Hearing Voices

"D'oh!"

If you know Homer Simpson, the fictional character on the animated television series *The Simpsons*, you instantly recognize this familiar burst of self-incrimination. He uses it whenever he catches himself doing something stupid. Try your best Homer imitation now. If you're good at it, you can actually feel the tension and tightness that this mere syllable creates in your body and mind. It's as if your heart and whole inner self recoil into a closed fist. If you can sense this tightness, I'll bet that your heart rate and blood pressure just shot up as well. Of course, this is only a momentary surge. Yet just imagine the damage this way of treating yourself could do over a lifetime. Homer is lucky to be a cartoon character: He need not experience the physical wear and tear that inevitably trails this trademarked emotional habit.

Nearly everyone hears voices, in the form of inner self-talk. What do you say—either out loud or silently to yourself—when things go wrong? Do you berate yourself, speaking to yourself in a harsh, scolding tone? Does your own inner critic, like Homer, have its own particular catchphrase? Being your own worst critic is only one form of negative self-talk. Other forms abound. Maybe your own self-talk is decidedly more anxious. Maybe you worry too much, second-guessing your every action, expecting the worst at every turn. Or perhaps the voices you hear keep your mind running in circles, questioning over and again why things have happened to you as they have, ruminating over every unpleasant episode.

How many times each day do you saddle yourself with needless negativity in one form or another? You might find the answer to this question especially illuminating. To discover it, get one of those old-school handheld counters and keep it in your pocket for a day. Tick it off every time your inner critic, inner worrywart, or inner ruminator speaks up. Your total for the day counts up the number of times your body and mind have tightened into a defensive, closed-off stance. True, some of this inner negativity is inevitable. There is no such thing as a negativity-free life. Yet just like your number of reps in weightlifting, the number of times that you speak negatively to yourself each day builds up a hardness in you.

Maybe speaking harshly or pessimistically to yourself is not your problem. Perhaps instead, your own particular modus operandi is to praise yourself excessively, giving yourself inner high fives and pats on the back for any accomplishment, while at the same time turning a blind eye to your shortcomings. Whereas other people can't seem to shake the habit of self-denigration and self-flagellation, focusing too much as they do on the negative, maybe your love-limiting habit comes in the form of excessive self-praise and self-aggrandizement, focusing too exclusively on the positive.

Sound surprising? If so, it may be helpful to remind yourself that knowing a little bit about virtually any topic can sometimes be a dangerous thing. This is certainly true for positive psychology. This fact often takes people by surprise because, as a scientific specialty, positive psychology seems utterly innocuous. What could be dangerous about trying to be happy? Yet if positive psychology is absorbed solely at a surface level, it can sometimes morph into a way of being in the world that is as thwarting to love as is persistent self-criticism or self-doubt. Appreciating this danger requires absorbing the subtle differences between what I call eyes-open positivity and eyes-closed positivity.

True positivity springs from your full embodiment of positive emotions. It comes from a deeply felt sense of safety. By nature's design, it expands you. Your body relaxes into it. Your torso literally stretches outward. Muscle tension melts away. With your torso expanded and your head held high, you see more of what surrounds you. Your peripheral vision expands, allowing you to take in more detail than you typically do. Your mind follows suit and it, too, expands. Conceptual boundaries, once sharply delineated and guarded, begin to soften, allowing objects and ideas that at one time seemed altogether separate to melt into a common pool of oneness. When positivity is genuine—when it is truly embodied and heartfelt—it becomes virtually inseparable from this sort of physical, sensory, conceptual—and indeed spiritual—openness. I call this *eyes-open positivity*. When positivity is truly genuine, your eyes, mind, body, and heart blossom open, wide open.

Then there's another form of positivity altogether, a kind that you put on, like an artfully applied mask. This form of positivity can be well-meaning, to be sure. People often come to it having learned a bit about the science of positive psychology, enough to make them resolve to be more positive themselves. Despite this good intention, this form of positivity can be a slippery form of self-deception. You can sometimes yearn so badly to be happy that you fool yourself into believing that you are.

A telltale sign that betrays this form of positivity as a counterfeit state is that it remains above the neck. It shows up in the channels that you can most readily control—your words, your facial expressions, and your self-talk. But it doesn't take root in your body or in your heart, and so it doesn't fully flower into openness. The physical, sensory, conceptual, and spiritual openness that is the hallmark of genuine emotional positivity is simply absent. I call this *eyes-closed positivity* because its outlook on the world is self-protective, not immersive. Indeed, it can be quite narrow and rigid. Although it arises out of your sincere yearning for good feelings, it can also reflect an abiding ignorance about what the full experience of positivity means and entails.

Making matters more complicated, eyes-closed positivity is a double-edged sword. At times it can actually be useful. No doubt you've heard the phrase: "Fake it 'til you make it." At times, that can be great advice. My caveat, though, is while you're faking your positivity, you're merely seeking a springboard into the real thing. You are not reaping the benefits of genuine positivity.

The other side of the sword is blunt and causes far more damage. Eyes-closed positivity cuts you off from precious opportunities to access true positivity. This happens when you strive to find bliss in your safe cocoon, mistaking it as the end, not the means.

Although self-praise and other forms of positive self-talk can *seem* like good strategies for increasing your well-being, whether or not they are depends on whether you "walk the talk." Put differently, knowing whether your self-talk is positive or negative simply isn't enough. The positivity you harbor for yourself needs to be fully embodied. Indeed, all true emotions *are* embodied. "Wishful thinking" positivity, by contrast, remains forever imprisoned within your mind. It does you little good up there, remaining just talk.

The embodied positive regard in which you hold yourself has all the markers of a truly positive emotion: It opens you, relaxes you, and helps you see the larger tapestry of life in which you are embedded. It doesn't tempt you to shun negative feedback or failure. Rather, it supports you, like a well of reserved resources, when you need to take a close look at the hard facts of your life. Above all, genuine, heartfelt self-love is flexible and grounded in reality.

These critical ingredients are missing from much of the positive self-talk prescribed in the self-help industry: flexibility, openness, and realism. Absent these attributes, positive self-talk can morph into cold-blooded narcissism. It becomes inner chatter that in fact serves to insulate you from healing connections with others. It drugs you into thinking that while you've got your own life together, most other people decidedly do not, and therefore they're hardly worth your time. Smugness can prevent you from being a true friend to yourself.

The key to knowing whether self-correction or self-congratulations are in order is to assess the degree to which either is commensurate with your actual circumstances. This is where the classic tools of cognitive behavioral therapy can work wonders. What evidence backs up your self-talk? Is any evidence being ignored or distorted? Are there parts of the bigger picture that you are conveniently keeping out of view, whether negative or positive? The idea is to check your self-talk against the full reality of the situation as evenhandedly as you can.

Whatever your tally of self-criticism or self-aggrandizement amounts to, this same number represents the opportunities you have each day to practice something altogether different: gentleness instead of harshness, openness instead of tightness, flexibility instead of rigidity, an inner smile instead of that all-too-familiar inner scowl. This is what learning to be a true friend to yourself entails.

Try This Micro-moment Practice: Narrate Your Day with Acceptance and Kindness

Your inner voice narrates your experience—your days, and indeed, your life. Your self-talk can feel unbidden and completely outside of your control. Yet truth is, it isn't. Like any habit, with awareness and effort, you can change it. After you've witnessed your own self-talk for a day or two, and perhaps tallied instances of your inner harshness or inner Pollyanna, try countering any unfriendly or rigid tendencies with a more accepting, kind, or loving tone. When you notice a shortcoming, instead of berating yourself for it, try gently reminding yourself that other people also struggle with that same shortcoming. Like them, you're human, you're learning. Like everyone else, your aspirations and shortcomings are all intertwined in one jumbled skein of experience. This skein will never be all goodness and light, without imperfections or darkness, either now or in some distant, yearned-for future. At the same time, wallowing in your shortcomings—or defensively hiding them out of view—distorts reality. Simply accepting them, allowing them to exist and inform you, can be a radical act of self-love. Meditation teacher and clinical psychologist Tara Brach's phrase "radical acceptance" can be a useful touchstone for this. Embrace all aspects of yourself, especially when your first impulse is to either turn away from or scold yourself for them. Put differently, experiment with leaning in toward your shortcomings, with eyes and heart open. Find a way of rephrasing your self-talk such that you become a friend to yourself.

It can help to imagine how someone more practiced in love and compassion might respond to you at this moment. My own touchstone for accessing love and acceptance has become an experience I had upon the tremendous honor of first meeting His Holiness the Dalai Lama. I'd been invited to participate in a scientific discussion with His Holiness as part of the grand opening of Richard Davidson's Center for Investigating Healthy Minds at the University of Wisconsin–Madison. I'd been briefed on the ritual aspects of the event: Following Tibetan custom, on parting, His Holiness would greet us each individually in turn. We were each to bow when he stood before us, and then he would drape a *khata*, a ceremonial white silk scarf, around each of our necks. I knew all this, and indeed I'd witnessed this ritual countless times. And yet, when the Dalai Lama stood before me, I froze. I simply stared into his eyes and absorbed the warmth and benevolence of his demeanor. I did this for too long. I'm sure it was only a few seconds too long, but it was too long nonetheless. What happened next was an exquisitely subtle and loving nonverbal gesture: a slight movement of His Holiness's face that gently moved me along, as if to say "You're doing this [ritual] wrong, but I love you anyway." It was an experience completely new to me. I was simultaneously corrected and loved, and in a public setting, no less. What was especially new to me was the silence of my inner critic, that part of me that would typically scold myself for such a public gaffe. Instead, I gently thought to myself, I bet this happens from time to time. Some people become awestruck in the presence of the Dalai Lama. It happened to me. He's experienced this before and helped me along without judgment.

This last piece is key: without judgment. That's what full acceptance feels like. It is loving connection without judgment, without the unreachable conditions of perfect actions or perfect speech. Acceptance—full, radical acceptance—does not hold out for some improvement in your character or your abilities. However you find yourself right here and right now is enough. However broken you feel, however incomplete, however inadequate. No matter which of your aspirations yet remain out of your reach, you are worthy of your own kindness, your own acceptance.

Who better to practice this level of acceptance with than yourself? You know yourself better than anyone. You know all about your own unmet aspirations and your own shortcomings. To narrate your day with acceptance and kindness means keeping those unmet aspirations and shortcomings in full view, while also taking in your noble qualities. For you—just like everyone else—are a unique mixture of good and bad, of success and failure. Being a friend to yourself means accepting all those parts of yourself, without judgment or harshness, and without sweeping the unsavory aspects of yourself out of view.

When I shared my "frozen khata" experience with an audience at the Environmental Protection Agency some months later, someone voiced "I wish all bosses were like that!" She longed to have a boss who could point out her mistakes while also maintaining full acceptance of her. That is a nice image to uphold, especially when thinking of the times when we are responsible for pointing out someone else's missteps—whether those of a child or an employee. Yet how does your inner boss treat you? If you find that you boss yourself around with a harsh tone, remind yourself that there's another, more loving way to treat yourself. As Walt Whitman reminds us, you exist as you are, and that is enough.

Erika's Story

I see a powerful reminder of how self-acceptance is foundational for positivity resonance in the stories that my good friend Erika has shared with me about her experiences as an amateur musician. For the past few years, she's enrolled in a summer camp to expand her musical abilities under the tutelage of some of her favorite professional musicians.

She'd learned about this particular camp from a friend who'd attended it himself, a fellow Deadhead she'd jammed with for years. True to his forewarnings, the camp experience was not only immensely rewarding but also immensely challenging. Although she'd played guitar for years, she felt self-conscious in the presence of so many great musicians. She was sure she was among the least skilled students at camp, some of whom were actually career musicians themselves. She reinforced her insecurities by ruminating on certain facts: She'd not been classically trained; she only played a few hours each week; she'd only picked up music theory on her own; and so forth. Although she absorbed the wondrous experiences that the camp offered, she fretted periodically about how she'd be able to solo in front of all those brilliant musicians when she was called to do so. I'm sure you can recognize aspects of the classic imposter syndrome script here. We all read from it when we take up the challenge to push ourselves to the next level.

The camp was designed to be a safe haven for musical exploration. Campers were encouraged to place their full trust in others and to create an encouraging and supportive atmosphere for everyone. In light of inner self-judgments, however, this is easier said than done. Any form of self-consciousness can rob you of the chance to fully immerse yourself in learning something new and can derail peak flow experiences. Erika knew that if she wanted to get the most out of this camp, she'd need to let go of her self-doubts and self-judgments. She credited her longtime meditation practice for helping her keep such thoughts at bay, and for reminding her that her ultimate goal—in both music and life— was to be ever happier, lighter, and more playful. As she described it, it took her both radical self-acceptance and radical presence to "let go" and "lighten up."

Having worked hard to cultivate a more accepting and lighthearted attitude toward herself, when she was called up to solo on that last day of camp, Erika thoroughly enjoyed it. She also played differently from that day forward. She became "truly open and ready" to take her music to the next level, to learn how to listen deeply to other musicians as they played together, and to improvise with them in fresh ways. Building on these experiences, when Erika returned to camp the following summer, she had what she called one of the "peak musical experiences" of her life in a small workshop on "Chemistry." The band member who led the workshop emphasized that musical chemistry didn't come from musical skill alone. Even two great musicians can completely miss out on it. Hearing Erika recount the take on musical chemistry she'd absorbed here, I couldn't stop seeing it as an amplified form of positivity resonance: The bodily vibes that resonate between and among people during micro-moments of love could be amplified and made audible by musical instruments. After the band member's brief discussion of his own experiences and observations of musical chemistry, each student in turn took a chance to improvise with him as he played the drums. While some musical connections emerged, they were all getting the sense that true chemistry is hard to predict. Then Erika took her turn. She started off introducing an idea by playing a few notes in a particular way on her guitar. Her teacher responded on drums. They each listened, they each responded, and eventually they started playing, playfully, together at the same time. It was immensely enjoyable "the way a good conversation would flow, we were on the same page and could finish each other's ideas." They played together like this for only three to four minutes, yet when they finished and looked up at each other the teacher pronounced to the class, "Okay, now that's chemistry."

Full self-acceptance is what allowed Erika to make the most out of the safety that the camp created. She's found that lightening up on herself has been essential for getting the most joy out of her music, which comes especially when she's jamming and improvising with fellow musicians. It's a lesson that she finds applies to the rest of life as well. Truth is, however much they may try, other people can't make you feel safe. Only you can do that. When you do, you spring open countless opportunities to forge fresh instances of that elusive state we call chemistry.

Love 2.0: The View from Here

Loving is a skill. It takes practice. When you set the goal of learning to love yourself, you'll find ever-present opportunities to practice this new skill, because you're never further than arm's reach, or perhaps better said, heart's reach. Just like all forms of positivity resonance, however, self-love first requires safety and connection. Beating yourself up with the continual harshness of self-criticism is no way to make yourself feel safe in your own company. Likewise, if your self-assessments are unflappably sunny, unhinged from reality, or otherwise blind to your ingrained bad habits, you can hardly feel safe either. A true friend, after all, is the one who tells you the truth. He or she affirms you realistically and often, and yet does not abandon you or grow silent when a negative assessment is prudent. Creating a sense of safety within your own skin is just the same. To access self-love, disengage from harshness in your self-talk, but not from reality. Affirm your positive qualities, but refrain from delusion and self-deception. Be your own compassionate truth-teller.

Love's second precondition is connection. This is no less true for self-love than for positivity resonance with others. Truly loving yourself requires that you slow down enough to truly meet yourself heart to heart, letting the heart of your *I* resonate with the heart of your *me*. Allow time to reflect on your inherent strivings for goodness. Tune in to the messages your body sends you. You can't simply rush from one activity to the next, attending forever outward, and expect to fall into self-love. Indeed, you might let rushing about serve as your cue to switch gears.

Self-love, we've seen, is not the same as having an inflated, narcissistic view of yourself or high self-esteem. These often hinge on good outcomes, making you rigidly guard against negative feedback. When bad news crashes through, it sends you into a free fall. Self-love, by contrast, is steadier, more peaceful. This inherent calm arises because it's not predicated on good outcomes. You can learn to be a friend to yourself through thick and thin, through good times and bad. Indeed, it's in the toughest times that harboring compassion toward yourself makes the biggest difference. Practice standing by your own side during hard times, with openness and goodwill, and you'll appreciate the steady security self-love offers you. It safeguards you from plunging into despair.

Self-love buys you even more. It's the currency in which all other forms of positivity resonance trade. When your reserves of self-love are low, you can scarcely meet the gaze of others, seeing yourself as either beneath or above them. A chasm forms between you and others that slashes your odds of forging true connections. Yet when you practice and bank self-love, you become rich with emotional reserves. You're more able to recognize sources of goodness in others, to see and fulfill others' yearnings to connect, no matter their circumstances. The next chapter describes how to do just that.

CHAPTER 7

Loving Others, in Sickness and in Health

WHAT IS RICH? ARE YOU RICH ENOUGH TO HELP ANYBODY?

—Ralph Waldo Emerson

L ove, in its old-school version, seems to love similarity. Study upon study bears this out. People are most drawn to others who share roughly their same level of physical attractiveness, their same degree of financial wealth, their same physical abilities, their same lot in life. Each person, then, tends to have a small, circumscribed set of "loved ones" whose beauty, wealth, health, and ability are not too different from their own. Your attraction to similar others seems to keep the playing field level.

Yet attraction like this also stratifies. Seeking similarity in your companions invites endless social comparisons as you continually size people up, judging whether they're worse off or better off than you. When you judge others as having it worse than you, you may even feel relief at your own relative good fortune. Or maybe you feel some form of aversion: pity for their plight, fear that their unfortunate lot in life may one day be your own, or unspoken anger at them for bringing their misfortune on themselves. Regardless of which emotions emerge as you look down on others, the distinctions you've already made between you and them—and the judgments that go with it—create a gulf between you, a gulf that erodes your potential for authentic love.

A similar gulf forms when you judge others as better off than you. When you see others as having more than you—more beauty, more wealth, more happiness—you come to see yourself as relatively disadvantaged. This can stoke fires of envy, or of self-pity. In looking up to others in this comparative way you stratify your social world into haves and have-nots. Most poignantly, though, you limit your own opportunities to experience the healing powers of positivity resonance.

For some people—and you may be one of them—social comparisons like this happen constantly. When encountering someone new, without a moment's thought, you size him or her up, placing the person on a rung above or below you. Although this habit may seem innocuous, it fuels an often imperceptible greed that constricts love's radius. Greed thrives on the illusion that good fortune is a scarce commodity, that another's gain is your loss, and vice versa. It leads to a guarded stance toward others that creates and reinforces distance. Greed makes you cling tightly to your own good outcomes, fearing anything that might make you lose a foothold on the rung on which you find yourself. You look down at those below you with pity, fear, or irritation, and up at those above you with envy or desperation. You grab at opportunities to get more "goods" for yourself, with little regard for whom you may be pushing aside or harming along the way. Through the mere act of ranking others, greed slithers in to create a false social topography that utterly denies the inherent sameness and oneness across all people.

The truth is that there's no such ladder. When it comes to the things that matter most, others are neither beneath you nor above you. Time and again, studies show that the happiest among us are the ones who've simply shed this pernicious habit of social comparison. When you learn to see others through the lens of sameness, instead of through the lenses of downward and upward comparisons, you come to recognize that others' difficulties are also your own difficulties, either at present, or at some past or plausible future moment. You also recognize that their good fortune doesn't subtract from your own, and it does you no harm whatsoever to celebrate it. Indeed, you multiply your own riches when you do so.

Love's boundaries, as we've seen, need not be constricted, its vision need not be myopic. Love is both open and caring. While love like this obeys the bedrock preconditions of safety and connection, and is in part defined by some form of shared positivity, it does not hinge at all on you and another sharing precisely the same positive emotional state. Given the many factors that shape each person's emotions, an exact matching of inner experience would be exceedingly rare and can hardly be expected.

Fortunately, love doesn't require the absence of unpleasantness or misfortune. Nor does it require the presence of any certain form of pleasantness or good fortune. Awareness of these fundamental truths opens the entire spectrum of human experience as opportune moments to cultivate positivity resonance. Whether in sickness or in health, good fate or bad, love remains possible. In this chapter, I share techniques for accessing two forms of love that may perhaps be less intuitive to you: loving through and despite another's suffering, and loving through and despite another's good fortune.

Compassion: Meeting Suffering with Love

By nature's design, we all recoil from pain. Suppose you're cooking dinner with brand-new cookware and mistakenly pick up that fancy, all-metal, oven-ready pot lid, forgetting to use a pot holder. It's only natural that you drop the lid in a clamor as you yank your hand away. The haste of your recoil probably spares several layers of skin. And so it may seem with suffering of all sorts. Your first instinct may often be to look, leap, or pull away, or otherwise hang back. Increasing your distance from the source of pain can seem like the best way to spare yourself the added suffering that may come from being too close to it.

Compassion does just the opposite. It moves toward suffering, not away from it. It seeks connection, not distance. Compassion is what rouses the father who, without a moment's thought, rushes toward his bloodied child after a playground accident, scooping her up in his arms to comfort her and attend to her wounds. It fuels the hospice volunteer, who reads poetry to the gentleman she met just last week who's facing imminent death from colon cancer. It can move you to gently place your hand on a coworker's arm, as you absorb her recounting of the difficulties her family is now enduring. Indeed, the latest evidence from studies of primates (both human and nonhuman) suggests that compassionate responding like this is just as natural, just as hardwired, and just as beneficial to our species as is our evolved instinct to recoil from burning sensations and other forms of physical pain.

Compassion *is* love. It flowers when you recognize some kind of physical or emotional pain within the other person. I dare say that no human experience is purely 100 percent good. Life experiences are instead virtually always some rich amalgam of good and bad. Think of it as a vibrant tapestry, in which the gilded threads of love and good fortune are interwoven among the darker threads of pain, sorrow, and loss.

Equally true, no human experience is purely 100 percent bad, nor need it be. Even the heaviest of human experiences—sudden grief or joblessness, natural or human-orchestrated disasters and other brushes with mortality—can be lightened appreciably when you recollect simple truths such as "this too shall pass" or "I'm not in this alone." Indeed, such braiding of adversity with hope and love, of destructive with more reassuring emotions, is the secret to resilience. Resilient people are the ones who bend without breaking and who eventually bounce back from even the most difficult life challenges. Instinctually, they can see some form of light in the darkness they face. In study after study, my collaborators and I find that it is precisely this infusion of positive emotions into negative emotional terrain that drives resilient people to bounce back.

Perhaps you come by this sort of resilience naturally. For whatever reasons, you may have little trouble finding the value in difficult experiences, even if it's only to discover the depths of your inner fortitude or your social support. But maybe resilience doesn't come to you naturally. Maybe you flounder in the wake of upsets and struggle to regain your footing. Rest assured, people can and do become more resilient in time. All it takes is practice. With repeated practice, you can build new emotional habits that fuel a newfound and well-earned resilience. You, too, can bounce back from the many adversities you endure. And when you do, you'll also discover a renewed capacity to offer positivity resonance to others, helping others to heal, grow, and bounce back as well. The place to start is with your own suffering.

Try This Micro-moment Practice: Use Your Own Suffering as a Cue to Connect

Whenever pain, suffering, or any form of adversity weaves its way into your own experience, take that very moment as a cue to practice compassion, to take tender care of yourself. Depending on the exact nature of your circumstances, your self-care may be swift, like yanking your hand away from a burning hot surface, or slow, like taking time to read or write poetry when you feel lost, numb, or otherwise disoriented. In either case, bring your full awareness to your painful predicament, putting a metaphorical (or literal) hand on your own shoulder as you witness your experience of it. The kindness and awareness that you give yourself draws more of the gilded threads into the tapestry of your own experience. There's no need to deny or suppress difficult feelings. Simply allow the good and the bad to sit side by side, so that they can inform and influence each other. In doing so you plant seeds of hope: Even as you fear the worse, you yearn for better.

Remind yourself that whatever painful predicament you now endure is—at this very moment—being faced by others as well. When it comes to suffering, after all, there's scarcely anything new under the sun. While the particulars of your predicament may be unique, the bones of it are not. At one level or another, you'll be able to recognize the shared elements in your difficult circumstances, whether it's physical pain, social injustice, uncertainty about your own or another's health, a crushing influx of demands, rejection, or a disorienting lack of direction. Take a step back from your own suffering and imagine yourself connected with others who suffer similarly. This is the first step toward compassion. No matter who or where these others may be, no matter whether you know them, you're connected to them through your shared experience of this difficulty.

It's only natural, when you suffer, to yearn for your distress to pass. Although this wish may already be intense, I suggest you make it larger still. Let that wish expand horizontally, to encompass both you as well as others who suffer similarly. As you do, articulate some version of the following wish to yourself:

May I, together with all those who suffer [this], find peace.

Experiment with self-compassion in this more encompassing manner and you coax yourself out of the narrowband focus that all but defines your own difficult passages. As your awareness expands, you become less self-absorbed, more open and attuned to the suffering of others. This broadened perspective often provides the toehold you need to reverse the downward spiral that threatens to drag you into despair or self-pity. It begins to lift you on the warm winds of an upward spiral. It also conditions your heart to become more oriented toward others, more attuned to their difficult passages. You are no longer alone.

With repeated practice, you un-numb yourself. Your awareness of others' suffering grows sharper and clearer. Indeed, whenever you become aware that the other person with whom you connect suffers, love and compassion become one and the same. Given the ubiquity of suffering in this world, the appropriateness of compassion is wide-spread. Even so, when you can trust simple truths like "this too shall pass" and "we're in this together," you won't be overcome by the weight of others' suffering. You're better able to offer a steady source of comfort to the suffering person you're with.

In time, you can untether your awareness of another's suffering from your own suffering. Knowing that you have suffered, or could suffer, similarly can be enough. This is the wisdom of sameness, of shared humanity. Let this be the foundation for your compassion. Resilience doesn't just reside within people. It also resides within the vast web of our collective social connections. Each time you offer compassionate attention to another, you build up this resource, this resilience, not just in that very moment for that particular person, but also across your entire community, in enduring ways.

Compassion's Aim

Your aim in offering compassion to others is modest. You simply offer an infusion of warmth and light, however small, into the chilly darkness that your companion is now facing. You don't pretend to be an alchemist, magically turning his or her entire tapestry into gold. You simply offer up a single gilded strand, a single warm gesture. Indeed, an alchemist's bravado would surely backfire, leaving your companion wounded by the added harm that comes from having the grave realities of his or her current circumstances ignored. Difficult experiences, most often, can't simply be erased. They can only be met with the respect of openness and the warmth of goodwill.

As you practice compassion, maintain an awareness of your own current resources. Take in and take on only as much of another's pain as you can responsibly hold. Becoming more open to pain is a process, often a difficult one. So don't force it. Take baby steps. Know that even a small increase in your openness to another's pain changes both your own heart and the situation the other faces for the better. Opening too far to pain, or too fast, can push you beyond that sweet spot of positivity resonance that you seek. When that happens, you altogether miss your intended aim of simply being with the other through this difficult passage. You instead collapse under the weight of your own pain, losing your ability to offer support to others. Although "Be open" can be a great motto in many circumstances, like any piece of good advice, it can also be taken too far.

You'll soon find that when you connect with those who suffer, when you sit beside them with kindness, clear eyes, and acceptance, you'll quite naturally be drawn to care, help, or give. The warm and tender feelings in your heart inspire you to do whatever you can to relieve the other person's suffering. Put another way, compassion doesn't just sit there. It motivates action. Those actions may be seemingly small—like listening attentively or taking over a chore—or more heroic—like hosting a fund-raiser or taking on a position of leadership to advocate on behalf of those less fortunate. Let your new appreciation for the other's predicament guide you in selecting the wisest course of action, knowing that—as with alternative medicine—the smallest interventions sometimes have the biggest effects.

Compassion, then, meets the negativity of suffering with the positivity of love, acceptance, and concern. When love moves toward suffering in this way, it raises the ratios of positivity to negativity for all involved. These newly raised positivity ratios spur on healing, growth, and resilience when and where it's needed most.

Laura's Story

My friend Laura works as a doula. Pregnant women hire her to support them during labor and childbirth, and into their postpartum stages. While other professionals who attend a birth focus primarily on a safe childbirth, a doula's aim is to "mother the mother," continuously offering her timely information, emotional support, and physical assistance throughout that miraculous and often tumultuous journey, helping her to feel safer, and more comfortable and confident. Studies show that the continuous support that a doula provides can improve health outcomes for both the mother and the baby.

More than a decade ago, Laura's mother was diagnosed with breast cancer and had a mastectomy. At that time, she had declined the recommended courses of radiation and chemotherapy, even though she was informed that without them she might live only months. Because Laura's mom had defied medical expectations by living well year after year, Laura "never knew what to expect" and "learned to adopt an 'in the moment' mind-set." She knew that especially with respect to her mother's life expectancy, "it did little good to plan." So when, about a dozen years after the mastectomy, she learned that her mother's cancer had spread to her bones and was terminal, Laura continued to address her mother's dying one moment at a time. As her mom's physical limitations increased, Laura made a room for her in her own small apartment so that she could better care for her. Eventually, with help from her sister, hospice workers, and countless others, Laura was piecing together round-the-clock care for her dying mom. Laura had attended countless home births over the years. This was her first home death. She'd made a career out of caring for mothers while they faced difficult passages, and here she was doing the same for her very own mom, albeit for a very different kind of passage.

Toward the end, her mother's pain, confusion, and frailty intensified to the point where she'd wake up terrified, hallucinating, unsure whether she was dead or alive. To meet the challenge of caring for her mother during these difficult weeks, Laura drew on many of the same resources she used in her doula work, which she said are "hard to describe, because they don't come from words." A first step, she shared, is to know that "you can't fix someone else's pain" but can only "be fully present with it, with awareness and calm." Laura's caring for her mom before she died translated into sleeping at her mother's side while holding her hand. That way, Laura could meet the first signs of her mother's agitation with "total presence and reassurance." Just as in her doula work, she knew it was important "not to get swept up in another person's issues" but instead to simply "be present" and "stable in yourself" and let them know they're "not in this alone." This can take courage, especially when the other person is experiencing fear as well as pain. Being present in this way during the difficult transitions of labor and childbirth often calls on Laura to be bold. As she put it, she may need to "get in her face," which can mean getting down on the floor so that she can position her own face just inches from the birthing mother's face. From this close range she gently insists, "Open your eyes and look at me. Breathe with me. I'm here with you." She drew on similar courage in caring for her mother, often reminding her that she could "talk later, for now, just breathe with me." Laura has found that to connect and be helpful to someone in dire emotional or physical pain requires that she "be fully present, one moment at a time, which can at times stretch into hours." When the suffering eventually subsides, as it always does, the ensuing shared sense of calm—or in the case of childbirth— success, can be "beautiful," even "exhilarating."

Laura's descriptions underscore the importance of connection. True compassion, just like positivity resonance more generally, demands the physical copresence of bodies. For Laura, touch, eye contact, and "breathing together with the other" have been "huge" resources. They can be for you, too, when you wish to connect with someone who's suffering. As Laura put it, compassion like this "doesn't come from words." It comes instead from being physically and emotionally present, concerned and grounded. That's the stance from which you can most readily turn toward pain, rather than away from it, while offering up one more gilded strand for the other to weave into the dark tapestry of the trying time they now face. When compassion flowers, you're not simply giving of yourself to another, you are also stretching open your own heart. A positivity resonance emerges that changes you both.

Try This Meditation Practice: Compassionate Love

Retreat to a quiet place where you won't be disturbed. Sit comfortably, with both of your feet flat on the floor. Straighten your spine, bringing the top of your skull skyward and your shoulder blades down and together, creating room in your rib cage for your heart and lungs to expand more readily.

Take a few slow and deep breaths. Bring your awareness to the subtle rocking of your heart with each in-breath and each out-breath. Call forth your intention for this practice session. Perhaps it's to slow your pace and soften your heart so that you can be a true friend to someone who suffers, a source of comfort and reassurance. Know that all people, everywhere, suffer adversity from time to time. Just as all people yearn to be free of suffering. In this moment, as you sit relatively free from your own suffering, you yearn to be a ready resource to others.

Throughout this session, keep bringing your awareness to your heart. Witness how this practice affects your body. Know that your body sensations deserve your awareness as much as the phrases or thoughts that emerge from your mind.

Gently call forth an image of someone who is currently facing ill fortune or otherwise suffering. Without getting mired in these difficulties, explore their scope. Then, lightly remind yourself of this person's good qualities, and how much you would wish to ease his or her pain or lighten his or her load. Say the following classic phrases, or your own versions of them, slowly and from your heart.

May you find safety, even in the midst of pain (or misfortune, difficulties).
May you find peace, even in the midst of pain.
May you find strength, even in the midst of pain.
May you find ease, even in the midst of pain.

Repeat these ancient wishes one by one, with each breath you take. Let each phrase infuse and soften your heart. Visualize yourself simply standing beside this person, recognizing his or her courage in the face of whatever difficulty life now delivers.

As your practice deepens, experiment with new ways to soften and expand your heart's capacity. Shift your focus to new people who are suffering, whether they're people you know well or not. Keep in mind that your aim is not to make this or any other person's pain or adversity magically disappear. Rather your aim is to condition your own heart to move in toward others' suffering when you see it, to open up to it a bit more, so that you may offer comfort and strength, rather than to turn away in self-protection.

If you find that the words of this practice stand in the way of your ability to call forth true tenderness, try simplifying your focus. Draw on images. Visualize before you the difficulty that this other person faces, whether it's physical or emotional pain or uncertainty. Imagine what this difficulty might look like. Give it a color and a shape. Where do you see it in relation to the person on whom you focus? Next, visualize your own heart as it yearns to be compassionate. Imagine that this is your well of healing positivity. Imagine its color, shape, and movements. Is it bright or golden? How much does it expand? Now, with these visual details painted in your mind's eye, imagine that as

you breathe in, you inhale the other person's ill fortune, lifting a portion of it away from him or her. As you inhale, let this ill-fortune enter
in and be transformed by your steady, loving heart, pausing for just a
moment before you exhale to witness this change. Then, as you breathe
out, imagine that you are giving some thread, however small, of good
fortune to this person, relief from his or her pain or suffering. Visualize
this process of hope and change with each breath you take. Breathe in
pain. Add your own compassionate wishes to the mix, and breathe out
a small infusion of comfort. Breathe in threats, softening them by adding your love into the mix, and breathe out safety. Breathe in despair;
breathe out peace. Breathe in feelings of being overcome, and breathe
out strength. Breathe in the suffering person's difficulties, and breathe
out ease.

As you end this practice session, know that you can access this
growing supply of compassion anytime you wish.

Try This Micro-moment Practice: Create Compassion in Daily Life

You can also practice compassion informally. Opportunities to do
so are plentiful in the full buzz of daily life, as you walk from your car
to your office, as you stand in the checkout line, or sit in a meeting.
Why not replace random mind-wandering with simple mental activities that build your capacity to connect with others compassionately?
The only investment you make is in the currency of emotional energy,
not time or money. All it takes is a willingness to retrain your heart
and mind to see others differently.

Here's how to dive in: In these "found" moments, take in the faces
and body postures of others. These need not be people with whom you
are currently interacting. Mere passersby are great targets for informal practice. Think of it as harmless people-watching, albeit with

respectful distance and loving intent. Consider your commute. On the train, in the car, or in the parking lot, instead of staying wrapped up in your own thoughts, take time to notice the people around you. Imagine the ways—small or large—that they might be suffering right now. It can be helpful to remember that no situation is 100 percent good (or bad). Each moment, for each person walking this earth, contains some unique blend of good and bad fortune. As Armistead Maupin writes, describing Mona's Law in the book series Tales of the City: You can have a great job, a great apartment, and a great relationship, but never all three at the same time.

With this awareness in mind, take a close look at those others with whom you cross paths. Look for nonverbal signs, however small, of their suffering—a grimace, a furrowed brow, a heavy sigh, or slumped posture—any clue that this other person is carrying some burden on his or her shoulders or in his or her heart. Witness this suffering with your whole body, not just with your eyes and your mind. See if you can feel in your own body and your own heart the heavy load that this person endures. All people suffer. At some level, whatever flavor of difficulty another faces will feel somewhat familiar to you. Lightly let your heart and mind reflect on that source of shared pain for a moment. Next, into this moment of empathy, extend a simple wish for the person's release from pain and suffering. Try saying one or more of the following classic phrases, silently, in your own mind and heart, directing your good wishes to this particular person:

May your difficulties [misfortune, pain] fade away.
May you find peace [ease, strength].
May your burdens be lifted.

As with all phrase-based practices, it's not the words you choose that matter, but rather the feelings these words evoke. Experiment: Try new phrasings until you find a phrase or two that truly moves you, or leads to a subtle shift in the physical sensations of your heart.

Remember, you're not engaging any sort of magical thinking by doing this. Shifting your stream of consciousness toward compassion is no metaphysical trick that instantly whisks away all suffering from this other person's experience. Your aim with this informal practice is far more humble and realistic. It is simply to condition your own heart to be more open and concerned about the pains and predicaments others inevitably face. Put differently, although your focus is completely on other people in this practice, the person who is most changed by it is you.

Celebration: Meeting Another's Good Fortune with Love

At times it can seem all but overwhelming to truly open to the suffering of others. Standing beside and becoming one with those who suffer takes courage, which can, over time, become depleted. But it can also be replenished, for courage is a forever renewable resource. Fortunately, opportunities to recharge your resources for compassion abound. The secret is to be ready for chances to forge yet another variant of love: celebratory love. This lets you connect with others who are experiencing good fortune.

Moments of bad fortune, with attendant opportunities to suffer, seem plentiful in this world. Yet, statistically speaking, moments of good fortune, with attendant opportunities for positive emotions, outnumber them by a wide margin. One rigorous examination of people's day-to-day lives concludes that good events outnumber bad events by margins of about 3 to 1. Put differently, for every episode of bad fortune that you encounter, odds are you also encounter three or more episodes of good fortune to balance it out. Plus, it's the frequency, not the magnitude of good events, that predicts your overall well-being. The key, of course, is to notice and be open to the good events just as much as you take in the bad. Set aside the mental time travel of worry and rumination. Awaken to the present moment. If you do, you'll discover that most moments in life offer at least some good fortune to be relished, whether it's fresh air, a welcomed meal, or the opportunity for companionship.

The discovery that good events in people's lives are more plentiful than bad events can be especially comforting. You might even say that the world conspires to offer up just the right ratio of positivity to negativity for you to thrive. My earlier research identifies 3 to 1 as a key tipping point in people's emotional experiences. It's the ratio of positive to negative emotions that marks the divide between languishing and flourishing, or between just getting by and becoming ripe with abundant energy, connections, and contributions.

It can be tempting to think that good events, almost by definition, translate into good feelings. Yet that's not always the case. Whether or not good events create moments of joy, gratitude, serenity, or love hinges on whether people recognize and lean in to such events, or instead brush them off or even fail to notice them altogether. Back in chapter 1, I mentioned that variation in the extent to which people seek out good events is what my graduate student Lahnna Catalino and I call *prioritizing positivity*. The more you prioritize your own positivity, the more readily you convert good events into good feelings. Indeed, Lahnna and I have discovered that people who score higher on our measure of this tendency even receive more emotional uplift from a hug.

Just as you can be tempted to turn away from others' suffering in an attempt to limit your own, you may also be tempted to pull away from others' good fortune, believing that—in some way—their good fortune subtracts from your own. This distancing may come in one of three flavors. One is resentment or envy, characterized by obsessive counterfactual thinking, "Why them, and not me?" You ask yourself, over and again, "Why did they get accepted, and not me?" Of course, you can replace "accepted" in that internal rant with other forms of good fortune, like "a raise," "that praise," "that lover," "that car," or any other social or material good. Implicit in this reaction are the inter-twined and erroneous beliefs that "they are not worthy" of their good fortune, but instead "I am"—a narcissistic self-aggrandizement that squelches loving connections of all sorts. Another flavor of distancing is self-diminishment, seeing yourself as somehow perennially unlucky, or unworthy of the good fortune that others enjoy, a self-deprecating preoccupation that, like envy, prevents positive connection with fortu-nate others. Yet a third flavor of distancing is utter indifference, seeing other people's good (or bad) fortune as completely irrelevant to one's own self-absorbed circle of concern. In this mode of being, you're emo-tionally disconnected from what's going on in other people's lives.

By contrast, when you awaken to the insight that everybody, just like you, yearns to be happy, and that for each person, suffering and good fortune inevitably come and go, you can learn to take others' good fortunes as events to cherish and celebrate. These moments cre-ate abundant opportunities to reduce social distance and be open, to forge positivity resonance.

Several randomized controlled trials in positive psychology have confirmed that learning to cherish your own good fortune—for instance, by counting up at least three blessings each day—can boost your gratitude, which in turn strengthens your social bonds and cre-ates abiding happiness, even physical health. Think of celebratory love as gratitude's more generous cousin. It leverages the known benefits of gratitude across a far wider range of gifts—encompassing not just those bestowed on you but also those bestowed on everyone else. The math is simple: If you cherish the good fortunes of others as dearly as you cherish your own, you vastly multiply your opportunities for love and happiness. Just as "Happy Hour" forever begins anew because it's always five o'clock somewhere, you can be nearly continually uplifted through shared joy, love, and connection because good fortune is always happening somewhere. You need only open your eyes and heart to it.

People everywhere need others to lean on. Social support is a lifeline. My guess, though, is that when you visualize offering social support to someone, you imagine another person as weak or suffering in some manner. In your mind's eye, you might visualize your friend in the hospital, your neighbor's child having just fallen off his bicycle, or your coworker near tears under the strain of crushing demands. Yet the latest research documents that offering social support when things go *right* is a more efficient way to build relationships than offering it when things go wrong. In fact, it's precisely those moments in which you celebrate another's good fortune that let him or her know you truly care and instill faith that you'll lend a hand during tougher times ahead.

It can take practice, however, to recognize and respond to others' good fortune in this healthy, life-giving and relationship-strengthening way. You may need, after all, to break long-standing habits of resentment, self-diminishment, or indifference. Try the next activity to open your heart to celebratory love.

Try This Meditation Practice: Celebratory Love

Find a location where you can sit undisturbed. Place your feet flat on the floor and adjust your position and posture until your body feels both alert and open. Lengthen your spine as if it were an antenna. Lift your heart as if you were offering it up as a gift.

Take a few slow and deep breaths, bringing your awareness to each as it rises and falls. Then bring your awareness to your intention for this practice session. Perhaps it's to learn to be an even better friend, or to reduce pernicious envy and instead learn to celebrate others' successes. Know that good events—both seemingly minor and major—are abundant in other people's lives. Sometimes, all it takes is to awaken from the trance of self-absorption to see this abundance pouring forth.

Throughout the session, bring your awareness to your heart region from time to time. Take time to notice how your practice is affecting your body, even your face. As ever, the sentiments and bodily sensations you create are more important than the particular phrases you repeat to yourself.

Now, gently call forth the visual image of someone for whom you know something good has happened. This good event may be big or small. Perhaps this person's family has been expanded to include a healthy newborn child. Or maybe he or she got a raise or had an important project at work meet with success. Or maybe this person is simply feeling healthy and strong, and enjoying a sense of ease in daily life. No matter the circumstances, let your mind slowly absorb the scope of this person's good fortune, knowing that, like all events—good and bad—this, too, shall fade with time. Then, lightly remind yourself of how people worldwide yearn to be happy, and that—at this particular moment, for this particular person—this universal wish is coming true. Into this context, say the following classic phrase, or your own version of it, speaking from your heart:

May your happiness and good fortune continue.

Repeat this ancient wish over and again, with each new breath you take. Let the phrase infuse and soften your heart and your face. Visualize yourself supporting this person, celebrating his or her unexpected good fortune, coaxing whatever goodness he or she experiences to linger just a bit longer.

As your practice deepens, try out new ways to soften and expand your heart's capacity. Take in new people, ranging from those you know well to those you don't know at all. Remember that your aim is not to make this or any other person's good fortune last forever. That's hardly possible. All things pass, and it does no good to expect otherwise. Instead, your aim is simply to condition your own heart to appreciate others' blessings when you become aware of them, to open to them, so that you may lovingly celebrate with them.

Try This Micro-moment Practice: Create Celebratory Love in Daily Life

Personally, I find informal practice of celebratory love to be especially powerful. As I walk to my campus office from where I park, I cross paths with many people—students, staff, faculty, and visitors alike. Likewise, when I'm able to take my lunch, or a short break, on one of the many park benches in my campus's nearby arboretum, I like to people-watch. Instead of being indifferent to others nearby, or simply sizing them up out of idle curiosity, I purposely try to notice signs of good fortune. Is this person smiling? Is there a spring in this person's step? Does he or she seem to be moved by a purpose or a passion? Is something going right for him or her in this moment? Even without knowing anything about what this person's particular good fortune may be, I silently offer my wish for him or her: "May your good fortune continue." This can be an especially moving mental exercise when I sharpen my earnestly supportive intentions. There's no need for me to interrupt the person or intervene in any way. I simply bask in his or her blessings and wish him or her the best. Sometimes I picture myself cheering this person on or giving him or her an imaginary high five. I'm often struck by how readily this shift in perspective will put a smile on my face and awaken my feelings of connection with others.

You can even deploy silent celebration to transform any minor irritation you might feel at another's actions into a more buoyant, light-hearted moment. Any of us, despite our generally benevolent attitudes, can grow somewhat impatient with others, even if their only crime is that they march to their own drummer. Perhaps it's the cashier who tends the long, slow line in which you wait, who chats for a bit too long with each customer, or the restaurant patron at the next table who in her enthusiasm speaks too loudly, or the free spirits who hula hoop in your town square, obstructing your shortcut. For me, it seems like just about every day, while I'm at work in my office, I find my flow of thoughts interrupted by "the campus whistler," an older gentleman who walks throughout campus and town enjoying music on his headphones while whistling in full force. He's actually a fantastic whistler. Yet once you've heard him once or twice, it gets easy to begrudge his next arrival. I'm not the only one to react this way. My colleague shared with me that when she held her class outside one uncommonly fine day in February, for a moment their discussion was pierced by the campus whistler strolling nearby. Her students groaned and grumbled. Sometimes, when others enjoy themselves in unusual ways, your first reaction can be judgmental. Take two, however, can be more charitable. My campus whistler is joyful after all. When I allow myself to savor this unique musical moment and wish him continued enjoyment, I create my own joy as well.

Try it for yourself. See if you notice any new radiance or levity within your heart, or any additional softness or openness within your face. As you experiment with celebratory love, notice how readily you can turn these feelings of loving connection on and off just by bringing in others' presumed good fortune into your awareness. Notice how others respond to you. Does the face and openness with which you meet the world make a difference?

Love 2.0: The View from Here

The facts are that all people face both good and bad fortune every year, if not every day. When you look out at others, even without speaking with them or knowing anything specific about them, you can be virtually certain that they are simultaneously blessed by good fortune, however small or large, and also burdened by bad fortune, again, however small or large. Each person we encounter, then, simultaneously merits both our compassionate love and our celebratory love. Love, upgraded as positivity resonance, comes in many flavors. It bends toward compassion when suffering is salient, and toward celebration when good fortune is salient. Above all, love is connection. In connection, you are far more likely to recognize what other people are going through, and meet them where they are, sincerely wishing them the very best.

In the next chapter, I'll ask you to stretch the scope of your love even wider. Beyond the special people in your life, and even beyond those with whom you interact regularly, I hope to convince you that love's reach is virtually unbounded. Experimenting with unbridled loving is perhaps the most challenging and rewarding of all.

CHAPTER 8

Loving Without Borders

TO LOVE ONE PERSON WITH A PRIVATE LOVE IS POOR
AND MISERABLE; TO LOVE ALL IS GLORIOUS.

—Thomas Traherne

In a world replete with threats, uncertainties, and ceaseless distractions, the urge can be strong to simply look out for oneself. If you're like most who grew up in Western culture, you've absorbed countless versions of this message. I know I did. The messages, both direct and indirect were clear: Be self-sufficient, independent, pay yourself first. You can't necessarily count on anyone else to look after your needs, so you need to learn to take care of yourself. Indeed, entire economic systems are built upon this premise of self-interest. Many economists have assumed, first and foremost, that people direct all their available rationality toward maximizing their own self-interests. To be sure, a healthy dose of independence and concern for self is no doubt required for success in any culture. Even so, one unfortunate side effect of rugged individualism can be a thick cocoon of self-absorption that all but blinds you to the concerns, gifts, and welfare of others.

Becoming more aware of the inherent value of positivity resonance can help you break free from this life-limiting cocoon. Indeed, study after study suggests that positive emotions, in and of themselves, unlock your ability to really see other people. When feeling good, then, you're far more likely to approach each new person as an opportunity for connection and growth. Love, viewed in this way, knows no borders. When love is as modest as a shared interest, a shared inspiration, or a shared hope, you have no reason to withhold it from anyone.

I again draw from the ancient wisdom of LKM in this chapter. As does LKM, I gently encourage you to stretch open your heart wider than you ever thought possible. I first invite you to experiment with extending warmth and goodwill to everyone you know and then to stretch that positive vibe even further to encompass everyone you don't know. Once you set your sights, mind, and heart on these larger aims, you'll find countless ways to forge tender, loving connections with everyone, without a single exception.

These are not just idle wishes, empty intentions, or a futile form of magical thinking. In wishing people on the other side of the planet to be happy and peaceful, you need not believe that your wishes somehow metaphysically travel the world to change the course of their day. The point is to change *your* day, by conditioning your heart to be soft, open, and caring toward each new person you encounter, regardless of how remote the prior connection between you may have been. This chapter features both formal and informal practices to help you extend the reach of your love, even in the face of uncertainty or ambiguity.

Redefining love as those micro-moments of positivity resonance you can share with nearly anyone breaks open extraordinary opportunities.

To be sure, extraordinary opportunities pose extraordinary challenges, not only to see the chances for loving connection but also to be ready for them. Micro-moments, by definition, are fleeting. If you blink—or slip into self-absorption—you miss out. Even so, merely seeing opportunities to connect, without being prepared to act, can make you lonelier. To build community and escape painful isolation, you need to teach your heart to be ready. Hone your skills for capitalizing on those life-giving micro-moments so that, as the river of fresh opportunities for love flows toward you, you'll be poised to jump in.

Try This Meditation Practice: Loving All

Retreat to a place in which you can sit undisturbed. Ground yourself by placing your feet flat on the floor, and adjust your posture until your body feels both alert and open. Lengthen your spine and lift up your rib cage. Since emotional states are deeply embodied, seek out the posture that feels attuned to expanding love.

Start, once again, by drawing a few slow and deep breaths, resting your awareness on each one as it moves through your lungs and through your body.

Next, bring your awareness to your intention for this session. Articulate this intention silently to yourself. Perhaps it's to awaken yourself to the vast sea of possibilities for love, or to find joy in connecting with all the people you'll encounter today.

As you practice, remember to lightly bring your awareness to your heart region. Pay attention to any shifting sensations in your body and face. These physical aspects of your experience matter more than the particular phrasings you choose.

Now, gently call forth the image of a whole swath of people. This might be all the people in your part of town or your region of the country. To do this, you might visualize the view you'd have flying low over your stretch of earth. Although you can't see individual people, you're aware that they are there, underneath nearly every rooftop, carrying out the activities of their day, perhaps eating, resting, working, worshipping, or simply moving from one place to another. Expand your awareness to encompass this whole community. Know that it includes people you know quite well, those you know just a bit, as well as those you don't know at all. You can be sure that each and every one, like you, has at one time or another yearned for something more in their life, for happiness, for connection, and for an abiding sense of peace. Let your awareness of this fundamental similarity between you and all others infuse the space between your heart and each of theirs. You share the same wishes, the same earth. You breathe the same air.

With your various connections to all these people in mind, silently say to yourself the following ancient phrases, or your own versions of them, offering these wishes from your heart:

May you all feel safe and protected.
May you all feel happy and peaceful.
May you all feel healthy and strong.
May you all live with ease.

Offer each wish in time with the rise and fall of each of the slow and full breaths that you take. Let your goodwill toward all those in your neighborhood, town, or region infuse and soften your heart.

When you are ready, gently expand the scope of your focus further still. You might choose to visualize your entire country or continent, offering your goodwill to everyone residing there, recognizing again that this includes people you know personally as well as an immense sea of those you do not know. Silently repeat the phrases with this now larger expanse of people held gently within your awareness.

Another way to experiment with loving all is to divide the sum of all people into two mutually exclusive and encompassing categories. No need to bring in heavy analytic thinking here. Simply call up any division that makes sense to you, such as "all children" paired with "all adults" or "all girls and women" paired with "all boys and men" or "all those who suffer" paired with "all those currently free of suffering." You can bring in your own touch of creativity at this stage, perhaps choosing to focus on "all those who are sleeping" paired with "all those who are awake" or "all those on whom the sun shines" paired with "all those in the darkness of night." The key is to leave no person out, to encompass all within your consideration. Then, repeat the classic phrases for each subset of your focus, calling forth your heartfelt goodwill.

> May all children feel safe.
> May all children feel happy.
> May all children feel healthy.
> May all children live with ease.

As you extend these wishes, gently coax yourself to truly feel the sentiment that underlies that simple word *all*. Give this one word just a bit more emphasis than the other words, to nudge your heart just a bit wider with each wish you offer.

> May all adults feel safe.
> May all adults feel happy.
> May all adults feel healthy.
> May all adults live with ease.

As you end this practice session and move on into your day, know that each person you encounter has already been the focus of your loving intention today. Use that awareness to forge new micro-moments of connection.

Unlock Your Opportunities for Focusing on Others

Outside the formal practice of LKM for all people, it can be heart-stretching simply to notice how much of your attention each day is devoted to your own concerns. There's nothing inherently wrong with self-concerns. You are responsible, after all, for navigating yourself through your day, and at times doing so can require planning or strategic self-presentation. Problems arise only when you get swept up in swirls that appear to run on indefinitely. It can seem, sometimes, as if you've entered a hall of mirrors, completely alone. All you see reflected back at you is yet another view of the same self-concern, and you can no longer find the way out. Redirecting your focus toward others *is* the way out.

Your intent, of course, matters. Focusing on others comes in many forms, not all of which are generous. It can be yet another selfish act. I spent several years early in my career cataloging the psychological damage done to girls and women who face the message that they can be reduced to how they look. The question an objectifying stance asks is, "What can you do for me?" By contrast, a genuine wish to understand and appreciate who this other person is asks, "Who are you?" and trusts that taking steps to find out will reveal inherent goodness. From this openhearted perspective, caring sentiments surface quite effortlessly.

One way to become more mindful of the degrees of your focus on self versus others is to revisit a typical day—your yesterday—and comb through it episode by episode. In doing so, you uncover the sheer number of untapped opportunities for creating micro-moments of positivity resonance. This added awareness can then inspire you to begin turning toward these recurrent opportunities, rather than let them slip away unnoticed.

Try This Micro-moment Practice: Reconstruct Your Yesterday to Uncover Opportunities for Love

Here I walk you through how you can adapt an assessment technique developed by a former collaborator and mentor of mine, Nobel

Prize–winning psychologist Daniel Kahneman, author of the best-selling book *Thinking, Fast and Slow*. It's called the "Day Reconstruction Method," or DRM for short. You can use it to review and evaluate your daily habits of mind as well as your emotions, both actual and possible.

You should know up front that this activity takes time to complete, up to an hour. It's the insights from it that you can use in later micro-moments. To get started, you'll need either your journal, or some other pad of paper, and a calculator. Or, you can register to use the free online tools that you can find at www.PositivityResonance.com.

Once you're situated—either at your computer or with paper and pencil handy—your task is to remember everything you did yesterday. It can be difficult to recall the details of a whole day. That's why the DRM exercise breaks this process down into steps. The first step is to record the times at which you woke up and went to sleep. Then, starting from when you awoke and proceeding sequentially throughout all your waking hours, divide your day up into a string of contiguous episodes. Give each episode a number and a short descriptive name, like "1—stretching my body," "2—out for a walk," and "3—eating breakfast." Write down the approximate times each episode began and ended, avoiding large gaps or overlaps in time. You can think of episodes like scenes within a play. Whenever the characters in, or the setting or purpose of, your daily activities change, call that a new episode. You can, of course, skip past small behind-the-scenes moments, like blowing your nose or using the bathroom. Still, the key is to map out your day in its entirety. With typical episodes lasting between ten minutes to two hours, you may find that your day yesterday can be broken down into fewer than ten or as many as thirty episodes.

Now, here's the variant on the DRM that can be useful for spotting and unlocking opportunities for focusing on others, with the potential that such moments hold for love. For each and every episode in turn, record your responses to the following questions as accurately and honestly as you can:

Name of episode: _____

Duration of this episode (in minutes): _____

1. For what proportion of time during this episode (from 0 to 100 percent) were other people present, either face-to-face or by phone (do not include asynchronous communications, like e-mails, voice mails, or texts). _____

2. For what proportion of time during this episode (from 0 to 100 percent) were you able to focus on the other(s) in respectful and meaningful ways? _____

3. For what proportion of time during this episode (from 0 to 100 percent) were you able to attune to and connect with the other(s)' experiences? _____

4. For what proportion of time during this episode (from 0 to 100 percent) did you feel energized by the company of others? _____

5. For what proportion of time during this episode (from 0 to 100 percent) did you experience a shared flow of thoughts and feelings between you and the other(s)? _____

6. For what proportion of time during this episode (from 0 to 100 percent) did your interactions reflect a smooth coordination of effort between you and the other(s)? _____

7. For what proportion of time during this episode (from 0 to 100 percent) did you experience a mutual sense of being invested in the well-being of the other(s)? _____

As you progress through the first three of these seven questions for each episode, the proportions of time that you identify are likely to become progressively smaller. Questions 1 and 2 capture the prerequisites for sharing micro-moments of positivity resonance with others; first, the presence of others, and next, respectful and meaningful focus on others. Whereas question 3 captures the gestalt sense of connection (first introduced in chapter 5), the remaining questions capture the three key facets of positivity resonance in turn—shared positive emotions (questions 4 and 5), biobehavioral synchrony (question 6), and mutual care (question 7).

Now comes the scoring. While the online tools take care of this chore for you, if you're completing this exercise on paper, here's when a calculator comes in handy. First, add up the total number of minutes across all your recorded episodes. This number should come close to representing the total time you were awake yesterday. Then, for each episode, convert your responses to questions 1 through 7 into the unit of minutes. Do this by multiplying the number that represents each episode's duration (in minutes) by the proportion of time you indicated in your response (in other words, 20 percent would mean multiplying by .20, 5 percent by .05). Next, add up the total minutes, separately for each question, across all episodes. That is, for question 1, find the total number of minutes, across all your waking hours, during which you were surrounded by others. Likewise, for question 2, find the total number of minutes, across all your waking hours, that you meaningfully focused on others, and so on. Odds are the gap between these two numbers is large. This gap represents your untapped potential, in a typical day, for creating conditions conducive to positivity resonance.

Next, continue on to find the total number of minutes, across all your waking hours yesterday, that you sensed either the gestalt sense of positivity resonance (question 3) or one of three facets of it (questions 4 and 5, followed by questions 6 and 7). The gap between each of these numbers and your total number of minutes spent in the presence of others (question 1) represents your untapped potential for love, a number likely to be quite large. By contrast, the more modest gap between each of these numbers (for questions 3 through 7) and your total number of minutes spent with respectful and meaningful focus on others (question 2) represents how easily you were able to convert these opportunities into micro-moments of love.

With this rundown before you, consider now the opportunity costs for self-absorptions like surfing the Internet. That kind of behavior is normal and inevitable, and at times even rejuvenating. But think about what other kinds of experiences you are crowding out. What do you miss out on? More love?

Jeremy's Story

In my home office, I have three framed letters—two from my own sons and a third from a couple of children whom I may never meet. The two from my boys are cherished Mother's Day gifts. Each lists what it takes to be their mom, ranging from "make the best pancakes" and "cheer me on" to "enjoy talking to me" and "teach me about what she teaches." The third is written in blue marker on green construction paper and decorated with glitter glue and cartoon drawings. It reads: "Dear Dr. Fredrickson, Thank you for teaching Mr. Wills to be + [positive], [heart] Tisha and Kelly."

Mr. Wills is Jeremy Wills, one of my former students. A few years back, he'd enrolled in an upper-level undergraduate seminar of mine, on positive psychology, before which he'd never given a second thought to positive emotions.

A few months ago, as I was thick into crafting part I of this book, I ran into Jeremy as I was walking across campus at the University of North Carolina at Chapel Hill. He was back in town for a short stretch between jobs. He'd been a wonderful contributor in my class years back, so open and thoughtful, and I enjoy catching up with him when I can. It was during this sidewalk conversation, which stretched into what must have been half an hour, that Jeremy told me he had a letter to pass on to me from some of his own former students. Having heard just a little bit about those students, and his experiences as their teacher, I knew I needed to hear more. I asked if I might interview him for this book and he agreed. His and his students' stories, as it happens, provide a clear and poignant illustration of why and how positivity resonance matters, and how you can tap into it, even in the most difficult of group circumstances.

After graduation, Jeremy had taken a coveted position at Teach For America, the nonprofit modeled after the Peace Corps that enlists thousands of future leaders, just out of college, to bring low-income communities fresh teachers for two or more years. Jeremy had been drawn to Teach For America because he yearned to make real differences for social change. A few years earlier, as a volunteer classroom assistant in the struggling city schools in neighboring Durham county, he'd become keenly aware of the irony of sitting in "ivory tower" classrooms in his own elite university, discussing in abstract terms how, generation after generation, social inequalities get replicated through entrenched inequities in education and wealth, when just down the road sat a middle school student who struggled to read "Go dog go." Getting to know one of these kids in particular, and noting the poignant gap between his aspirations (for example, "to design video games") and his academic ability, Jeremy discovered up close and personal that "the problem had a face." As he put it, "Someone somewhere did something to him that prevented him from learning or didn't give him the opportunity and that's a problem that no one should have to deal with."

Teach For America (TFA) offered Jeremy the chance to roll up his sleeves and help to close the achievement gap by working directly with struggling kids in low-income classrooms. After a few months in TFA's teaching training, and a short stretch into his first placement in a poor rural county in North Carolina, his assistant principal took note of his extraordinary patience and high expectations for even the lowest-performing kids in the high school. She offered him his own math class.

He'd take charge of about a dozen chronically failing "special ed" kids, some with IQs in the fifties or with behavioral problems so severe that if "you look [at them] the wrong way, you could have a desk flipped." He was excited to take on this challenge. His idealism ran high. He admits that at first he thought he would simply "waltz in" and fix the problem of social inequality, one classroom at a time.

But the reality of the problem hit him hard. Even though Jeremy spent four or more hours each day preparing lesson plans, complete with guided notes, tactile instruments, and every teaching tool about which he'd read, it soon became clear that he was utterly failing his students. Behavior management, or dealing with kids' outbursts, hardly turned out to be the problem. As he put it, "The kids were despondent." Getting them to say anything "was like pulling teeth." They wouldn't make eye contact with him. When they talked at all, they just mumbled. The worst was when he'd distribute a math test. Many would just put their heads down on their desktops. They wouldn't even look at it, wouldn't even try. "There was no life in the classroom."

Jeremy described this new teaching assignment as "humbling" and "stressful." It was "overwhelming" to be "directly responsible for kids' academic success, which then translates to their overall health, earning potential, and career." Although this had been his dream postcollege placement, he began to dread going into his classroom. On top of that, he wasn't sleeping well. He'd wake up "almost out of breath." His hair started falling out. He'd even lost his taste for fun. He found he no longer enjoyed heading back to Chapel Hill to hang out with his college buddies, playing ping-pong or darts over a few beers like old times. "I was just a shell of myself because I had all these worries."

Coming to terms with his failure as a teacher—the painful mismatch between his high hopes and his daily experiences with disengaged adolescents—was the toughest thing he'd ever experienced. He knew something had to change. Even his body was telling him he simply couldn't go on like this much longer. After wading through his own despondency for a while, he began to recall the previously abstract ideas he'd encountered that now seemed especially relevant to his painful predicament. He remembered ideas discussed during his orientation training for Teach For America, about classroom climate and getting students to invest in their own education. He also recalled catching an interview I'd given on our local public radio station, as well as the opening story from my first book, which described how a parent who woke up to positivity changed the course of her day, her life, and the lives of those around her. Then he thought back to the class he took with me at Carolina. There he'd learned about the sizable asymmetries between negative and positive emotions. What struck him most was that negative emotions shout out and drag on, whereas positive emotions are "like the quiet kid in the room that no one ever pays attention to." This helped him remember that if he could cultivate and savor those quiet and fleeting positive emotions—and help his students do the same—then together they could leverage feeling good to build their resources and resilience. He admitted to me that before he fell into the funk of this all-time low point of his life, all of these ideas had merely remained abstract to him, interesting ideas, to be sure, but they didn't feel real. Now, together with the support of his supervisors and TFA mentors, they were forming a lifeline.

He realized that what needed to change first and foremost was his own attitude. As he put it, "I was not celebrating education in any way." True, he'd been given a difficult assignment. But he realized that if he made the effort to look at his situation in another way, he could also see that he'd been given "a rare opportunity to actually change these kids' lives in a positive way, to actually rekindle their love for learning." He began to see teaching as "a bi-directional relationship. They may be pretty despondent, but look at me. I am certainly not the life of the classroom when I walk in!"

That's when he decided to take a break from teaching basic math to build real relationships with and between his kids. "I said let's get to know each other, so we played games." He asked the students to share something about themselves, how many brothers or sisters they had, their thoughts about their town, anything to break the ice. He asked them to write stories about themselves, telling "who they were, what their worst experiences in life had been, what made them happy." After one kid was bold enough to share his own story, "the stories poured out." He said it was like penguins lining up along "the edge of an iceberg" all peering down at the water, and then "one jumps in and if it's safe then everyone else jumps." The kids began to open up, telling of dads who weren't around or moms who were struggling to feed the family on food stamps. They shared their fears, alongside their hobbies and hopes. Ty had built his own stock car and had recently won two thousand dollars racing it. Tisha shared that she wanted to be a nurse. They learned to trust their classmates and to honor what each shared.

He even devoted a few class sessions to basic lessons from the science of positive emotions, which he attributed to "Dr. Fredrickson" back at Carolina. He asked them to recall a time that they felt down or upset. They shared stories of breakups and other failures. He encouraged them to notice how feeling down, just by itself, becomes self-defeating, because it zaps their energy and confidence. He also asked them to notice that feeling good can sometimes escape awareness altogether, but that these good feelings could do quite a lot for them. Celebrating the good feelings that they were learning to create in the classroom—by listening to and supporting their classmates—could renew their energy, give them confidence, and build the resources they needed to face tough math problems. Together as a class, they drew on this discussion of emotions to create extended analogies to tough situations in sports. They talked, for instance, about how a baseball player, up at bat in the bottom of the ninth with the tying run on second base, needs to have confidence and to be able to visualize his own success and give it his all. He told them that math class was just like that, that they'd need to marshal up their own resources and confidence to persevere and give each step of a math problem their all.

One by one, Jeremy helped his students tie this particular math course to what they wanted to do in life. He helped Tisha see how, as a nurse, she'd need math to measure blood pressure or dispense a particular dosage of medicine. "She was like, 'You need math for that?' and I said, 'Yeah! You think you are just going to stick someone with a needle?'" With Ty, Jeremy talked about engineering, tire pressure, and rotations per minute and speed, and emphasized all the math that these ideas involved. "He was like 'Really? I need math? I didn't know any of this. . . . '" Jeremy went on to tell me, "I think that was the big key . . . that we tied the course to something positive and we even talked about how they felt. Like, does it make you happy when you think about your career or what you want to do? And they were like, 'Yeah!' Well, then math should make you happy too because it is going to get you there!"

After days and weeks of "conversating," as they called it, these twelve lowest-achieving students bonded in Jeremy's math class. Along the way, he encouraged them to celebrate one another by sharing what they found interesting in one another's stories. He also encouraged them to help each other through difficult steps on math problems and cheer on one another's successes, however small. Then, instead of mumbles, silence, and no eye contact, "if Tisha got something right, they would shout 'You go, girl!' " and eventually "the kids were celebrating one another's success without me, and that was huge." He described the classroom now as "full of life." He said, "I know it sounds cliché, but you could say 'the sun rose on a dark day,' [and] they would just shout out answers and it got to the point where they were almost too willing and it was incredible." The atmosphere Jeremy and his students created was "almost celebratory" and truly interactive, like a church in which shouts of "Hallelujah!" come from any pew. Or, as Jeremy summed it up: "It was like a party, except with math."

This huge emotional turnaround paid dividends. Ty got an A and told his mom, for the first time ever, that he liked math. The kid with the IQ in the fifties passed the class. Another went from the fourteenth to the forty-fourth percentile. "I remember she told me, 'Mr. Wills, I am going to pass, I'm going to pass,' and she did and that was what was incredible." Indeed, more than 80 percent of Jeremy's special ed kids passed the state's standardized math test. When you compare that to the 50 percent pass rate of the regular ed kids in the same high school, you begin to see how remarkable this transformation was. One grand-mother called to find out whether her granddaughter passed, and when Jeremy told her she did, "she was like, 'Hallelujah! Thank the Lord Jesus!!'"

Understandably, Jeremy was immensely gratified. With poignancy he shared that "when I think about how someone, somewhere down the line, did something horrible to make these kids not like learning and to see their love of learning rekindled was almost like, sort of this . . . I don't know . . . it is very hard to describe . . . it is almost surreal. When you see the look on their face when they start to believe in themselves again. . . ." He admits that it didn't work for everyone, but for most it did. "I can safely say that a lot of them walked out of that classroom as far more confident and capable people than they walked in."

As for Jeremy himself, once his classroom climate began to turn around, he began to sleep better. He felt that he had more energy to give. He not only felt better, but his hair stopped falling out. He said to me, "I feel like a far more capable and confident person because of it." The experience taught him both how and why to be optimistic. He drew on what he learned in TFA and in my course to "overcome prob-ably the most difficult challenge" of his life in ways that have "applica-bility throughout life." He called it "incredible" and went on to say, "It is one thing to learn [positive psychology] on paper, and another thing to actually implement it and see real success from it."

After Jeremy shared his and his students' stories with me during this interview, I shared with him a sketch of the ideas I'd been developing for this book, especially my definition of positivity resonance and its precon-ditions. As he took in these new ideas, he nodded his head in recognition. He too began to appreciate what I'd picked up back in our sidewalk con-versation: that the inner changes he'd made in himself—his rekindled hope, his eagerness to savor and celebrate even the smallest of successes, and most especially, his openness to experiment with new ways to lead—created new connections and resources within his classroom. Drawing on what he'd absorbed all those years earlier about the science of positive emotions, together with the values TFA had instilled in him, Jeremy came to see the abstract idea of "classroom climate" as the accumulation of the many real micro-moments of positivity resonance his students cre-ated. It was the energy within these micro-moments—the celebrations and the feelings of connection and camaraderie—that sparked newfound capacity and resilience in these previously lowest-performing students. Jeremy admitted that at first "the kids thought it was lame and stupid to celebrate things." They had to be exposed to the facts about emotions, like he'd been, before they would buy into the new classroom climate he was trying to instill. Even then, their more positive climate was some-thing that they all had to nurture. "It wasn't anything quick . . . it wasn't one person, we all bought into this idea, we all were conscious, we all made an effort, and the fruits of our labor were clearly on display. It was just life changing."

Dear Tisha and Kelly, I'd like to write: Thank you for letting me see how you taught yourselves and your classmates to be so positive. My warmest wishes to you both!

Try This Micro-moment Practice: Redesign Your Job Around Love

Although positivity resonance can and certainly does unfold com-pletely on its own, without any added thought or intervention, frankly speaking, quite often it doesn't. Long-held habits of mind and social interaction often conspire to tempt you to focus on vexing problems or to otherwise judge or hang back from others, perhaps especially at work. The on-the-job changes Jeremy made took courage. He had to make the hard choice to forgo teaching about positive numbers in favor of teaching about positive emotions. Plus, just as he taught math experientially, he also taught about emotions experientially. Teaching in abstractions would surely have taken less time but could hardly have yielded the turnaround results that he sought. So he created games and other means through which his students could open up and connect, and feel safe both to take risks and give their all.

Take some time to do what Jeremy did. Review your own job, your own work routines, your own work attitudes. Which parts of your job do you carry out with, or in the presence of, others? For what proportion of time, during those moments, do you make a conscious effort to connect? Do you slow down enough to really listen and make eye contact? Do you, like Jeremy, allow yourself and others to go "off topic" in ways that build relationships, resilience, and other resources? Maybe you don't simply need more time, a bigger budget, or higher technology for your work team to meet its highest aspirations. Perhaps you, too, can unlock more individual and collective capacity within your team through positivity resonance. How might you devote more of your energy toward cultivating moments of connection? What new rituals or habits could you create to bring more love into your workday? What metrics would help you and coworkers know whether this investment pays off?

On Love, Science, and Spirituality

I'm an emotions scientist, not a scholar of religion. To date, I've written exactly one paper that has religion in its title, and that was merely a commentary offering my two cents on why religious involvement predicts good health. Yet my own and other people's efforts to describe the mystical and ultimately ineffable vistas that love opens up is what first drew me to explore how love and spirituality interrelate. So when I was invited by Boston University's Danielsen Institute to develop a series of lectures on how the science of emotions relates to spiritual development and religious well-being, I was immediately drawn in by the opportunity to dive in further. I delivered those lectures in early 2010. That experience planted seeds in the garden of thoughts and theories that have since grown into this book.

Philosophers, religion scholars, and psychologists alike have long pointed to the gulf that inevitably exists between your embodied experiences and the words that describe them. Your emotional experiences, in particular, can be unspeakably extreme, sweeping you away on free falls into hellish abysses or flights to exalted peaks. At either altitude, the air can get so thin that words turn back, no longer able to reassure you. Words pigeonhole your experiences, yet words are at times your only way to communicate what you've been through to others. They offer up reassuringly fixed concepts and categories that become the basis for our shared understandings, our cultures and institutions. Words are the planks in the bridges that cultures have built to span the chasm between individual, spiritual, and emotional experiences and our shared belief systems. Through the further application of words, rituals, and decrees, some of these shared beliefs evolved into organized religions, cultural institutions that claim to explain—and create—those profound and indescribable spiritual experiences, like love, that visit us all from time to time.

I've been particularly drawn to religious writings that shine a spotlight on experiences of oneness and connection, because those are part of the signature of love. In these moments, borders seem to evaporate and you feel part of something far larger than yourself, be it nature, eternity, humanity, or the divine. This is the "oceanic feeling" that Sigmund Freud dismissed as a regression to the infantile sense of being merged with your mother, but that William James and many others have held up as the bedrock of people's embodied experiences of spirituality. Following in James's footsteps, I take spirituality to revolve around expansive emotional moments like these. Consistent with the idea that words fail to capture the essence of spirituality, in his 1902 classic, *The Varieties of Religious Experience*, James wrote: "Feeling is the deeper source of religion, and . . . philosophical and theological formulas are secondary products, like translations of a text into another tongue."

More than a century after James equated spirituality with emotions, Karen Armstrong opened her 2009 book, *The Case for God*, with a vivid and harrowing description of what it feels like to make your way down some sixty-five feet below ground level—at times crawling on your hands and knees in complete darkness—to explore the ancient caves on the border of France and Spain where you can view the elaborate paintings created by our Stone Age ancestors some seventeen thousand years ago. She concludes:

> Like art, the truths of religion require the disciplined cultivation of a different mode of consciousness. The cave experience always began with the disorientation of utter darkness, which annihilated normal habits of mind. Human beings are so constituted that periodically they seek out [what the Greeks called] ekstasis, a "stepping outside" the norm. Today people who no longer find it in a religious setting resort to other outlets: music, dance, art, sex, drugs, or sport. We make a point of seeking out those experiences that touch us deeply within and lift us momentarily beyond ourselves. At such times, we feel that we inhabit our humanity more fully than usual and experience an enhancement of being."

To Armstrong, religion is doing, not belief. It's the effort you put into repeatedly cultivating such peak, unbounded epiphanies that stretch open your heart and mind, and make you more attuned to boundless possibilities.

As Armstrong notes, religion isn't the only path to expanded modes of consciousness. Back in chapter 4 I drew on that age-old metaphor about swinging open the doors of perception, first used by William Blake, and then more than 160 years later by Aldous Huxley. Your own commonplace experiences of positive emotions can open those doors as well, expanding your outlook on life and setting off spiritual experiences. At times that expanded outlook is hardly noticeable at all, whereas at other times it can take you by surprise, like a powerful gust of wind that clears away debris and allows you to see things with fresh eyes. The point I wish to make here is that your experiences of love and connection need not overwhelm you to open your perceptual gates. Scientific evidence now documents that far less intense positive emotional experiences reliably open those same doors and raise spirituality. By regularly engaging in the kinds of formal and informal practices I offer throughout part II of this book, you can learn to infuse your day and your life with more of the expanded and spiritual modes of consciousness of which James, Armstrong, Huxley, and countless others write.

Toward this end, consider the spiritual lessons from Buddhism. In his acclaimed 1995 book, *Living Buddha, Living Christ*, Vietnamese monk Thich Nhat Hanh wrote that he resonated with how a Catholic priest once described to him the Holy Spirit as "energy sent by God." Nhat Hanh shared that this phrasing both pleased him and deepened his conviction that the most reliable way to approach the Christian Trinity was through the doorway of the Holy Spirit. Integrating this with his Buddhist perspective, he likened the Holy Spirit to mindfulness and its fruits: understanding, love, and compassion. When you purposely tune in to the present moment, this view holds, and see and listen deeply in an open, accepting manner, you open a door to divine oneness. As does Armstrong, then, Nhat Hanh sees both Christian and Buddhist spirituality in the doing. From this vantage point, love, compassion, and other deeply moving spiritual experiences become holy states that you can cultivate through your own intentional efforts to be present, grounded, and mindfully aware of both yourself and others.

Learning to trust that your deepest emotions can lead you somewhere good is what my collaborator and American Buddhist writer Sharon Salzberg calls faith in her 2002 spiritual memoir by the same name. Faith, or alternatively trust or confidence, is the usual translation of the ancient Pali word *saddha*, which Salzberg points out literally means "to place the heart upon." Like Armstrong and Nhat Hanh, Salzberg emphasizes that faith is a verb, an action—something you do—not a received definition of reality or belief system that explains away life's mysteries. In Buddhism, to have faith is to open your heart to your experiences, or as Salzberg puts it, to be willing "to take the next step, to see the unknown as an adventure, to launch a journey." Faith is a way of leaning in toward your feelings of love and oneness, trusting that—somehow—they will nourish you and lead you closer to your spiritual higher ground. Faith, according to Salzberg, is "an active, open state that makes us willing to explore." It draws you out of the safe and familiar territory of labels and constructs, and into the more challenging and always changing flux of your own inner experience.

From what I've highlighted so far, you won't be surprised to learn that I especially resonate with how my friend and Harvard psychiatrist George Vaillant, an expert in adult development, defines spirituality. In his 2009 book, *Spiritual Evolution*, he equates spirituality with positive emotions, noting that these states are what connect you to others, to the divine, and over time help you attain wisdom and maturity. Succinctly, he concludes, "Love is the shortest definition of spirituality I know." I see no need to improve upon this definition.

To be sure, casting spirituality as an altered state of consciousness is hardly new. Viewed one way, it's simply another description of the human practices that yield exalted emotional states in the first place. Descriptions like these didn't take us very far in the past precisely because they remained on the same "soft" side of the opposition between subjective and objective ways of knowing. Religion has long anchored the subjective side, whereas science anchored the other. Likewise, the languages of poetry and emotions marked one pole, whereas mathematics and reason marked the other. Spirituality, poetry, and emotions were all deemed soft and subjective, whereas science, mathematics, and reason were all deemed hard and objective. Historically, the two poles simply didn't have anything to say to each other.

But just as borders melt away when you feel that elemental oceanic feeling, today these old oppositions no longer hold water. In particular, the new and amply objective science of emotions allows us—for the first time—to systematically explain transcendent spiritual experiences and unravel their poetic mystery. We no longer need to stop at calling the varieties of religious experiences altered states, *ekstasis*, or oceanic. We can instead examine them through the lenses of the science of positive emotions.

These new scientific lenses reveal facts that can be deeply moving. Those potent, boundary-blurring and heart-expanding experiences of positivity resonance that you share with others are not merely an academic concept or a poetic flourish. Positivity resonance changes your biochemistry in ways scientists are only just now beginning to grasp. As these moments become more and more typical of your daily experience, they even alter the foundational rhythms of your heart, increasing your vagal tone, resulting in a closer synchrony between the actions of your heart and the actions of your lungs. High levels of vagal tone, scientists have now firmly shown, are linked not only to greater social attunement but also to more efficient self-regulation and improved physical health. In this way, love and health cocreate each other in your life. At the same time, this reciprocal, upward spiral dynamic between micro-moments of love and lasting changes in your health forges a path toward your higher spiritual sense of oneness. It may well be these cell-nourishing moments of positivity resonance that, according to Karen Armstrong, "touch us deeply within and lift us momentarily beyond ourselves" and, according to Sharon Salzberg, embody the "active, open state" of faith "to take the next step."

Love 2.0: The View from Here

I've encouraged you, throughout this chapter, to take the next step toward loving all, without borders. I hope that I've convinced you that this step is indeed glorious, as Thomas Traherne promised in the opening chapter quote. This is the step that will take you closer to your highest aspirations, your highest spiritual ground. It will open you up to create more and better opportunities for flourishing and for physical health.

All your waking moments give you opportunities to practice opening your heart. You choose the best way for you to do this. It may well be best to meet your new ideal of "loving all" by adopting the more modest aspiration of "loving one more" and then renewing this more achievable aspiration time and again. Your goal can be to see past the borders that traditionally constrain love, and to exclude no one. By nature's design, your genetic and psychological makeup grant you the capacity to recognize, protect, and cherish your kin and the other special loved ones to whom you have bonded. Just as surely, however, evolution has also designed you to benefit from sharing micro-moments of love with even the most distant and dissimilar other. Don't miss out on your chance to give love . . . and health . . . and oneness . . . freely, to all.

CHAPTER 9

A Closing Loving Glance

I NEVER KNEW HOW TO WORSHIP UNTIL I KNEW HOW
TO LOVE.

—Henry Ward Beecher

After spending months building the case for this book for why it's worth upgrading your view of love, I've become convinced that this simple call opens the door to an endless process. The work of science, after all, is never done. Even though the latest discoveries about love's impact on your body, brain, behavior, and future prospects can fill volumes and fill you with amazement, it's equally humbling to recognize how little we actually know about love's full impact. New discoveries about love's power will continue to unfold. As they do, you and I alike will be called to upgrade our views of love, time and again, to reimagine this life-stretching experience from the ground up once more. Whatever your prior beliefs about love, my hope is that I've piqued your curiosity to begin to see love as your body experiences it, as positivity resonance that can momentarily reverberate between you and virtually anyone else. Before these reverberations fade, they initiate biochemical cascades that help remake who you are, both in body and in mind.

It's also worth considering whether you've unwittingly placed constraints on your own experiences of love by following cultural norms. These constraints may have been holding you back from reaching your full potential for health and happiness, and from making deeper contributions to the lives of others. Beyond sharing the latest science on love, my aim in this book has been to release you from these constraints. The task of upgrading love remains incomplete without self-reflection and self-change.

Years ago, when I sat in a silent meditation retreat sponsored by the Mind and Life Institute held at the retreat center cofounded by my friend and collaborator Sharon Salzberg, one of our teachers shared a joke with us. It went something like this: On learning of a friend's new (or renewed) devotion to meditation practice, an observer quipped, "Practice, practice, practice! All you ever do is practice! When's the performance?" After a muted wave of chuckles rolled through the meditation hall, our teacher went on to say that there is indeed a performance scheduled; it's called "Your Daily Life."

This is the mind-set about the practices in part II that I urge you to adopt. Whether you choose to shift your focus with formal meditation or with the informal micro-moment practices I've offered, I can guarantee you that merely dabbling in them one or two times will lead to no appreciable changes. You well know that engaging in one bout of vigorous physical exercise, or eating one stem of broccoli, will not do anything to improve your health. Your path to physical, emotional, and spiritual vitality is no different. So find activities that speak to you, and identify the recurring cues that might trigger you to do them. Let the micro-doses of positivity that these activities bring draw you to practice, practice, practice. Let these practices help you build new and life-expanding habits, habits that little by little remake you and the course of your day and your life from the inside out.

Love 2.0: An Emotion Is Born?

Even as I have been writing this book, the equivalent of a scholarly earthquake has been shaking the foundations of the science of emotions. The question at the root of this rattler is ages old, yet repeated most cogently now by my fellow emotions scientist Lisa Feldman Barrett with the force of considerable data. What Barrett and her collaborators (including one of my newest Carolina colleagues, Kristen Lindquist) have asked is simply, what is an emotion? William James himself devoted considerable attention to this very question back in 1884.

In the current era, a typical scientific answer to this question describes a momentary emotional state—like anger, fear, or joy—as an organized set of responses to some new circumstance you face—like an insult, a clear danger, or sudden good fortune. These coordinated responses show up as discrete and identifiable changes in your facial movements and cardiovascular activity, in your subjective experience and action urges, and so on, all presumably orchestrated by discrete and identifiable changes in your brain. A hidden assumption is that the unique states of anger, fear, and joy are given to you by the basic design of your body and brain, as sculpted over millennia by Darwinian natural selection.

Barrett's answer to the question, what is an emotion?, equally compatible with the premise that you inherited your basic emotional architecture from a long line of human ancestors, is that your experiences of anger, fear, and joy are not, in fact, biological givens, handed to you, preformed, by specific hardwired locations or circuits in your brain. Instead, she argues for considerably more flexibility in what makes for an emotion. Posing an assumption-shaking challenge to the field we share, Barrett contends that your brain comes preset only with the capacity to represent what she calls *core affect*, the more amorphous pleasure or displeasure of your bodily states, along with some degree of arousal. What makes for a specific experience of anger, fear, or joy, then, is your ability to weave together your appreciation of your body's current state of pleasure or displeasure with your conceptual understanding of what's happening to you in that very moment. In other words, higher-order mental processes—like memory, learning, knowledge, and language—are the more basic "ingredients of mind" that combine together with "core affect" to create the various recipes for states like anger, fear, or joy. Although aspects of Barrett and colleagues' "constructionist" view of emotions can be traced back to earlier scientists, theirs is the first to be backed by modern neuroscientific evidence.

What does this mean for love? What does it mean for you? Plenty. For millennia, your ancestors felt energized by markedly good feelings when they interacted and connected with others. Those were the moments that made them feel part of something much larger than themselves, more energized, alert, and alive than they felt in other, more ordinary moments. Piecing together the commonalities across the many and varied situations that gave rise to such powerfully energizing good feelings led your ancestors to come up with words, rituals—and indeed whole religions—fashioned to represent and cultivate those longed-for feelings, in themselves and in others.

Having such words and rituals makes a big difference. Research coming out of Barrett's lab and other labs, including my own, demonstrates that even the particulars of people's bodily experiences hinge on the labels and ideas each person holds about emotions. For instance, inspired by Barrett's work, Lindsay Kennedy and Bethany Kok, working in my PEP Lab, were drawn to test whether the bodily effects of anger depend on whether the person experiencing it believes anger to be an emotion, as is typically the case, or whether he or she is led to believe that anger is *not* an emotion, but instead "an instinctual response to an imbalance of resources." Fitting with Barrett's view, people's understandings of the unpleasant state that they were just then experiencing shaped their bodily response: Those who took anger to be an emotion showed the typical jumps in heart rate and blood pressure, whereas those for whom the idea that anger is an emotion was debunked had an appreciably more muted cardiovascular response.

This means that the mere act of reading this book may well have added a new and powerful emotion to your repertoire of interpersonal experiences. How you come to think about love actually stands to reshape the way your body experiences it. A global poll, released on Valentine's Day, 2012, revealed that most married people, or those similarly coupled, identify their significant other as their most important source of happiness. Likewise, nearly half of all single people say they yearn to find their own happiness by finding their own special person to love. While these numbers certainly varied culture by culture, they strike me as a worldwide collapse of imagination. Thinking of love purely as the romance or commitment that you share with one special person—as it appears most on earth do—surely limits the health and happiness you derive from micro-moments of positivity resonance. Put differently, your beliefs about what love is become self-fulfilling prophecies. If, for instance, you think love can in fact also bloom between you and the utter stranger with whom you connect for only a few minutes at the airport, then it more readily can. If, by contrast, you think love can bloom only between you and a special, predesignated one, then you've severely limited the prospects for yourself and that kindly person at the airport. Think of the old-school view of love as pouring a thick layer of cement over a garden that has been planted with a thousand flower bulbs. Although any single flower might still push its way through cracks in the cement and bloom nevertheless, the odds are severely stacked against it. Yet by upgrading your view of love to recognize its full scope, you break up and remove this cement to let a thousand flowers bloom.

Positivity resonance exists, whether you adopt a new view of love or not. It remains the ancient life-giving, soul-stretching state that your body craves. The difference you get with an upgrade is whether you are awake to the thousands of opportunities that surround you for fulfilling this craving. When you awaken to this new understanding of your heart's potential, a new and life-changing emotion is born within you.

Do-It-Yourself Gene Expression?

Also in the span of time that I've written this book, my research team and I have been making new discoveries about how your experiences of love may be either amplified or muffled by the expression of certain genes within your cells. As sketched back in chapter 3, we've already discovered that people with higher cardiac vagal tone somehow extract a larger and more immediate positive jolt out of their efforts to practice the style of mediation, LKM, that I've featured prominently in part II. Even more inspiring, we found that practicing LKM actually raises people's vagal tone such that positive feelings and higher vagal tone feed each other over time.

In our most recent experiment, we obtained blood samples from study volunteers before they tried out meditation for the first time. By the flip of a coin, they tried either LKM or a different style of mediation, one that does not aim to cultivate loving feelings. Before and immediately after their assigned guided meditation, we asked them to rate the extent of their positive feelings. We then processed the blood samples in my collaborator Karen Grewen's lab at Carolina, and later shipped them to my newest collaborator, Steve Cole, the director of UCLA's Social Genomics Core Laboratory. Using sophisticated computational techniques, Cole analyzed each person's RNA to determine whether any differences in gene expression uniquely predicted whether people had especially positive reactions to LKM.

A compelling pattern of differences emerged. While it's too soon to say exactly what this pattern of differences means, it is consistent with the more general hypothesis that my team has been testing: that certain biomarkers, like cardiac vagal tone, inflammation, gene expression patterns, and perhaps even body mass index, can either amplify or muffle the good feelings you get when you try to cultivate love. To the extent that love in turn reshapes these biomarkers—a prediction we're poised to test in the coming year—upward spiral dynamics ensue, in which love and health dynamically cocreate each other. How, then, your DNA gets translated into your cells next season may to some degree be up to you. By practicing healthy patterns of emotional expression, you may be able to sculpt healthy patterns of gene expression. Countless times in this book I've suggested that your body was designed for love's positivity resonance and indeed cries out for it. My team is currently homing in on ever more precise statements about which of your genes, differentially expressed in your cells, contribute to this cry the loudest.

Pilot Yourself

How can you tune in to your body's cravings and hear its subtle cries for love? It hardly sounds possible. Actually, becoming attuned to these cellular messages may be easier than you think. By nature's design, you come equipped with a ready indicator of whether or not you're meeting your body's basic needs. Feeling good is that indicator. What's more, the biochemistry of your brain has been carefully orchestrated by natural selection to keep close track of the contexts in which your good feelings arise, even when you're busy thinking of other things. That's because good feelings trigger a cascade of neurochemicals that makes you like whatever caused it. It's as if feeling good sets off a localized firework that comes to cover the people and objects in its radius with enduring glitter dust. The new sparkle draws your eye and pulls you back toward them, impulses that operate even outside your conscious awareness. Think of this as your innate and automatic positivity-fueled navigation system. If you follow it, you'll find yourself enticed back, time and again, to circumstances that enliven you most, including those life-giving micro-moments of positivity resonance.

You do, of course, need to keep your wits about you as you tune in to positivity's navigation system. Sure enough, peddlers are forever standing by to tempt you to find your bliss in commercial goods and services, both legal and illegal. Such commerce is often carefully engineered to set off the emotional fireworks that create brand loyalty, and even addictions. With conscious effort, you can override these impulses. If you couldn't, you'd be a hapless product of past conditioning. Yet overriding hedonist impulses isn't always a wise move. Discerning which pleasure-seeking urges actually represent healthy pursuits, like the age-old cellular cry to connect, is foundational to emotional intelligence. All it may take is to step out of the marketplace, and to trust the wisdom inherent in your body to draw you to connect with others in meaningful ways.

Infants and toddlers follow their positivity instincts as a matter of course. Yet once impulse control becomes possible, all bets are off as to when and whether people of any age will tune in to and prioritize their own good feelings. Evidence suggests that it isn't until midlife or beyond that people develop true wisdom about positivity's quiet cues. This delay may well reflect the strong supporting role that families and educational institutions play in the lives of younger people. Many families and schools are organized around ways to help younger people find ready sources of positivity resonance. Parents and teachers, coaches and resident assistants, provide scaffolding to support positive connections between and among young people. When you were growing up, for instance, far beyond providing you shelter, meals, and clothing, your parents likely stoked your opportunities to share positivity-laced moments with them and others. At first it was simply through tickles and grins, and later it was through setting up playdates and creating family rituals around mealtime, bedtime, weekends, and holidays. Many schools, colleges, and universities strive to provide similar structural support. Through icebreakers and other experiential activities, both within and outside classrooms, through sporting and artistic events, these places create entire webs of people, institutional practices, and rituals that may have provided additional external support for the positivity resonance that nourished you through your youth.

Jeremy, whose story I told in chapter 8, likened all this structural support to an external navigation system. As he put it, "Your path up through college is kind of decided for you and then it is like the navigation system turns off and you have to pilot yourself and that's when it gets scary." Being released into the so-called real world, absent the scaffolding to support ready connection, can leave recent graduates wondering why their life suddenly seems less sparkly, their days more life-draining than life-giving.

Adapting to this stark change can be like learning to cook for yourself. After decades of having your every meal prepared by parents, and then by dining hall staff, you needed to learn to put the right balance of micronutrients on your plate each day. While the effects getting the balance wrong may not have shown up for months, or even years, you've felt those effects nonetheless, in terms of unhealthy changes in weight or health. Think of love as another key micronutrient. How long will it take before you learn to put the right amount of it in your daily diet? It can take years, even decades, for people to learn this vital life lesson: That in the "real world" you are responsible for feeding yourself your own recommended daily value of love.

It easily took me two decades to internalize this message, and I still struggle at times to truly live by it. My natural tendencies toward introversion, combined with my socialized tendencies toward workaholism, set me on a life trajectory that was hardly sustainable. By my early forties, my relationships and health began to suffer. I've since learned to plan my day and week around love and other opportunities to feel good. I also stay open to those impromptu chances to forge meaningful connections with the people at work and in my community, and even with complete strangers when I'm away from home. Two decades is a long time. I even had the benefit of seeing the facts about positivity stack up on my desk. My wish for you is that it doesn't take you this long.

We now know that whether you truly embrace this life lesson—whether you learn to prioritize and kindle your own sources of love each day—matters a lot: It makes you far more likely to flourish, which not only makes your own life more rewarding but also adds value to those around you. Or, as Jeremy put it, "You can work as hard as you want, but if you are not connecting, you are not going to be successful or happy." Fortunately, you already have what it takes to "pilot yourself." Your inborn navigation system, running on positivity, is always available for you to consult, even if at times its readout is rather faint. Consult it wisely and you can pilot yourself in the direction of love, health, and happiness.

Love 2.0: The View from Here

Love, I've argued, is our supreme emotion. It governs all that you feel, think, do, and become. It lifts you toward the higher spiritual altitudes of oceanic oneness. And from these new and higher vantage points, you can better see and appreciate your connections to the larger fabric of life as well as your place and influence within it.

Love is also deeply personal. It unfurls within and throughout your mind and body like a wave, cresting with each new micro-moment of connection—that smile, that laugh, or that knowing and appreciative glance that you share with another. Yet even as these micro-moments are deeply personal and fleeting, they've also been targets of increasing scientific scrutiny. So now, for the first time, you can know and appreciate love not only through a personal, subjective lens but also through a scientific, objective lens. Through this scientific lens, you can better see and appreciate how your body and brain were made for love, and made to benefit from loving. Learn to seek love out more frequently and it can elevate you, your community, and our world far beyond what you and I can today envision.

Opportunities for love abound. It's up to you to nourish yourself with them.

Acknowledgments

The ideas about love that you'll encounter here have been gestating in my mind and heart for years. Fittingly, they first arose through my connections with others. Some of these connections have been fleeting, others long-standing. Some have been mutual connections, with ideas forged through rich conversations and collaborations, others have been more one-sided, as I've privately mulled over and expanded on the words of other scholars.

For the foundational idea that love is best seen as any positive emotion shared within a safe, interpersonal connection, I thank Carroll Izard. His 1977 book described love as moments of shared joy and shared interest, and convinced me that any accounting of the positive emotions should not omit love. What little I wrote about love in my first presentation of the broaden-and-build theory owed a great deal to Izard's influence on my thinking.

A deeper shaping of my views on love comes from the pioneering work on high-quality connections by my friend and University of Michigan colleague, Jane Dutton. I've long been inspired by her ways of seeing and describing the connective tissue that binds and energizes people in long-standing relationships and one-time encounters alike. Apart from her inspiring theoretical work, Jane is also an inspiring person, and I am thankful that our friendship has withstood the strain of my move from Ann Arbor.

Other scholars whose work has deeply influenced my thinking about love and related ideas include Lisa Feldman Barrett, Kent Berridge, John Cacioppo, Laura Carstensen, Sy-Miin Chow, Steve Cole, Michael D. Cohen, Mike Csikszentmihalyi, Richie Davidson, Paul Ekman, Ruth Feldman, Shelly Gable, Eric Garland, Karen Grewen, Melissa Gross, Uri Hasson, Julianne Holt-Lunstad, David Johnson, Danny Kahneman, Dacher Keltner, Corey Keyes, Ann Kring, Bob Levenson, Kathleen Light, Marcial Losada, Batja Mesquita, Paula Niedenthal, Susan Nolen-Hoeksema, Keith Payne, David Penn, Chris Peterson, Bob Quinn, Cliff Saron, Oliver Schultheiss, Leslie Sekerka, Marty Seligman, Erika Rosenberg, Robert Vallerand, George Vaillant, and David Sloan Wilson. Although these people span the spectrum from my dearest friends to those I've yet to meet, the theoretical and empirical contributions of each have inspired me to build upon them.

Although I described love as shared positive emotions as early as 1998, I did not take these ideas up empirically until coaxed to do so by the students and post-docs working with me in my Positive Emotions and Psychophysiology Lab (aka PEP Lab). Former University of Michigan graduate students Christian Waugh and Kareem Johnson, for instance, were the first to pursue the idea that positive emotions inspire people to think more in terms of "we" than "me," and my first wave of students at the University of North Carolina at Chapel Hill have each taken these ideas further in their own signature way. Bethany Kok, for instance, forged her expertise in the vagus nerve and has expanded my appreciation of it. Lahnna Catalino discovered that some people, more than others, lean toward their moments of positivity and positivity resonance and thereby reap more from them. And Tanya Vacharkulksemsuk steadily developed a most compelling research program on nonverbal behavioral synchrony and helped me see how and why two or more people moving "as one" matters.

My thinking on positivity resonance has also been indelibly marked by two brilliant PEP Lab post-docs, with whom I've had countless conversations about ideas of mutual fascination. Stephanie Brown, a former post-doc at Michigan (now faculty member at SUNY Stony Brook), crafted (with her father) one of the most convincing evolutionary accounts of social bonds I've read to date. She was also the first to turn me on to the idea that the human body appears to have two basic modus operandi, one centered on *self survival*, often governed by negative emotions and fight-or-flight tendencies, and a second attuned to *species survival*, owing a great deal to positive emotions and calm-and-connect tendencies. Likewise, Sara Algoe, a former post-doc (and current faculty colleague) at Carolina, brought considerable firepower in relationship science to the PEP Lab and helped me to see the profound effects of mutual care (aka mutual perceived responsiveness) within positive relational processes. I am often awed by her ability to unravel complex dyadic processes, and I aspire to continue to learn from her exemplary work.

Other past and present members of the PEP Lab who have shaped my thinking include Carrie Adair, Christine Branigan, Daryl Cameron, Lisa Cavanaugh, Michael Cohn, Anne Conway, Zan Isgett, Keenan Jenkins, Matt Keller, Lindsay Kennedy, Laura Kurtz, Greg Larkin, Yi-Chen Lee, Janna Lembke, Aly Light, Roberta Mancuso, Paul Miceli, Joe Mikels, Keiko Otake, Elise Rice, Tori Schenker, Kandace Thomas, Eddie Tong, Michele Tugade, Patty Van Cappellen, and Tor Wager. Dr. Kimberly Coffey deserves special note, for it is her quantitative talents that make PEP Lab discoveries ever more powerful. I offer special heartfelt thanks to Ann Firestine, for her legendary drive and talent to do whatever it takes to superbly manage our various PEP Lab projects. Since the day she joined us, she has single-handedly elevated PEP Lab productivity to new heights.

Of course, the research that streams out of the PEP Lab would not have been possible without the many people who've donated their time and thoughts to science as participants in our studies. I thank each of them for being the bedrock of this book. Nor would this work have emerged without those at the U.S. National Institutes of Health who have found sufficient merit in my hypotheses to award grant funds to support their test. Over the years, my lab has been the fortunate recipient of grants awarded by the National Institute of Mental Health and the National Institute of Nursing Research, and now also the National Cancer Institute. My work has also been supported by the James Graham Kenan Foundation for Distinguished Professors at the University of North Carolina at Chapel Hill, and, more generally, I am grateful for the support I've long received from colleagues, administrators, and staff at UNC–CH. These people are what make Carolina an astoundingly congenial and productive place to work. Go, Heels!

The path toward getting these new ideas on love from my mind into yours began when Brian McCorkle invited me to serve as a Templeton Research Fellow for a series on religious and psychological well-being at the Danielsen Institute at Boston University. With funding from the Metanexus Institute and the John Templeton Foundation, the Danielsen Institute invited me to deliver a series of six lectures at BU in early 2010. With appreciation, then, I acknowledge Brian and my hosts at the Danielsen Institute for planting the seeds for this book and supporting me to write it.

Richard Pine, of Inkwell Management, is my agent and so much more. He stepped in to serve as my initial editor, helping me to shave off the excesses of academic language and theory. *Love 2.0* would not exist without him. Also of Inkwell, I thank Lyndsey Blessing and Charlie Olsen, for helping get my ideas translated for foreign language readers.

Caroline Sutton, of Hudson Street Press and the Penguin Group, has been an extraordinary editor. She was quick to see my strengths and weaknesses as a writer and to work with them with respectful equanimity. Also of Hudson Street Press and the Penguin Group, I thank John Fagan, Liz Keenan, Courtney Nobile, Ashley Pattison, and Brittney Ross for shaping and promoting *Love 2.0* in their various ways.

It's one thing to study love and another thing to live it in the moment, wholeheartedly. I humbly admit to being more novice than expert when it comes to putting these ideas into action. Yet I've been blessed with many teachers, formal and informal, who have guided and inspired me to live with more heart each day. Among my formal teachers, I call out Sharon Salzberg, Guy Armstrong, Mark Coleman, and Sally Armstrong for the teachings they offered during a weeklong silent retreat on loving-kindness meditation that I sat in January 2010 at the Insight Meditation Society in Barre, Massachusetts. That experience was nothing short of soul-stirring. I also thank Rita Benn, Jeff Brantley, Mary Brantley, Jon Kabat-Zinn, Yun Lu, Sandra Finkel, Libby Outlaw, Jaime Powell, and Sharon Salzberg (again) for helping me to learn, both as a scholar and a human, about the practice of meditation. I've also learned so much about love, compassion, forgiveness—and color—through my lifelong friendship with my sister, Jeanne Gallaher. Plus I thank those who shared with me their heartfelt experiences of living with love through difficult passages—Donna, Erika, Laura, and Jeremy. I hope that their stories, which I present in part II of this book, will move and inspire you as much as they move and inspire me.

Still my most cherished teachers—my two sons, Crosby and Garrett, alongside my husband and soul mate, Jeff Chappell. We four have now been joined by my boys' two "kitty boys"—Zeus and Apollo—who seem to know an awful lot about positivity resonance already. Every day I learn something new from my family about how to open my heart to love.

Singularly most inspiring and important of all, Jeff has, from the day we first met in that strawberry patch, taught me how love really works and opened my eyes to the poignant limits of my entrenched ivory tower habits. His natural gifts for seeing and acting from his heart, together with his courageous honesty, have taught me, year by year, to fully trust his instincts and wisdom, so much so that he was always the first to read and critique each word and chapter of this book. Just like our beloved ocean, my love for Jeff crests and renews endlessly, reinforcing our lifelong bond.

Recommended Reading

Brach, Tara (2003). *Radical Acceptance: Embracing Your Life with the Heart of a Buddha*. New York: Bantam.

Brantley, Mary and Hanauer, Tesilya (2008). *The Gift of Loving-Kindness: 100 Mindful Practices for Compassion, Generosity and Forgiveness*. Oakland, CA: New Harbinger.

Cacioppo, John T. and Patrick, William (2008). *Loneliness: Human Nature and the Need for Social Connection*. New York: W. W. Norton.

The Dalai Lama (2001). *An Open Heart: Practicing Compassion in Everyday Life*. Boston: Little, Brown.

de Waal, Frans (2009). *The Age of Empathy: Nature's Lessons for a Kinder Society*. New York: Three Rivers Press.

Ehrenreich, Barbara (2009). *Bright-Sided: How the Relentless Promotion of Positive Thinking Has Undermined America*. New York: Metropolitan Books.

Fredrickson, Barbara L (2009). *Positivity: Groundbreaking Research Reveals How to Embrace the Hidden Strength of Positive Emotions, Overcome Negativity, and Thrive*. New York: Crown.

Germer, Christopher K. and Siegel, Ronald D. (eds.) (2012). *Wisdom and Compassion in Psychotherapy: Deepening Mindfulness in Clinical Practice.* New York: Guilford.

Lyubomirsky, Sonja (2008). *The How of Happiness: A Scientific Approach to Getting the Life You Want.* New York: Penguin.

Neff, Kristin (2011). *Self-Compassion: Stop Beating Yourself Up and Leave Insecurity Behind.* New York: William Morrow.

Nhat Hahn, Thich (2007). *Living Buddha, Living Christ* (10th anniversary ed.). New York: Riverhead Books.

Salzberg, Sharon (2002). *Faith: Trusting Your Own Deepest Experience.* New York: Riverhead Books.

Salzberg, Sharon (2011) *Real Happiness: The Power of Meditation.* New York: Workman.

Index of Practices

Notes

Chapter 1

3 **The Eskimos had fifty-two names for snow:** Margaret Atwood (1972). *Surfacing.* New York: Simon and Schuster.

5 **having at least one close relationship like this is vital to your health and happiness, to be sure:** James S. House, Karl R. Landis, and Debra Umberson (1988). "Social relationships and health." *Science* 241(4865): 540–45. See also Ed Diener and Martin E. P. Seligman (2002). "Very happy people." *Psychological Science* 13(1): 81–84.

8 **the two anchor points for my broaden-and-build theory of positive emotions:** I first introduced the broaden-and-build theory to the scientific community in 1998. It has since become the most widely cited scientific explanation for why we humans have positive emotions in the first place. Barbara L. Fredrickson (1998). "What good are positive emotions?" *Review of General Psychology* 2: 300–319; see also Barbara L. Fredrickson (2001). "The role of positive emotions in positive psychology: The broaden-and-build theory." *American Psychologist* 56: 218–226.

8 **my first book, *Positivity*:** *Groundbreaking Research Reveals How to Embrace the Hidden Strength of Positive Emotions, Overcome Negativity, and Thrive* (2009). New York: Crown.

9 **lies within momentary experiences of connection:** My focus on connection is inspired in part by the work of my colleague Jane Dutton, who has persuasively

highlighted the importance of "high-quality connections" within organizations. She and I share the view that good interpersonal connections have vital physical correlates that contribute to health, although she and I differ on whether it's fruitful to identify such moments as instances of love. See her 2003 book, *Energize Your Workplace*. Jossey-Bass. See also Emily D. Heaphy and Jane E. Dutton (2008). "Positive social interactions and the human body at work: Linking organizations and physiology." *Academy of Management Review* 33(1): 137–162.

10   **casting love as shared positive emotion doesn't go nearly far enough:** In *Positivity* (2009), I only scratched the surface by identifying love as any positive emotion shared within a safe interpersonal connection.

10   **crosses emotions science with relationship science:** From emotions science, I draw the view that love, like all emotions, is a momentary, biobehavioral response to changing circumstances, whether real or imagined. In other words, love is not lasting. I depart from traditional emotions science, though, by elevating love above other emotions, calling it our supreme emotion. There is no precedence for this in emotions science, which takes specific, discernable emotions—fear, anger, joy, pride—as roughly equal-status categories, each holding value for human survival in its own unique way. Under this democratic logic, no emotion is set apart as on an altogether different plane or scale of importance, not even love. That's an idea I draw from relationship science, which unabashedly positions love relationships as larger, more special than ordinary relationships. Yet as I've suggested already, I part company with traditional relationship scientists by not defining or confining love to enduring or intimate relationships.

10   **invested in this other person's well-being:** Kevin E. Hegi and Raymond M. Bergner (2010). "What is love? An empirically-based essentialist account." *Journal of Social and Personal Relationships* 27(5): 620–36. Not all attention paid to others is so benevolent. Earlier in my career, I articulated and investigated the damage caused by a very different form of other-focus, one I now see as the polar opposite of love. This was sexual objectification, which you could describe as investment in the *physical appearance and sexuality* of another person for *one's own* sake, one's own pleasure. See Barbara L. Fredrickson and Tomi-Ann Roberts (1997). "Objectification theory: Toward understanding women's lived experiences and mental health risks." *Psychology of Women Quarterly* 21(2): 173–206. See also Barbara L. Fredrickson, Lee Meyerhoff Hendler, Stephanie Nilson, Jean Fox O'Barr, and Tomi-Ann Roberts (2011). "Bringing back the body: A retrospective on the development of objectification theory." *Psychology of Women Quarterly* 35(4): 689–96.

11   **a yearlong interdisciplinary faculty seminar on integrative medicine:** This was spearheaded by Dr. Rita Benn, director of education at the University of Michigan's Integrative Medicine Program. Encouraged by my friend and colleague Professor Jane Dutton, I joined the Integrative Medicine Faculty Scholars Program in 2004–5. It was through this program that I was introduced to the work of Sandra Finkel, a longtime meditation instructor who eventually became my research collaborator.

12   **warmed their connections with others:** Barbara L. Fredrickson, Michael A. Cohn, Kimberly A. Coffey, Jolynn Pek, and Sandra Finkel (2008). "Open hearts build lives: Positive emotions, induced through loving-kindness meditation, build consequential personal resources." *Journal of Personality and Social Psychology* 95(5): 1045–1062.

12   **these connections that most affected their bodies, making them healthier:** Bethany E. Kok and Barbara L. Fredrickson (2010). "Upward spirals of the heart: Autonomic flexibility, as indexed by vagal tone, reciprocally and prospectively predicts positive emotions and social connectedness." *Biological Psychology* 85: 432–36. See also Bethany E. Kok, Kimberly A. Coffey, Michael A. Cohn, Lahnna I. Catalino, Tanya Vacharkulksemsuk, Sara B. Algoe, Mary Brantley, and Barbara L. Fredrickson (in press). "How positive emotions build physical health: Perceived positive social connections account for the upward spiral between positive emotions and vagal tone." *Psychological Science.*

12   **a steady diet of love influences how people grow and change:** See the randomized controlled trial that my colleagues and I presented in Fredrickson et al. (2008).

13   **Your upward spirals lift you higher and faster:** Lahnna I. Catalino and Barbara L. Fredrickson (2011). "A Tuesday in the life of a flourisher: The role of positive emotional reactivity in optimal mental health." *Emotion* 11(4): 938–50. Stay tuned also for Lahnna Catalino's emerging doctoral dissertation work on prioritizing positivity.

14   **age, measured as time since birth, provides no guarantees for maturity or wisdom:** See work by Paul B. Baltes and Ursula M. Staudinger (2000). "Wisdom: A metaheuristic (pragmatic) to orchestrate mind and virtue toward excellence." *American Psychologist* 55(1): 121–136.

Chapter 2

15   **Love is brief, but frequently recurring:** François de la Rochefoucauld (1959). *Maxims.* Translated by Leonard Tancock. London: Penguin Books.

16   **you can revive them later through conversation:** Bernard Rimé (2009). "Emotion elicits the social sharing of emotion: Theory and empirical review." *Emotion Review* 1(1): 60–85.

17   **or cheer at a football game:** Some scholars have singled out experiences of mass euphoria as unique. Jonathan Haidt and colleagues, for instance, suggest that such experiences reveal that humans, similar to hive creatures like bees, at times follow a "hive psychology" in which they benefit from losing themselves within a much larger social organism, like the crowd at a football game, music festival, or religious revival. While I share Haidt's appreciation of the self-transcendence that can emerge from the "group love" experienced in small or large crowds, unlike Haidt, I see this as an extension of the oneness that also emerges within micro-moments of positive connection experienced within pairs. For additional descriptions of "group love" see the 2006 book by Barbara Ehrenreich, *Dancing in the Streets: A History of Collective Joy.* Metropolitan Books.

18   **think of emotions as largely private events:** I qualify this statement as referring to those of us raised in Western culture because scientists who have studied emotions across cultural boundaries challenge this view. They find that people in other cultures don't necessarily subscribe to the notion that emotions belong to specific individuals. In cultures that originate in East Asia or the Middle East, for instance, people are more likely to say *"We're* angry" rather than *"I'm* angry." See work by Batja Mesquita (2001). "Emotions in collectivist and individualist contexts." *Journal of Personality and Social Psychology* 80(1): 68–74. Relatedly Rimé (2009) contends that "an individualist view of emotion and regulation is untenable" (p. 60).

19   **love belongs not to one person, but to pairs or groups of people:** My conceptualization of positivity resonance has parallels to the idea of "resonant leadership" as described by Richard Boyatzis and Annie McKee in their 2005 book by the same name (Harvard Business School Press). Yet one place where my conceptualization differs from theirs concerns where resonance is located. Boyatzis and McKee locate the origin of resonance in leaders and suggest that followers depend on leaders to move and inspire them. By contrast, I view resonance as a property of the pair or group. For a related perspective, see Wilfred Drath's 2006 book review of *Resonant Leadership* in *Personnel Psychology* 59(2): 467–71.

19   **It can even energize whole social networks:** See work by James H. Fowler and Nicholas A. Christakis (2009). "Dynamic spread of happiness in a large

social network: Longitudinal analysis over 20 years in the Framingham Heart Study." *British Medical Journal* 338(7685): 1–13. See also the book these two wrote about their research for a general audience: Nicholas A. Christakis and James H. Fowler (2009). *Connected: The Surprising Power of Our Social Networks and How They Shape Our Lives.* New York: Little, Brown.

19   **Your innate threat detection system even operates outside your conscious awareness:** See work by Joseph LeDoux, as described in his 1998 book, *The Emotional Brain: The Mysterious Underpinnings of Emotional Life.* New York: Simon and Schuster.

20   **The main mode of sensory connection, scientists contend, is eye contact:** Newborns show an immediate preference for eye contact, as well as innate skills for establishing it with the adults who come within their visual range, leading scientists to describe eye contact as the "main mode of establishing communicative context between humans." This quote is drawn from page 9602 of Teresa Farroni, Gergely Csibra, Francesca Simion, and Mark H. Johnson (2002). "Eye contact detection in humans from birth." *Proceedings of the National Academy of Science (USA)* 99(14): 9602–5. I learned of Farroni and colleagues' work through a fascinating article by Paula Niedenthal and her colleagues, who build the case that because eye contact automatically triggers embodied emotional simulations, infants' prescient skills for making eye contact can be viewed as evolved adaptations that help infants wordlessly and accurately convey their ever-shifting emotional needs to engaged caregivers. See Paula M. Niedenthal, Martial Mermillod, Marcus Maringer, and Ursula Hess (2010). "The Simulation of Smiles (SIMS) model: Embodied simulation and the meaning of facial expressions." *Behavioral and Brain Sciences* 33(6): 417–80.

21   **can substitute for eye contact:** Voice only, such as over the telephone, seems to offer another avenue for positivity resonance to emerge. Unlike other forms of mediated communications, voice-only conversations carry real-time bodily information through acoustic properties. See Klaus R. Scherer, Tom Johnstone, and Gundrun Klasmeyer (2009). "Vocal expression of emotion." In *Handbook of Affective Sciences,* edited by Richard J. Davidson, Klaus R. Scherer, and Hill H. Goldsmith, pp. 433–56. New York: Oxford University Press. See also Jo-Anne Bachorowski and Michael J. Owren (2008). "Vocal expressions of emotion." In *The Handbook of Emotions,* 3rd ed., edited by Michael Lewis, Jeanette M. Haviland-Jones, and Lisa Feldman Barrett, pp. 196–210.

And for classic experiments with monkeys on the importance of touch, or contact comfort, for love and healthy development, see Harry F. Harlow (1958). "The nature of love." *American Psychologist* 13(12): 673–85.

21 **A smile, more so than any other emotional expression, pops out and draws your eye:** D. Vaughn Becker, Uriah S. Anderson, Chad R. Mortensen, Samantha L. Neufeld, and Rebecca Neel (2011). "The face in the crowd effect unconfounded: Happy faces, not angry faces, are more efficiently detected in single- and multiple-target visual search tasks." *Journal of Experimental Psychology: General* 140(4): 637–659.

21 **fifty different types of smiles:** Paul Ekman (2001). *Telling Lies: Clues to Deceit in the Marketplace, Politics, and Marriage.* 3rd ed. W. W. Norton. In the early 1990s, Paul Ekman codirected (with the late Richard Lazarus) the NIMH-funded postdoctoral program in which I was first trained as an emotions scientist. He's since gone on to become one of the most influential psychologists of all time. See http://www.paulekman.com/.

21 **disadvantage in trying to figure out what she really feels or means:** Niedenthal et al. (2010).

21 **allows you to simulate:** Franziska Schrammel, Sebastian Pannasch, Sven-Thomas Graupner, Andreas Mojzisch, and Boris M. Velichkovsky (2009). "Virtual friend or threat? The effects of facial expression and gaze interaction on psychophysiological responses and emotional experience." *Psychophysiology* 46(5): 922–31.

21 **You become more accurate, for instance, at discerning what her unexpected smile means:** Marcus Maringer, Eva G. Krumhuber, Agneta H. Fischer, and Paula M. Niedenthal (2011). "Beyond smile dynamics: Mimicry and beliefs in judgments of smiles." *Emotion* 11(1): 181–87.

24 **certain facial movements universally express a person's otherwise unseen emotions:** Paul Ekman, Wallace V. Friesen, and Sonia Ancoli (1980). "Facial signs of emotional experience." *Journal of Personality and Social Psychology* 39(6): 1125–34. See also the 2005 volume edited by Paul Ekman and Erika L. Rosenberg, *What the Face Reveals: Basic and Applied Studies of Spontaneous Expression Using the Facial Action Coding System (FACS).* 2nd ed. Oxford University Press.

24 **evoked a positive emotion in the person who meets the smiling person's gaze:** Michael J. Owren and Jo-Anne Bachorowski (2003). "Reconsidering the evolution of nonlinguistic communication: The case of laughter." *Journal of Nonverbal Behavior* 27(3): 183–200. See also Schrammel et al. (2009).

24   **an implicit understanding—or gut sense—of the smiling person's true motives:** Niedenthal et al. (2010).

24   **and other evolutionary accounts:** Matthew Gervais and David Sloan Wilson (2005). "The evolution and functions of laughter and humor: A synthetic approach." *Quarterly Review of Biology* 80(4): 395–430.

27   **more stress, gaining more weight, and being diagnosed with more chronic illnesses year by year:** See a special report released in January 2012 by the American Psychological Association entitled "Stress in America: Our Health at Risk." For a dynamic and sobering visual graph of obesity trends in the United States, visit http://www.cdc.gov/obesity/data/trends.html.

27   **life expectancies have actually declined for kids today:** S. Jay Olshansky, Douglas J. Passaro, Ronald C. Hershow, Jennifer Layden, Bruce A. Carnes, Jacob Brody, Leonard Hayflick, Robert N. Butler, David B. Allison, and David S. Ludwig, D.S. (2005). "A potential decline in life expectancy in the United States in the 21st century." *New England Journal of Medicine* 352(11): 1138–1145.

27   **reflect the deeply encoded ancestral knowledge embedded within your DNA:** My perspective on the evolution of positivity resonance, as well as the positive social behaviors it inspires, is most compatible with multilevel selection theory as articulated by David Sloan Wilson and Edward O. Wilson (2007). "Rethinking the theoretical foundation of sociobiology." *Quarterly Review of Biology* 82(4): 327–48.

28   **strong bonds that they'd forged with those with whom their genetic survival was yoked:** Stephanie Brown and R. Michael Brown (2006). "Selective Investment Theory: Recasting the functional significance of close relationships." Target Article in *Psychological Inquiry* 17(1): 1–29.

28   **trigger biochemical changes that reshape the lenses through which those others are seen, increasing their allure:** Kent C. Berridge (2007). "The debate over dopamine's role in reward: The case for incentive salience." *Psychopharmacology* 191(3): 391–431.

32   **Under the right prenatal conditions:** Bridget R. Mueller and Tracy L. Bale (2008). "Sex-specific programming of offspring emotionality after stress early in pregnancy." *Journal of Neuroscience* 28(36): 9055–65. See also work by Frances A. Champagne (2009). "Epigenetic influences of social experiences across the lifespan." *Developmental Psychobiology* 52(4): 299–311. See also Elysia Poggi Davis, Laura M. Glynn, Feizal Waffarn, and Curt A. Sandman (2011). "Prenatal maternal stress programs infant stress regulation." *Journal of Child Psychology and Psychiatry* 52(2): 119–29.

33   **it coordinates biological synchrony as well:** Ruth Feldman, Ilanit Gordon, and Orna Zagoory-Sharon (2010). "The cross-generational transmission of oxytocin in humans." *Hormones and Behavior* 58: 669–76.

33   **developmental problems can persist for decades:** Lucy Le Mare, Karyn Audet, and Karen Kurytnik (2007). "A longitudinal study of service use in families of children adopted from Romanian orphanages." *International Journal of Behavioral Development* 31(3): 242–51.

33   **estimated to affect 10–12 percent of postpartum moms:** Vivian K. Burt and Kira Stein (2002). "Epidemiology of depression throughout the female life cycle." *Journal of Clinical Psychiatry* 63(7): 9–15.

34   **a disorder of the positive emotional system:** Aaron S. Heller, Tom Johnstone, Alexander J. Shackman, Sharee N. Light, Michael J. Peterson, Gregory G. Kolden, Ned H. Kalin, and Richard J. Davidson (2009). "Reduced capacity to sustain positive emotion in major depression reflects diminished maintenance of fronto-striatal brain activation." *Proceedings of the National Academy of Sciences (USA)* 106(52): 22445–50.

34   **less behavioral contingency between the two of you, and less predictability:** Adena J. Zlochower and Jeffrey F. Cohn (1996). "Vocal timing in face-to-face interaction of clinically depressed and nondepressed mothers and their 4-month-old infants." *Infant Behavior and Development* 19(3): 371–74.

34   **When synchrony does emerge, odds are it's laced not with positivity, but negativity:** Ruth Feldman (2007). "Parent-infant synchrony and the construction of shared timing: Physiological precursors, developmental outcomes, and risk conditions." *Journal of Child Psychology and Psychiatry* 48(3/4): 329–54.

34   **long-lasting deficits that can derail kids well into adolescence and beyond:** Lynne Murray, Adriane Arteche, Pasco Fearon, Sarah Halligan, Tim Croudace, and Peter Cooper (2010). "The effects of maternal postnatal depression and child sex on academic performance at age 16 years: A developmental approach." *Journal of Child Psychology and Psychiatry* 51(10): 1150–59.

34   **skills vital to developing supportive social relationships:** Feldman (2007).

35   **Couples who regularly make time to do new and exciting things together . . . have better quality marriages:** Arthur Aron, Christina C. Norman, Elaine N. Aron, Colin McKenna, and Richard E. Heyman (2000). "Couples' shared participation in novel and arousing activities and experienced relationship quality." *Journal of Personality and Social Psychology* 78(2): 273–84.

Chapter 3

39   **The soul must always stand ajar, ready to welcome the ecstatic experience:** Emily Dickinson (1960). *The Complete Poems of Emily Dickinson.* Edited by Thomas Johnson. Boston: Little Brown.

40   **the *social engagement system*:** Stephen W. Porges (2003). "Social engagement and attachment: A phylogenetic perspective." *Annals of the New York Academy of Sciences* 1008: 31–47.

43   **the degree to which your brains lit up in synchrony with each other, matched in both space and time:** Greg J. Stephens, Lauren J. Silbert, and Uri Hasson (2010). "Speaker-listener neural coupling underlies successful communication." *Proceedings of the National Academy of Sciences (USA)* 107(32): 14425–30. See also Uri Hasson (2010). "I can make your brain look like mine." *Harvard Business Review*, December.

43   **voice can convey so much emotion:** Scherer et al. (2009) and Bachorowski and Owren (2008).

44   **Your knowing is not just abstract and conceptual; it's embodied and physical:** Niedenthal et al. (2010).

45   **Brain coupling, Hasson argues, is the means by which we understand each other:** You might be wondering how Hasson and his team can be so sure they've captured communication, a true transfer of information from one brain to another, and not simply matched responses to listening to the same sounds, like hearing your own voice, or the incomprehensible dialogue from a foreign-language film. They ruled this out by having listeners also hear a story in Russian (which none of them understood). In that case, virtually no neural coupling emerged.

45   **a single act, performed by two brains:** Hasson (2010), p. 1.

45   **the insula, an area linked with conscious feeling states:** A. D. (Bud) Craig (2009). "How do you feel—now? The anterior insula and human awareness." *Nature Reviews Neuroscience* 10: 59–70.

45   **people's brains come particularly into sync during emotional moments:** Uri Hasson, Yuval Nir, Ifat Levy, Galit Fuhrmann, and Rafael Malach (2004). "Intersubject synchronization of cortical activity during natural vision." *Science* 303: 1634–40.

46   **your awareness expands from your habitual focus on "me" to a more generous focus on "we":** This is work I described in my first book, *Positivity* (2009). See especially chapter 4.

47 **as if to prevent their pain from becoming your pain:** Yawei Cheng, Chenyi Chen, Ching-Po Lin, Kun-Hsien Chou, and Jean Decety (2010). "Love hurts: An fMRI study." *Neuroimage* 51: 923–29. See also work by Mary Helen Immordino-Yang, Andrea McColl, Hanna Damasio, and Antonio Damasio (2009). "Neural correlates of admiration and compassion." *Proceedings of the National Academy of Sciences (USA)* 106(19): 8021–26.

47 **stifled emotions . . . can also function as obstacles to positivity resonance:** For support for this idea, see work by Iris Mauss and colleagues. It suggests that stifled positivity erodes social connection and thereby limits well-being. Iris B. Mauss, Amanda J. Shallcross, Allison S. Troy, Oliver P. John, Emilio Ferrer, Frank H. Wilhelm, and James J. Gross (2011). "Don't hide your happiness! Positive emotion dissociation, social connectedness, and psychological functioning." *Journal of Personality and Social Psychology* 100(4): 738–48.

48 **oxytocin sparked the formation of a powerful social bond between them:** Jessie R. Williams, Thomas R. Insel, Carroll R. Harbaugh, and C. Sue Carter (1994). "Oxytocin administered centrally facilitates formation of partner preference in female prairie voles (microtus ochrogaster)." *Journal of Neuroendocrinology* 6: 247–50. See also work by Mary M. Cho, A. Courtney DeVries, Jessie R. Williams, and C. Sue Carter (1999). "The effects of oxytocin and vasopressin on partner preferences in male and female prairie voles (microtus ochrogaster)." *Behavioral Neuroscience* 113(5): 1071–79.

48 **oxytocin surges during sexual intercourse:** Marie S. Carmichael, Richard Humbert, Jean Dixon, Glenn Palmisano, Walter Greenleaf, and Julian M. Davidson (1987). "Plasma oxytocin increases in the human sexual response." *Journal of Clinical Endocrinology and Metabolism* 64(1): 27–31.

48 **a synthetic form of oxytocin, available as a nasal spray, for investigational purposes:** Synthetic oxytocin has now been approved for limited investigational use within the United States by the U.S. Federal Drug Administration.

49 **a double-blind research design:** This is the gold standard in human science: Neither the researchers nor the participants are aware of who receives which nasal spray—the spray with the drug or the chemically inert spray that serves as the placebo control.

49 **trusted their entire allotment to their trustee more than doubled:** Michael Kosfeld, Markus Heinrichs, Paul J. Zak, Urs Fischbacher, and Ernst Fehr (2005). "Oxytocin increases trust in humans." *Nature* 435(2): 673–76.

49 **the mere act of being entrusted with another person's money raises the trustee's naturally occurring levels of oxytocin, and that the greater the trustee's oxytocin rise, the more of his recent windfall he sacrificed back to the investor:** Paul J. Zak, Robert Kurzban, and William T. Matzner (2005). "Oxytocin is associated with human trustworthiness." *Hormones and Behavior* 48: 522–27. Interestingly, the effect of being trusted on circulating oxytocin and monetary sacrifice is far higher if trustees have just had a shoulder massage. See Vera B. Morhenn, Jang Woo Park, Elisabeth Piper, and Paul J. Zak (2008). "Monetary sacrifice among strangers is mediated by endogenous oxytocin release after physical contact." *Evolution and Human Behavior* 29: 375–83.

49 **more trusting—a whopping 44 percent more trusting—with confidential information about themselves:** Moira Mikolajczak, Nicolas Pinon, Anthony Lane, Philippe de Timary, and Olivier Luminet (2010). "Oxytocin not only increases trust when money is at stake, but also when confidential information is in the balance." *Biological Psychology* 85: 182–84.

49 **sharing an important secret from your life with someone you just met increases your naturally circulating levels of oxytocin:** Szabolcs Keri and Imre Kiss (2011). "Oxytocin response in a trust game and habituation of arousal." *Physiology and Behavior* 102: 221–24. The effect of telling secrets on oxytocin holds unless you are diagnosed with schizophrenia; see Szabolcs Keri, Imre Kiss, and Oguz Keleman (2009). "Sharing secrets: Oxytocin and trust in schizophrenia." *Social Neuroscience* 4(4): 287–93.

50 **The effects of oxytocin on trust turn out to be quite sensitive to interpersonal cues:** Moiri Mikolajczak, James J. Gross, Anthony Lane, Olivier Corneille, Philippe de Timary, and Olivier Luminet (2010). "Oxytocin makes people trusting, not gullible." *Psychological Science* 21(8): 1072–74. Likewise, oxytocin seems to especially promote trust with in-group members; see Carsten K. W. De Dreu, Lindred L. Greer, Gerben A. Van Kleef, Shaul Shalvi, and Michel J. J. Handgraaf (2010). "Oxytocin promotes human ethnocentrism." *Proceedings of the National Academy of Sciences (USA)* 108(4): 1262–66.

50 **under the influence of oxytocin, you attend more to people's eyes:** Adam J. Guastella, Philip B. Mitchell, and Mark R. Dadds (2008). "Oxytocin increases gaze to the eye region of human faces." *Biological Psychiatry* 63: 3–5.

50 **more attuned to their smiles, especially subtle ones:** Abigail A. Marsh, Henry H. Yu, Daniel S. Pine, and R. J. R. Blair (2010). "Oxytocin improves

specific recognition of positive facial expressions." *Psychopharmacology* 209: 225–32.

50   **a better judge of their feelings:** Gregor Domes, Markus Heinrichs, Andre Michel, Christoph Berger, and Sabine C. Herpertz (2007). "Oxytocin improves 'mind-reading' in humans." *Biological Psychiatry* 61: 731–33.

50   **view people on the whole as more attractive and trustworthy:** Angeliki Theodoridou, Angela C. Rowe, Ian S. Penton-Voak, and Peter J. Rogers (2009). "Oxytocin and social perception: Oxytocin increases perceived facial trustworthiness and attractiveness." *Hormones and Behavior* 56: 128–132.

50   **particularly sensitized to environmental cues linked to positive social connections—for instance, to words like** *love* **and** *kissing*: Christian Unkelback, Adam J. Guastella, and Joseph P. Forgas (2008). "Oxytocin selectively facilitates recognition of positive sex and relationship words." *Psychological Science* 19(11): 1092–94.

50   **the parts of your amygdala that tune in to threats are muted, whereas the parts that tune in to positive social opportunities are amplified:** Matthias Gamer, Bartosz Zurowski, and Christian Buchel (2010). "Different amygdala subregions mediate valence-related and attentional effects of oxytocin in humans." *Proceedings of the National Academy of Sciences (USA)* 107(20): 9400–9405. See also: Peter Kirsch, Christine Esslinger, Qiang Chen, et al. (2005). "Oxytocin modulates neural circuitry for social cognition and fear in humans." *Journal of Neuroscience* 25(49): 11489–93; and Predrag Petrovic, Raffael Kalisch, Tania Singer, and Raymond J. Dolan (2008). "Oxytocin attenuates affective evaluations of conditioned faces and amygdale activity." *Journal of Neuroscience* 28(26): 6607–15.

50   **If you were to face these difficulties under the influence of oxytocin, studies suggest:** Beate Ditzen, Marcel Schaer, Barbara Gabriel, et al. (2009). "Intranasal oxytocin increases positive communication and reduces cortisol levels during couple conflict." *Biological Psychiatry* 65: 728–731. See also work by Markus Heinrichs, Thomas Baumgartner, Clemens Kirschbaum, and Ulrike Ehlert (2003). "Social support and oxytocin interact to suppress cortisol and subjective responses to psychosocial stress." *Biological Psychiatry* 54: 1389–98.

50   **behaving kindly in these ways also raises your naturally occurring levels of oxytocin, which in turn curbs stress-induced rises in heart**

rate and blood pressure: Julianne Holt-Lunstad, Wendy A. Birmingham, and Kathleen Light (2008). "Influence of a 'warm touch' support enhancement intervention among married couples on ambulatory blood pressure, oxytocin, alpha amylase, and cortisol." *Psychosomatic Medicine* 70: 976–85. See also forthcoming experimental work by Stephanie L. Brown, early versions of which she presented in a talk at the Society for Experimental Social Psychology meeting in October 2011 entitled "Prosocial behavior and health: Towards a biological model of a caregiving system."

51   **reduces feelings of depression, and increases your pain thresholds:** Kerstin Uvnäs-Moberg, E. Bjorkstrand, Viveka Hillegaart, and S. Ahlenius (1999). "Oxytocin as a possible mediator of SSRI-induced antidepressant effects." *Psychopharmacology* 142(1): 95–101. See also work by Maria Petersson, Pawel Alster, Thomas Lundeberg, and Kerstin Uvnäs-Moberg (1996). "Oxytocin increases nociceptive thresholds in a long-term perspective in female and male rats." *Neuroscience Letters* 212(2): 87–90.

51   **the mammalian *calm-and-connect* response:** Kerstin Uvnäs-Moberg, Ingemar Arn, and David Magnusson (2005). "The psychobiology of emotion: The role of the oxytocinergic system." *International Journal of Behavioral Medicine* 12(2): 59–65. See also Kerstin Uvnäs-Moberg's 2003 book written for a general audience, *The Oxytocin Factor: Tapping the Hormone of Calm, Love and Healing.* New York: Perseus.

51   **Human greed, after all, runs rampant and can yield all manner of exploitation:** Compelling new insights on the nature of greed can be drawn from new experimental research on social class. See work by Paul K. Piff, Daniel M. Stancato, Stephané Côté, Rodolfo Mendoza-Denton, and Dacher Keltner (2012). "Higher social class predicts increased unethical behavior." *Proceedings of the National Academy of Sciences (USA)* 109(11): 4086–91.

51   **Oxytocin appears both to calm fears that might steer you away from interacting with strangers and also to sharpen your skills for *connection*:** Anne Campbell (2009). "Oxytocin and human social behavior." *Personality and Social Psychological Review* 14(3): 281–95.

51   **your gut instincts about whom to trust and whom not to trust become more reliable:** Niedenthal et al. (2010).

51   **oxytocin has been dubbed "the great facilitator of life":** Heon-Jin Lee, Abbe H. Macbeth, Jerome H. Pagani, and W. Scott Young, III (2009). "Oxytocin: The great facilitator of life." *Progress in Neurobiology* 88(2): 127–51.

52   **Without such engagement, however, no oxytocin synchrony emerges:** Ruth Feldman, Ilanit Gordon, and Orna Zagoory-Sharon (2010). "The cross-generation transmission of oxytocin in humans." *Hormones and Behavior* 58: 669–76.

53   **When a rat mom licks and grooms her pup, it increases the pup's sensitivity to oxytocin:** Frances A. Champagne, Ian C. G. Weaver, Josie Diorio, Sergiy Dymov, Moshe Szyf, and Michael J. Meaney (2006). "Maternal care associated with methylation of the estrogen receptor-a1b promoter and estrogen receptor-α expression in the medial preoptic area of female offspring." *Endocrinology* 147(6): 2909–15.

54   **your vagus nerve increases the odds that the two of you will connect:** Porges (2003).

55   **regulate their internal bodily processes more efficiently, like their glucose levels and inflammation:** Julian F. Thayer and Esther Sternberg (2006). "Beyond heart rate variability: Vagal regulation of allostatic systems." *Annals of the New York Academy of Sciences* 1088: 361–72.

55   **better able to regulate their attention and emotions, even their behavior:** Stephen W. Porges, Jane A. Doussard-Roosevelt, and Ajit Maiti (1994), "Vagal tone and the physiological regulation of emotion." *Monographs of the Society for Research in Child Development* 59(2/3): 167–86.

55   **especially skillful in navigating interpersonal interactions and in forging positive connections with others:** Kok and Fredrickson (2010).

56   **those with higher vagal tone experience more love in their daily lives, more moments of positivity resonance:** Kok and Fredrickson (2010).

56   **A handful of scientists were invited to a private meeting to brief His Holiness on their latest discoveries about the effects of mind-training:** Tenzin Gyatso, the Fourteenth Dalai Lama, had traveled from his home in Dharamshala, India, to Madison, Wisconsin, to participate in this event held on May 16, 2010, in conjunction with the grand opening of the Center for Investigating Healthy Minds, run by my colleague, Professor Richard Davidson. This day's dialogue, as have many of His Holiness's previous dialogues with Western scientists, was sponsored by the Mind and Life Institute. The exchange included scientists Dr. Antoine Lutz and Dr. Clifford Saron, in addition to Professor Davidson and myself. Also participating were contemplative scholars Thupten Jinpa, Sharon Salzberg, Matthieu Ricard, and Professor John Dunne.

57   **their vagus nerves began to respond more readily to the rhythms of**

their breathing, emitting more of that healthy arrhythmia that is the fingerprint of high vagal tone: Kok, et al. (in press).

57 **Having assets like these certainly makes life easier, and more satisfying:** Michael A. Cohn, Barbara L. Fredrickson, Stephanie L. Brown, et al. (2009). "Happiness unpacked: Positive emotions increase life satisfaction by building resilience." *Emotion* 9(3): 361–68.

58 **appears to usher in structural changes in brain regions that facilitate positivity resonance:** Pil Young Kim (2009). "The interplay of brain and experience in parental love." *Dissertation Abstracts International: Section B: The Sciences and Engineering* 70 (6-B): 3810.

59 **your inflammatory response becomes more chronic, less responsive to cues that a crises situation has subsided:** Steve W. Cole (2009). "Social regulation of human gene expression." *Current Directions in Psychological Science* 18(3): 132–37.

59 *feeling* **isolated or unconnected to others does more bodily damage than** *actual* **isolation:** Steve W. Cole, Louise C. Hawkley, Jesusa M. Arevalo, et al. (2007). "Social regulation of gene expression in human leukocytes." *Genomic Biology* 8: R189.

60 **you orchestrate the messages that your cells hear, the messages that tell your cells whether to grow toward health or toward illness:** Of course, other forces are at work as well. You do not hold sole responsibility (or blame) for your health or illness via the emotions you experience. In other words, please do not use this science to blame those who suffer from illnesses for their own fate. For a sharp critique of how science can be misused in this manner, see Barbara Ehrenreich (2009). *Bright-Sided: How the Relentless Promotion of Positive Thinking Has Undermined America.* New York: Metropolitan Books.

60 **just beginning to chart the ways that oxytocin and other ingredients that make up love's biochemistry trigger healthy changes in gene expression:** In ongoing research funded by the U.S. National Institutes of Health (R01NR012899) I've teamed up with Steve W. Cole, director of UCLA's Social Genomics Core Laboratory, to examine how learning loving-kindness meditation may alter people's patterns of gene expression. We are especially interested in changes that may occur in the cells that regulate inflammatory processes in the immune system.

61 **Your friend's coworker's sister's happiness actually stands to elevate your own happiness:** Fowler and Christakis (2009).

Chapter 4

63   **You are made in the image of what you desire**: Thomas Merton (1958). *Thoughts on Solitude*. New York: Farrar, Straus and Giroux.

64   **his controversial 1954 book,** *The Doors of Perception*: Published in the United States by Harper and Row and in the UK by Chatto and Windus.

65   **now confirmed by brain imaging experiments:** See the elegant brain imaging experiments reported by Taylor Schmitz, Eve De Rosa, and Adam K. Anderson (2009). "Opposing influences of affective state valence on visual cortical encoding." *Journal of Neuroscience* 29(22): 7199–207. See also work by David Soto, Maria Funes, Azucena Guzman-Garcia, et al. (2009). "Pleasant music overcomes the loss of awareness in patients with visual neglect." *Proceedings of the National Academy of Science (USA)* 106: 6011–16.

65   **a distinct brain area that reacts to human faces (the extrastriate fusiform face area, or FFA):** Nancy Kanwisher, Josh McDermott, and Marvin M. Chun (1997). "The fusiform face area: A module in human extrastriate cortex specialized for face perception. *Journal of Neuroscience* 17(11): 4302-11.

65   **a separate brain area that reacts to places (the parahippocampal place area, or PPA):** Russell Epstein, Alison Harris, Damian Stanley and Nancy Kanwisher (1999). "The parahippocampal place area: Recognition, navigation, or encoding?" *Neuron* 23:115-25.

65   **The results were clear:** Schmitz, et al. (2009).

66   **they are temporarily able to see and act on information that simply doesn't register for them while not listening to music:** Soto et al. (2009).

67   **to see things from their perspective:** Paul Miceli, Christian E. Waugh, Keiko Otake, Ahjalya Hejmadi, and Barbara L. Fredrickson (2012). "Positive emotions unlock other-focus." Unpublished data. See also Christian E. Waugh and Barbara L. Fredrickson (2006). "Nice to know you: Positive emotions, self-other overlap, and complex understanding in the formation of a new relationship." *Journal of Positive Psychology* 1(2): 93–106.

67   **the doors of perception widen further, in unique ways:** In addition to the common forms of broadening shared by different positive emotions, recent research by Dr. Lisa Cavanaugh suggests that distinct positive emotions may also broaden your awareness in distinct ways. For example, whereas the positive emotion of hope stretches your consideration of time to be more future-oriented, love appears to stretch your circle of moral concern to include more distant others. Lisa A. Cavanaugh (2009). "Feeling good and doing better: How specific positive emotions influence consumer behavior

and well-being." *Dissertation Abstracts International Section A: Humanities and Social Sciences* 70(3-A): 948.

67 **you come to view one another as part of a unified whole:** Waugh and Fredrickson (2006). See also work by John F. Dovidio, Samuel L. Gaertner, Alice M. Isen, and Robert Lowrance (1995). "Group representations and intergroup bias: Positive affect, similarity, and group size." *Personality and Social Psychology Bulletin* 21(8): 856–65.

67 **love stretches your circle of concern to include others to a greater degree:** Cavanaugh (2009).

67 **extend your trust and compassion to them:** Jennifer R. Dunn and Maurice E. Schweitzer (2005). "Feeling and believing: The influence of emotion on trust." *Journal of Personality and Social Psychology* 88(5): 736–48. See also classic work by the late Alice M. Isen and Paula F. Levin (1972). "Effect of feeling good on helping: Cookies and kindness." *Journal of Personality and Social Psychology* 21(3): 384–88.

67 **"investment in the well-being of another, for his or her own sake," as an essential, always-present fingerprint of love:** Quoted from page 621 in Hegi and Bergner (2010).

67 **attend more closely to other people's needs and help you vigilantly take in and evaluate incoming information so that you can protect them from harm:** Vladas Griskevicius, Michelle N. Shiota, and Samantha L. Neufeld (2010). "Influence of different positive emotions on persuasion processing: A functional evolutionary approach." *Emotion* 10(2): 190–206.

67 **leaves you with more positive automatic reactions:** Cendri A. Hutcherson, Emma M. Seppala, and James J. Gross (2008). "Loving-kindness meditation increases social connectedness." *Emotion* 8(5): 720–24.

67 **your everyday interactions with friends and coworkers become more lighthearted and enjoyable:** Fredrickson, et al. (2008).

67 **neuroscientific studies show that positive emotions open your perceptual awareness:** Schmitz et al. (2009).

68 **they also open your torso:** Melissa M. Gross, Elizabeth A. Crane, and Barbara L. Fredrickson (in press). "Effort-shape and kinematic assessment of bodily expression of emotion during gait." *Human Movement Science.*

68 **raising your cheeks to create (or deepen) the crow's feet at the corners of your eyes:** Together with raised lip corners, these crow's feet wrinkles have their own scientific label, the Duchenne smile, named in honor of the nineteenth-century scientist who first discovered the unique connection

between this type of smile and the sincere expression of good feelings. See Paul Ekman, Richard J. Davidson, and Wallace V. Friesen (1990). "The Duchenne smile: Emotional expression and brain physiology II." *Journal of Personality and Social Psychology* 58(2): 342–53.

68   **overreliance on posed expressions and still photographs:** Such limitations may well account for early claims that only one of the five or six basic, universal emotions was positive, identified variously as enjoyment or happiness. See work by Paul Ekman (1992). "An argument for basic emotions." *Cognition and Emotion* 6(3/4): 169–200.

68   **the unique nonverbal fingerprint of love:** Gian C. Gonzaga, Dacher Keltner, Esme A. Londahl, and Michael D. Smith (2001). "Love and the commitment problem in romantic relations and friendship." *Journal of Personality and Social Psychology* 81(2): 247–62.

69   **these four nonverbal cues—smiles, gestures, leans, and nods—both emanate from a person's inner experiences of love and are read by others *as* love:** Gonzaga et al. (2001).

69   **how they deliver direct criticism, which (as I describe in a later section) has been found to predict the long-term stability of loving relationships:** John M. Gottman, James Coen, Sybil Carrere, and Catherine Swanson (1998). "Predicting marital happiness and stability from newlywed interactions." *Journal of Marriage and the Family* 60: 5–22.

69   **these and other ways of keeping in time together forge deep feelings of group solidarity:** William H. McNeil (1995). *Keeping Together in Time: Dance and Drill in Human History.* Harvard University Press. See also Barbara Ehrenreich (2006).

70   **a colleague of mine urged my husband and me to attend the opening game of the football season, because "that's what we do here":** Thank you, Robert Sellors!

71   **when people move together as one orchestrated unit, they later report that they experienced an embodied sense of rapport with each other:** Tanya Vacharkulksemsuk and Barbara L. Fredrickson (2011). "Strangers in sync: Achieving embodied rapport through shared movements." *Journal of Experimental Social Psychology* 48: 399–402.

71   **it breeds liking:** Michael J. Hove and Jane L. Risen (2009). "It's all in the timing: Interpersonal synchrony increases affiliation." *Social Cognition* 27(6): 949–60.

71   **cooperation:** Scott S. Wiltermuth and Chip Heath (2009). "Synchrony and cooperation." *Psychological Science* 20(1): 1–5.

71   **and compassion:** Piercarlo Valdesolo and David DeSteno (2011). "Synchrony and the social tuning of compassion." *Emotion* 11(2): 262–66.

71   **success in joint action:** Piercarlo Valdesolo, Jennifer Ouyang, and David DeSteno (2010). "The rhythm of joint action: Synchrony promotes cooperative ability." *Journal of Experimental Social Psychology* 46(4): 693–95.

72   **the generation-spanning bonds you share with a parent or child were also forged through accumulated micro-moments of felt security and affection, communicated variously through synchronized gaze, touch, and vocalizations:** Ruth Feldman (2007). "Parent-infant synchrony: Biological foundations and developmental outcomes." *Current Directions in Psychological Science* 16(6): 340–45.

72   **nonverbal signs of unity forecast a shared subjective appreciation of oneness, connection, and an embodied sense of rapport:** Vacharkulksemsuk and Fredrickson (2011).

74   **couples who regularly do new and exciting (or even silly) things together have better quality marriages:** Art and Elaine's story is a fictionalized account based on the scientific facts derived from clever experimental work conducted by two highly accomplished (and married!) psychologists named Art and Elaine, together with their collaborators. See Aron, et al. (2000).

74   **bringing your own positive emotion to your partner:** Indeed, experiencing intense emotions, whether positive or negative, triggers the urge to talk about that emotional experience with others. See work by Rimé (2009).

75   **they also further fortify the relationship, making it more intimate, committed, and passionate next season than it is today:** Shelly L. Gable, Gian C. Gonzaga, and Amy Strachman (2006). "Will you be there for me when things go right? Supportive responses to positive event disclosures." *Journal of Personality and Social Psychology* 91(5): 904–17. See also Shelly L. Gable, Harry T. Reis, Emily A. Impett, and Evan R. Asher (2004). "What do you do when things go right? The intrapersonal and interpersonal benefits of sharing positive events." *Journal of Personality and Social Psychology* 87(2): 228–45.

76   **it forecasts becoming even more solid and satisfied with their relationship:** Sara B. Algoe, Barbara L. Fredrickson, and Shelly Gable (2012). "More than reinforcement: Expressions of gratitude reveal how and why gratitude functions for the dyad." Manuscript under review.

78   **good feelings nourish resilience:** Cohn, et al. (2009).

78   **They dismantle or undo the grip that negative emotions can gain on your mind and body alike:** Barbara L. Fredrickson and Robert W. Levenson (1998). "Positive emotions speed recovery from the cardiovascular sequelae of negative emotions." *Cognition and Emotion* 12(2): 191–220. See also Barbara L. Fredrickson, Roberta A. Mancuso, Christine Branigan, and Michele M. Tugade (2000). "The undoing effect of positive emotions." *Motivation and Emotion* 24(4): 237–58.

78   **resilience can be normative, or standard:** Sara B. Algoe and Barbara L. Fredrickson (2011). "Emotional fitness and the movement of affective science from lab to field." *American Psychologist* 66(1): 35–42. See also Ann S. Maston (2001). "Ordinary magic: Resilience processes in development." *American Psychologist* 56(3): 227–38.

78   **can be improved through experience and training:** In recent years, the great promise of the new science of resilience—and of positive psychology, more generally—has translated into massive efforts to increase resilience in people who perhaps need it most: those in the U.S. military who have faced an unprecedented number of repeat deployments across two extended wars. Increasingly, military personnel have returned from Iraq and Afghanistan with mental health problems, including depression, posttraumatic stress disorder, and suicidal tendencies. These problems compromise not only their own health and well-being but also the health and well-being of their spouses, their children, and other military family members. To address those pernicious problems and to raise the resilience and emotional fitness of *all* enlisted soldiers, the U.S. Army has collaborated with behavioral scientists to launch a multifaceted Comprehensive Soldier Fitness initiative. That effort, while noble, faces considerable challenges, to be sure. Yet to the extent that behavioral scientists are willing to translate and test theories of resilience within the crucible of military service and international conflict, both the military population and behavioral science itself will see mutual benefit. See Martin E. P. Seligman (2011). *Flourish: A Visionary New Understanding of Happiness and Well-being.* New York: Free Press.

79   **Even as kids, they were especially adept at using humor to get others to smile or laugh along with them:** Emmy E. Werner and Ruth S. Smith (1992). *Overcoming the Odds: High Risk Children from Birth to Adulthood.* Ithaca, New York: Cornell University Press.

79   **more sensitive and attuned parents help their children to develop their own store of self-soothing techniques:** Jennifer A. DiCorcia and Ed Tronick (2011). "Quotidian resilience: Exploring the mechanisms that

drive resilience from a perspective of everyday stress and coping." *Neuroscience and Biobehavioral Reviews* 35: 1593–1602.

79   **requires precisely that suite of personal and collective resources that micro-moments of positivity resonance serve to build:** John T. Cacioppo, Harry T. Reis, and Alex J. Zautra (2011). "Social resilience: The value of social fitness with an application to the military." *American Psychologist* 66(1): 43–51.

80   **John Gottman, perhaps the world's leading scientific expert on emotions in marriage:** For more infomation, see http://www.gottman.com

82   **"expertise in the fundamental pragmatics of life":** Paul B. Baltes, Judith Gluck, and Ute Kunzmann (2002). "Wisdom: Its structure and function in regulating successful life span development." In *Handbook of Positive Psychology*, edited by C. Rick Snyder and Shane J. Lopez, pp. 327–47. Oxford University Press. See also Robert J. Sternberg (1998). "A balance theory of wisdom." *Review of General Psychology* 2(4): 347–65.

82   **Spend just ten minutes in pleasant conversation with someone else and your performance on a subsequent IQ test gets a boost:** Oscar Ybarra, Eugene Burnstein, Piotr Winkielman, Matthew C. Keller, Melvin Manis, Emily Chan, and Joel Rodriguez (2008). "Mental exercising through simple socializing: Social interaction promotes general cognitive functioning." *Personality and Social Psychology Bulletin* 34(2): 248–259. See also Oscar Ybarra, Piotr Winkielman, Irene Yeh, Eugene Burnstein, and Liam Kavanagh (2010). "Friends (and sometimes enemies) with cognitive benefits: What types of social interactions boost executive functioning?" *Social Psychological and Personality Science* 2(3): 253–61.

83   **you'd be considerably more pragmatic and discerning if you could first discuss these dilemmas for a few minutes with someone whose perspective you really value . . . and then think about the situation a bit more on your own:** Ursula M. Staudinger and Paul B. Baltes (1996). "Interactive minds: A facilitative setting for wisdom-related performance?" *Journal of Personality and Social Psychology* 71(4): 746–62.

83   **positivity resonance unlocks collective brainstorming power:** David Sloan Wilson, John J. Timmel, and Ralph R. Miller (2004). "Cognitive cooperation: When the going gets tough, think as a group." *Human Nature* 15(3): 225–50.

83   **The more frequently older adults connect with others, the lower their risks for cognitive decline and Alzheimer's disease:** Robert S. Wilson, Kristin R. Krueger, Steven E. Arnold, Julie A. Schneider, Jeremiah F. Kelly, Lisa L. Barnes, Yuxiao Tang, and David A. Bennett (2007). "Loneliness and

risk of Alzheimer disease." *Archives of General Psychiatry* 64(2): 234–40. See also Teresa A. Seeman, Tina M. Lusignolo, Marilyn Albert, and Lisa Berkman (2001). "Social relationships, social support, and patterns of cognitive aging in healthy, high-functioning older adults: MacArthur studies of successful aging." *Health Psychology* 20(4): 243–55.

85   **physician can use knowledge of your vagal tone to forecast with some accuracy your likelihood of heart failure, as well as your odds of surviving such a catastrophic health event:** Steve Bibevski and Mark E. Dunlap (2011). "Evidence for impaired vagus nerve activity in heart failure." *Heart Failure Reviews* 16(2): 129–35.

85   **Your vagal tone also reflects the strength of your immune system, with a particular tie to chronic inflammation:** Richard P. Sloan, Heather McCreath, Kevin J. Tracey, Stephen Sidney, Kiang Lui, and Teresa Seeman (2007). "RR interval variability is inversely related to inflammatory markers: The CARDIA study." *Molecular Medicine* 13(3/4): 178–84. See also Thayer and Sternberg (2006).

85   **Past work discovered that chronic loneliness—a persistent yearning for more positivity resonance—compromises the ways a person's genes are expressed, particularly in aspects of the white blood cells of the immune system that govern inflammation:** Cole, et al. (2007).

85   **people who have diverse and rewarding relationships with others are healthier and live longer:** Lisa F. Berkman and S. Leonard Syme (1979). "Social networks, host resistance, and mortality: A nine-year follow-up study of Alameda County residents." *American Journal of Epidemiology* 109(2): 186–204. See also Sheldon Cohen and Denise Janicki-Deverts (2009). "Can we improve our physical health by altering our social networks?" *Perspectives in Psychological Science* 4(4): 375–78. For a recent meta-analysis of 148 studies, see Julianne Holt-Lunstad, Timothy B. Smith, and J. Bradley Layton (2010). "Social relationships and mortality risk: A meta-analytic review." *PLoS Medicine* 7(7): e1000316. doi:10.1371/journal.pmed .1000316.

86   **more damaging to your health than smoking cigarettes:** Holt-Lunstad, et al. (2010).

86   **fewer colds:** Sheldon Cohen, Cuneyt M. Alper, William J. Doyle, John J. Treanor, and Ronald B. Turner (2006). "Positive emotional style predicts resistance to illness after experimental exposure to rhinovirus or influenza A virus." *Psychosomatic Medicine* 68: 809–15. See also Sheldon Cohen,

William J. Doyle, David P. Skoner, Bruce S. Rabin, and Jack M. Gwaltney, Jr. (1997). "Social ties and susceptibility to the common cold." *Journal of the American Medical Association* 277(24): 1940–44.

86 **lower blood pressure:** Andrew Steptoe and Jane Wardle (2005). "Positive affect and biological function in everyday life." *Neurobiology of Aging* 26(1): 108–12.

86 **less often succumb to heart disease and stroke:** Julia K. Boehm and Laura D. Kubzansky (2012). "The heart's content: The association between positive psychological well-being and cardiovascular health." *Psychological Bulletin.*

86 **diabetes:** Judith Tedlie Moskowitz, Elissa S. Epel, and Michael Acree (2009). "Positive affect uniquely predicts lower risk of mortality in people with diabetes." *Health Psychology* 27(1): S73–S82.

86 **Alzheimer's disease:** Wilson et al. (2007). See also Seeman et al. (2001).

86 **and some cancers:** Janice K. Kiecolt-Glaser, Lynanne McGuire, Theodore F. Robles, and Ronald Glaser (2002). "Emotions, morbidity, and mortality: New perspectives from psychoneuroimmunology." *Annual Review of Psychology* 53: 83–107.

Chapter 5

91 **Love doesn't just sit there, like a stone; it has to be made, like bread; remade all the time, made new:** Ursula K. Le Guin (1971). *The Lathe of Heaven: A Novel.* New York: Scribner.

92 **Study after study shows that making concrete "if . . . then" plans like this dramatically increases people's success at self-change:** Peter M. Gollwitzer and Paschal Sheeran (2006). "Implementation intentions and goal achievement: A meta-analysis of effects and processes." *Advances in Experimental Social Psychology* 38: 69–119. See also Peter M. Gollwitzer, Paschal Sheeran, Roman Trotschel, and Thomas L. Webb (2011). "Self-regulation of priming effects on behavior." *Psychological Science* 27(7): 901–7.

92 **positive emotions are what most people feel most frequently:** John T. Cacioppo, Wendi L. Gardner, and Gary G. Berntson (1999). "The affect system has parallel and integrative processing components: Form follows function." *Journal of Personality and Social Psychology* 76: 839–55. See also Ed Diener and Carol Diener (1996). "Most people are happy." *Psychological Science* 7(3): 181–85.

92   **you can increase your ratio of positive to negative emotions even further by becoming more attuned to the sources of positive emotion in your midst:** I wrote part II of my first book, *Positivity* (2009), to share the science-backed tools that you can use to raise your own day-to-day positivity ratios and thrive. (To learn more, visit www.positivityratio.com.)

92   **Like bees and ants, we humans are ultrasocial creatures:** Jonathan Haidt, J. Patrick Seder, and Selin Kesebir (2008). "Hive psychology, happiness, and public policy." *Journal of Legal Studies* 37(2): S133–S156.

93   **Some of this tenderness, along with its associated impulse to show care and concern, is even released when you come across a kitten, puppy, or other baby animal:** Studies in fact show that the physical cues of cuteness, which include a large, rounded forehead and large eyes, release people's affectionate and caregiving impulses. Gary D. Sherman, Jonathan Haidt, and James A. Coan (2009). "Viewing cute images increases behavioral carefulness." *Emotion* 9(2): 282–86.

94   **Insincere smiles, by contrast, are either flashed more quickly, in less than a second, or worn for longer durations, like makeup or a mask:** Mark G. Frank, Paul Ekman, and Wallace Friesen (1993). "Behavioral markers and recognizability of the smile of enjoyment." *Journal of Personality and Social Psychology* 64(1): 83–93.

95   **Writing "On Friendship" Cicero made the case that without virtue, friendship is impossible:** Marcus Tillius Cicero (1884/2010). *De Amicitia (On Friendship) and Scipio's Dream.* Translated with an introduction and notes by Andrew P. Peabody (1811–1893). Charleston: Nabu Press.

95   **"for there are not so many possessed of virtue as there are that desire to seem virtuous":** Cicero (1884/2010), p. 67.

95   **"false statements . . . framed purposely to satisfy and please:"** Cicero (1884/2010), p. 67.

95   **Feigned positivity resonance creates a toxic insincerity that is damaging perhaps most severely to the person who initiates it:** Erika L. Rosenberg, Paul Ekman, Wei Jiang, Michael Babyak, R. Edward Coleman, Michael Hanson, Christopher O'Connor, Robert Waugh, and James A. Blumenthal (2001). "Linkages between facial expressions of anger and transient myocardial ischemia in men with coronary artery disease." *Emotion* 1(2): 107–15.

96   **"Unless you see an open bosom and show your own . . .":** Cicero (1884/2010), p. 66.

97   **we'd never seen improvements simply due to the act of regularly reflecting on feelings:** For instance, the following two prior studies showed

no upward drift in positive emotions over time in the absence of an intervention: Cohn et al. (2009); Fredrickson et al. (2008).

97 **increased feelings of social connection forecast changes in the functioning of people's physical hearts, as registered by increases in their vagal tone:** Kok and Fredrickson (2010).

97 **Bethany randomly assigned working adults to reflect daily either on their social connections in this manner or on the three tasks on which they spent the most time that day and to evaluate how "useful" and "important" those tasks had felt to them:** Bethany E. Kok (2012). Dissertation research in progress.

99 **reflecting on social connections with Donna:** This is not her real name.

100 **the "three good things" exercise commonly used in positive psychology:** Martin E. P. Seligman, Tracy A. Steen, Nansook Park, and Christopher Peterson (2005). "Positive psychology progress: Empirical validations of interventions." *American Psychologist* 60(5): 410–21. See also Christopher Peterson (2006). *A Primer in Positive Psychology.* Oxford University Press.

103 **wide array of benefits after just a few months of practicing LKM for an average of sixty minutes a week:** Fredrickson et al. (2008); Kok et al. (in press).

104 **striving too hard for happiness backfires:** Iris B. Mauss, Maya Tamir, Craig L. Anderson, and Nicole S. Savino (2011). "Can seeking happiness make people unhappy? Paradoxical effects of valuing happiness." *Emotion* 11(4): 807–15.

105 **whatever positive feelings you generate in LKM are likely to imbue the rest of your day with more positivity as well:** This comes from the data we gathered using the Day Reconstruction Method and published in Fredrickson et al. (2008).

105 **openness that can be readily spotted by those with whom you interact or cross paths:** Gross et al. (in press). See also Melissa M. Gross, Elizabeth A. Crane, and Barbara L. Fredrickson (2010). "Methodology for assessing bodily expression of emotion." *Journal of nonverbal behavior* 34(4): 223–48. See also Kathi J. Kemper and Hossam A. Shaltout (2011). "Non-verbal communication of compassion: Measuring psychophysiological effects." *BMC Complementary and Alternative Medicine* 11: 132.

105 **Since nonverbal gestures are contagious, your openness also allows others to become more open and relaxed:** Tanya L. Chartrand and Rick van Baaran (2009). "Human mimicry." *Advances in Experimental Social Psychology* 41: 219–74. See also Kemper and Shaltout (2011).

105 **You're more likely to see things in a good light, give the benefit of the doubt, and be optimistic about the future and others' potential:** Seunghee Han, Jennifer S. Lerner, and Dacher Keltner (2007). "Feelings and consumer decision making: The appraisal-tendency framework." *Journal of Consumer Psychology* 17(3): 158–68.

105 **Your intonation becomes more upbeat and inviting:** Leher Singh, James L. Morgan, and Catherine T. Best (2002). "Infants' listening preferences: Baby talk or happy talk?" *Infancy* 3(3): 365–94.

Chapter 6

113 **I exist as I am, that is enough:** Walt Whitman (1855/2009). *Leaves of Grass.* Nashville, Tennessee: American Renaissance.

115 **studies show that self-directed, self-compassionate love is far more vital to your health and happiness than is oft-touted high self-esteem:** Mark R. Leary, Eleanor B. Tate, Claire E. Adams, Ashley Batts Allen, and Jessica Hancock (2007). "Self-compassion and reactions to unpleasant self-relevant events: The implications of treating oneself kindly." *Journal of Personality and Social Psychology* 92(5): 887–904.

115 **Kristin Neff, a developmental scientist at the University of Texas at Austin who has pioneered scientific assessment of a form of self-love that she calls *self-compassion*, has found this to be the case:** For an accessible review of relevant research, see Kristin Neff's 2011 book, *Self-Compassion: Stop Beating Yourself Up and Leave Insecurity Behind.* William Morrow.

116 **Sharon Salzberg, cofounder of the Insight Meditation Society, in Barre, Massachusetts, is perhaps the leading Western teacher of LKM:** To learn more, please visit www.SharonSalzberg.com.

119 **American poet Galway Kinnell describes how Saint Francis gently put his hand on the forehead of a sow to remind her "in words and in touch" of her value:** This vivid poem was first published in 1980 in a volume entitled *Mortal Acts, Mortal Words.* Mariner Books.

119 **As you recognize your own value and value-added, . . . you open as a flower, "from within, from self-blessing":** This is another phrasing and idea drawn from Galway Kinnell's famous poem "Saint Francis and the Sow."

121 **Adopting this loving observers' perspective on yourself can offer an "appreciative jolt" that allows you to see—and truly feel—how it is**

that you add value to those around you: I borrow the phrase "appreciative jolt" from the work on reflected best-self portraits by my colleagues at the Positive Organizational Scholarship Center at the University of Michigan's Ross School of Business, which I describe in chapter 11 of *Positivity*. See also Laura Morgan Roberts, Jane E. Dutton, Gretchen M. Spreitzer, Emily D. Heaphy, and Robert E. Quinn (2005). "Composing the reflected best-self portrait: Building pathways for becoming extraordinary in work organizations." *Academy of Management Review* 30(4): 712–36.

128 **Try your best Homer imitation now:** If you don't know Homer Simpson, you can hear how he says this by looking up "D'oh!" on Wikipedia.

131 **These critical ingredients are missing from much of the positive self-talk prescribed in the self-help industry: flexibility, openness, and realism:** Research by David Sherman and colleagues suggests that self-affirmation works best when people are unaware of its possible beneficial effects. See David K. Sherman, Geoffrey L. Cohen, Leif D. Nelson, A. David Nussbaum, Debra P. Bunyan, and Julio Garcia (2009). "Affirmed yet unaware: Exploring the role of awareness in the process of self-affirmation." *Journal of Personality and Social Psychology* 97(5): 745–64.

132 **"radical acceptance":** Tara Brach (2004). *Radical Acceptance: Embracing Your Life with the Heart of a Buddha.* New York: Bantam.

138 **it's in the toughest times that harboring compassion toward yourself makes the biggest difference:** Leary et al. (2007).

Chapter 7

139 **What is rich? Are you rich enough to help anybody?:** Ralph Waldo Emerson (1888/2004). *Emerson in Concert: A Memoir Written in the "Social Circle" in Concord, Massachusetts.* Whitefish, Montana: Kessinger Publishing.

139 **People are most drawn to others who share roughly their same level of physical attractiveness:** For a summary of this classic work see the 1973 book by Zick Rubin, *Liking and Loving.* Holt, Rinehart and Winston.

140 **You grab at opportunities to get more "goods" for yourself, with little regard for whom you may be pushing aside or harming along the way:** Piff et al. (2012).

140 **the happiest among us are the ones who've simply shed this pernicious habit of social comparison:** Sonja Lyubomirsky and Lee Ross (1997). "Hedonic consequences of social comparison: A contrast of happy and unhappy

people." *Journal of Personality and Social Psychology* 73(6): 1141–57. See also Sonja Lyubomirsky, Kari L. Tucker, and Fazilet Kasri (2001). "Responses to hedonically conflicting social comparisons: Comparing happy and unhappy people." *European Journal of Social Psychology* 31(5): 511–35.

142 **compassionate responding like this is just as natural, just as hardwired, and just as beneficial to our species:** Stephanie D. Preston and Frans B. M. de Waal (2002). "Empathy: Its ultimate and proximate bases." *Behavior and Brain Sciences* 25(1): 1–20. See also Frans de Waal's 2009 book *The Age of Empathy: Nature's Lessons for a Kinder Society.* New York: Three Rivers Press.

143 **it is precisely this infusion of positive emotions into negative emotional terrain that drives resilient people to bounce back:** Barbara L. Fredrickson, Michele M. Tugade, Christian E. Waugh, and Gregory R. Larkin (2003). "What good are positive emotions in crises? A prospective study of resilience and emotions following the terrorist attacks on the United States on September 11th, 2001." *Journal of Personality and Social Psychology* 84(2): 365–76. See also Michele M. Tugade and Barbara L. Fredrickson (2004). "Resilient individuals use positive emotions to bounce back from negative emotional experiences." *Journal of Personality and Social Psychology* 86(2): 320–33. For a review, see chapter 6 in my 2009 book, *Positivity.*

144 **hope: Even as you fear the worse, you yearn for better:** I draw this description of hope from the late Richard S. Lazarus (1991). *Emotion and Adaptation.* New York: Oxford University Press.

144 **you're connected to them through your shared experience of this difficulty:** Simply recognizing these similarities can go a long way toward eliminating negativity toward foreigners. See Matt Motyl, Joshua Hart, Tom Pyszczynski, David Weise, Molly Maxfield, and Angelika Siedel (2011). "Subtle priming of shared human experiences eliminates threat-induced negativity toward Arabs, immigrants, and peace-making." *Journal of Experimental Social Psychology* 47(6): 1179–84.

147 **Studies show that the continuous support that a doula provides can improve health outcomes for both the mother and the baby:** Ellen D. Hodnett, Simon Gates, G. Justus Hofmeyr, Carol Sakala, and Julie Weston (2011). "Continuous support for women during childbirth." *Cochrane Database Systematic Reviews* 2: CD003766.

153 **One rigorous examination of people's day-to-day lives concludes that good events outnumber bad events by margins of about 3 to 1:** Shigehiro

Oishi, Ed Diener, Dong-Won Choi, Chu Kim-Prieto, and Incheol Choi (2007). "The dynamics of daily events and well-being across cultures: When less is more." *Journal of Personality and Social Psychology* 93(4): 685–98.

153 **it's the frequency, not the magnitude of good events, that predicts your overall well-being:** Ed Diener, Ed Sandvik, and William Pavot (2009). "Happiness is the frequency, not the intensity, of positive versus negative affect." In *Assessing Well-being: The Collected Works of Ed Diener*, edited by Ed Diener, pp. 213–31. Springer.

153 **My earlier research identifies 3 to 1 as a key tipping point in people's emotional experiences:** Barbara L. Fredrickson and Marcial F. Losada (2005). "Positive affect and the complex dynamics of human flourishing." *American Psychologist* 60(7): 678–86. See also chapter 7 in *Positivity* (2009) for more details on the origins and evidence for the positivity ratio tipping point.

154 **people who score higher on our measure of this tendency even receive more emotional uplift from a hug:** Lahnna I. Catalino, Kimberly A. Coffey, and Barbara L. Fredrickson (2012). "Prioritizing Positivity." Manuscript in preparation.

155 **Several randomized controlled trials in positive psychology have confirmed that learning to cherish your own good fortune—for instance, by counting up at least three blessings each day—can boost your gratitude, which in turn strengthens your social bonds and creates abiding happiness, even physical health:** Seligman et al. (2005). See also Robert Emmons's 2007 book, *Thanks!: How the New Science of Gratitude Can Make You Happier.* New York: Houghton Mifflin Harcourt.

156 **offering social support when things go *right* is a more efficient way to build relationships than offering it when things go wrong:** Shelly L. Gable, Courtney L. Gosnell, Natalya Maisel, and Amy Strachman (in press). "Safely testing the alarm: Close others' responses to personal positive events." *Journal of Personality and Social Psychology.*

Chapter 8

161 **To love one person with a private love is poor and miserable; to love all is glorious:** Thomas Traherne (1908/2007). *Centuries of Meditations.* Whitefish, Montana: Kessinger Publishing.

161 **positive emotions, in and of themselves, unlock your ability to really see other people:** Kareem J. Johnson and Barbara L. Fredrickson (2005). "We all look the same to me: Positive emotions eliminate the own-race bias in face recognition." *Psychological Science* 16(11): 875–81. See also Waugh and Fredrickson (2006).

166 **I spent several years early in my career cataloging the psychological damage done to girls and women who face the message that they can be reduced to how they look:** Fredrickson et al. (2011).

170 **Thank you for teaching Mr. Wills to be + [positive], [heart] Tisha and Kelly:** Not their real names.

178 **To date, I've written exactly one paper that has religion in its title, and that was merely a commentary offering my two cents on why religious involvement predicts good health:** Barbara L. Fredrickson (2002). "How does religion benefit health and well-being? Are positive emotions active ingredients?" *Psychological Inquiry* 13(3): 209–13.

180 **"Feeling is the deeper source of religion, and . . . philosophical and theological formulas are secondary products, like translations of a text into another tongue":** Quoted from page 470 of the 2002 edition of William James's 1902 classic, *The Varieties of Religious Experience: A Study in Human Nature.* New York: The Modern Library Classics.

180 **Like art, the truths of religion . . . more fully than usual and experience an enhancement of being:** Drawn from page 10 of Karen Armstrong's 2009 book, *The Case for God.* New York: Knopf.

181 **experiences of positive emotions can open those doors as well, expanding your outlook on life and setting off spiritual experiences:** Patty Van Cappellen and Vassilis Saraglou (2011). "Awe activates religious and spiritual feelings and behavioral intention." *Psychology of Religion and Spirituality.* Advance online publication. doi: 10.1037/a0025986.

182 **"to take the next step, to see the unknown as an adventure, to launch a journey" . . . "an active, open state that makes us willing to explore":** These two quotes from Sharon Salzberg are drawn from pages 12 and 67, respectively, of her 2002 book, *Faith: Trusting Your Own Deepest Experience.* New York: Riverhead Books.

182 **"Love is the shortest definition of spirituality I know":** George Vaillant (2009). *Spiritual Evolution: How We Are Wired for Faith, Hope, and Love.* New York: Three Rivers Press.

Chapter 9

185 **I never knew how to worship until I knew how to love:** Henry Ward Beecher (1869/2010). *Plymouth Pulpit: Sermons Preached at Plymouth Church, Brooklyn, Volume 4.* Charleston, NC: Nabu Press.

187 **What Barrett and her collaborators (including one of my newest Carolina colleagues, Kristen Lindquist) have asked is simply, what is an emotion?:** Lisa Feldman Barrett (2012). "Emotions are real." *Emotion.* See also Kristen A. Lindquist and Lisa Feldman Barrett (2008). "Constructing emotion: The experience of fear as a conceptual act." *Psychological Science* 19(9): 898–903.

187 **William James himself devoted considerable attention to this very question back in 1884:** William James (1884). "What is an emotion?" *Mind* 9: 188–205.

188 **Research coming out of Barrett's lab and other labs, including my own:** Barrett (2012); Lindquist and Barrett (2008). See also forthcoming publications by Lindsay Kennedy, Bethany Kok, and me.

188 **Those who took anger to be an emotion showed the typical jumps in heart rate and blood pressure, whereas those for whom the idea that anger is an emotion was debunked had an appreciably more muted cardiovascular response:** Kennedy, Kok, and Fredrickson. Manuscript in preparation.

189 **A global poll, released on Valentine's Day, 2012, revealed that most married people, or those similarly coupled, identify their significant other as their most important source of happiness:** http://af.reuters.com/article/commoditiesNews/idAFL2E8DDGDX20120214?pageNumber=1&virtualBrandChannel=0.

190 **By the flip of a coin, they tried either LKM or a different style of mediation, one that does not aim to cultivate loving feelings:** In this latest research, we compare learning loving-kindness meditation to learning mindfulness meditation, a similar practice albeit with less emphasis on cultivating positive emotions. This is work I am conducting with Steve Cole, Karen Grewen, Sara Algoe, Sy-Miin Chow, Kimberly Coffey, Ann Firestine, and others, which is funded by the National Institute of Nursing Research at NIH (R01NR012899).

191 **Feeling good is that indicator:** See classic work by Michel Cabanac (1971). "Physiological role of pleasure." *Science* 173(4002): 1103–7.

191 **That's because good feelings trigger a cascade of neurochemicals that makes you like whatever caused it:** Berridge (2007).

192 **Evidence suggests that it isn't until midlife or beyond that people develop true wisdom about positivity's quiet cues:** Catalino, Coffey, and Fredrickson. Manuscript in preparation.

Index